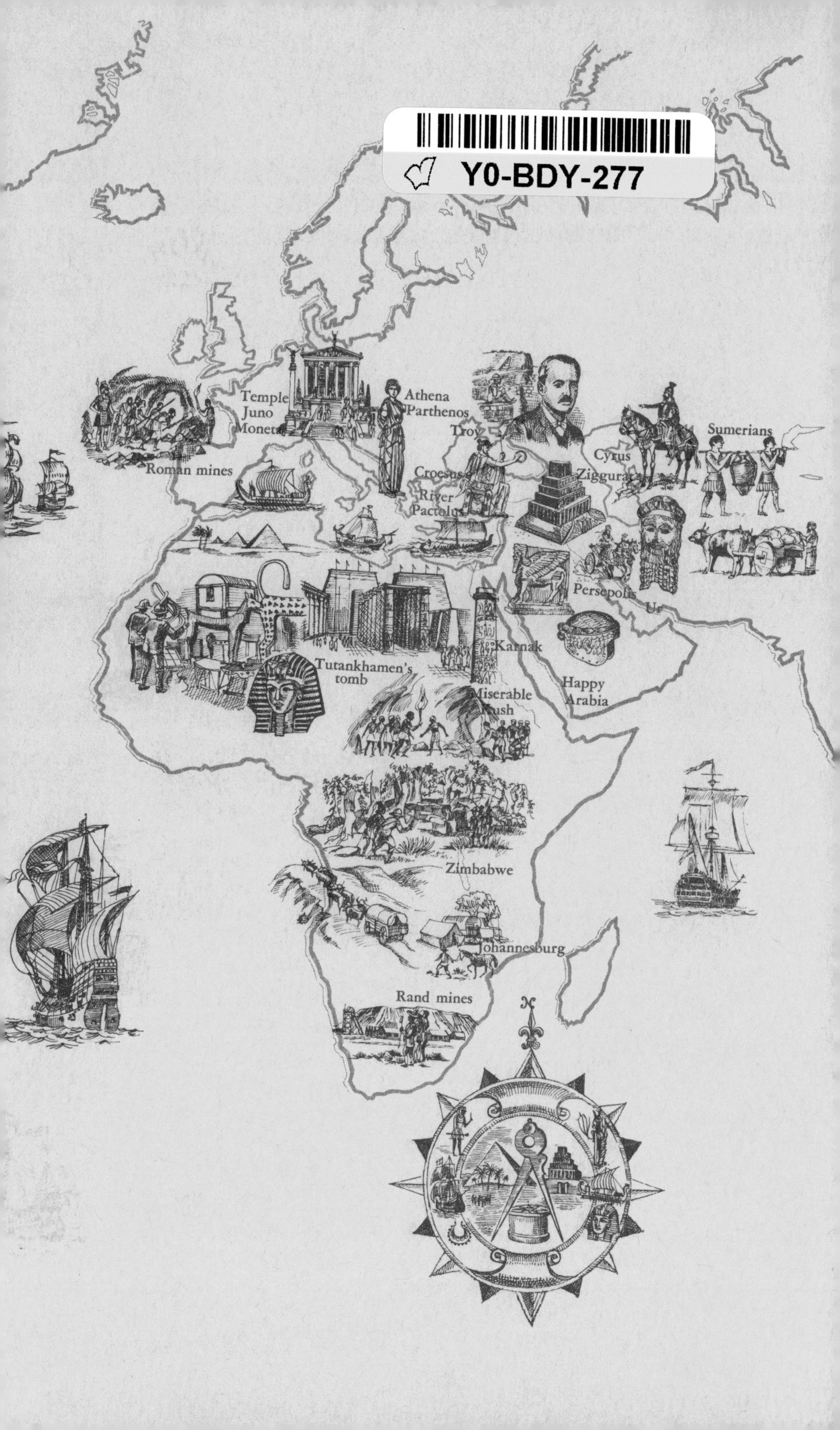
Temple
Juno
Moneta
Athena
Parthenos
Troy
Sumerians
Cyrus
Ziggurat
Roman mines
Croesus
River
Pactolus
Persepolis
Ur
Karnak
Tutankhamen's
tomb
Happy
Arabia
Miserable
Kush
Zimbabwe
Johannesburg
Rand mines

University of Illinois
HIGH SCHOOL LIBRARY

Gold!

Gold!

by Gina Allen

Thomas Y. Crowell Company

New York, Established 1834

Illustrations editor: Rhoda Tripp

Designed by Laurel Wagner

Manufactured in the United States of America

Library of Congress Catalog Card No. 64-23136

1 2 3 4 5 6 7 8 9 10

To my daughter, GINITA

Acknowledgments

I AM INDEBTED to my father, R. V. Hunkins, and to Darrell P. Ayer, Sr., of Lead, South Dakota, for a lifetime's education in the history of gold. The faults of the pupil lie not with the teachers.

In my research on gold the cooperation of the Homestake Mining Company, Lead, South Dakota, has extended over twenty years. Company officials have been most generous with pictures and publications. They have also provided me with repeated opportunities to view metallurgical processes and many hours of patient instruction.

For the opportunity of observing mining operations underground, I am most grateful to William Goodrich, former manager of the Bald Mountain Mining Company, Trojan, South Dakota. Tiffany and Company of New York City kindly permitted me to watch and learn from the goldsmiths in their workshops.

I have used material from speeches given by Donald H. McLaughlin, President, Homestake Mining Company, and L. L. Huelsdonk, Vice President, Best Mines Company, Inc., of California. I have also drawn on conversations with Jet Calhoon, Nathaniel P. Herz, Leonard Neary, Mr. and Mrs. John M. Sheedy, and my childhood friend, a prospector, Potato Creek Johnny.

Without the help and cooperation of family and friends, researching and writing the book would have been impossible. Mrs. Mayzie Cross devoted evenings and weekends to typing the manuscript. For ideas, assistance, encouragement, and patience I wish particularly to thank my husband, Ted Allen, my daughter, Ginita, my agent, Mrs. Ann Elmo, and my dear friend Mrs. Ofelia Martinez Mediano.

Contents

CONTENTS

Illustrations

Child of the Sun *the divine metal of earliest civilizations*

AT DAWN

FOR THOUSANDS OF YEARS, from the Orient to Egypt, the ancient world glittered with gold. Above the walls of man's first cities gold shone from temple spires and from towers raised to the sun.

The most spectacular of these dazzling structures were the staged pyramids, or ziggurats, that dotted the valleys of the Tigris and Euphrates rivers fifty centuries before Christ. Built first by the Sumerians, they were conquered and rebuilt through millennia as invaders swept into the rich land, taking over gods and gold and the arts of civilization.

The highest ziggurat rose almost seven hundred feet above the walls of ancient Babylon. Topped with gold mounted on a platform of silver, it could be seen for miles on every side, guiding travelers and attracting enemies for twenty centuries. The Israelite captives who helped rebuild it in the sixth century B.C. called it the tower of Babel.

This soaring, slave-made mountain was the home of the god Bel-Marduk, originally a sun god. The tower was built in seven stages, perhaps to represent the seven days of the week and the seven heavenly "planets" known to the priest astronomers who studied the stars from its commanding height. Like a tiered wedding cake it rose above the city, each ascending platform colored to match its corresponding planet. The highest, made of the sun's own metal, was the great god's private dwelling.

On the lowest level Bel-Marduk, in the form of a golden idol, half human, half animal, received his mortal worshipers. The idol sat on a throne of gold, rested his golden feet on a golden footstool, and presided over the golden table on which the pious could leave their golden offerings.

The Greek historian Herodotus recorded one estimate of the weight of the gold contained in the idol and the furnishings of the lower chamber as more than twenty-six tons. Its value today would be thirty million dollars.

There was as much gold again in the platform that topped the tower, though Herodotus never saw it. Only those who served the god were allowed to climb to his golden home. There everything Bel-Marduk might need was of gold, except the food placed daily on the golden table and the maiden who awaited his pleasure each night.

About 1525 B.C., Bel-Marduk lost much of his treasure to another god worshiped as Amen-Ra in far-off Egypt. It happened when the divine son of Amen-Ra, the Egyptian pharaoh, Thutmose I, riding in a chariot of pale gold, called electrum, led his armies eastward, wherever gold beckoned. He conquered much of the Near East, leaving monuments to his victories and taking back the spoils of battle.

Like the people whose gold he captured, Thutmose would use the metal for religious purposes. Gold was divine. Long before it became the symbol of royalty or a medium of exchange in the market place, men searched for it, mined it, stole and fought over it, that they might make it into idols or offer it to the gods.

None were more devout than the Egyptians who used four fifths of the world's gold to please their two thousand gods. Thutmose's daughter, Hatshepsut, who succeeded him on the throne of Egypt, was femininely particular about the quality of the gold she offered the gods.

Because she heard that the finest gold could be obtained from Punt, which may have been on Africa's eastern coast, she sent ships for it and other rare commodities. The hazardous voyage took years. When the expedition returned, she was disappointed to find that some of the gold had a green tinge.

Nevertheless, she had the picture story of the historic venture recorded in bas-relief on the walls of the temple she had planned and built at Deir el-Bahri. There the sculptors reproduced the long ships, propelled through strange waters by means of sails and oars, returning laden with gold, ebony, ivory, monkeys, and exotic trees, plants, and flowers.

"Never have like things been brought back for any king since the beginning of the world," says the temple inscription.

At Karnak the queen erected two granite pillars, each peaked lavishly with gold. They were placed so that they could be seen for miles along the Nile. When the sun set behind them, they glowed like torches of fire and "their radiance fills the two lands," the queen boasted in her inscription.

"To gild them I have given gold measured by the bushel, as though it were sacks of grain," she had her scribes record. "You who after long years shall see these monuments will say, 'We do not know how they can have made whole mountains of gold.' "

Today Hatshepsut's towers have been stripped of their gold, as have the ziggurats of Mesopotamia. One of the Karnak monuments has fallen but the other still stands, naked, but beautifully proportioned.

Like the gold of Sumeria and Babylonia, Hatshepsut's offering was made to the sun, the oldest of the gods, the source of all life, and the father of gold, which resembled the heavenly parent in color, sheen, and durability. This relationship of gold with the sun was recognized by the Greek poet Pindar when he called gold the "child of Zeus," who, like Jehovah, was originally a sun god. The tradition is still with us.

As late as the sixteenth century of our own era learned men were explaining that metals entered the earth through emanations from heavenly bodies, an idea that was as old as the Sumerian ziggurats. Wrote Calbus of Freiberg, a German doctor and metallurgist, in 1527: "Every metallic ore receives a special influence from its own particular planet. Thus gold is of the Sun or its influence, silver of the Moon, tin of Jupiter . . . . Thus gold is often called the sun."

In the first hieroglyphs, or sacred signs, gold was represented by a necklace. Long afterwards, the sign became a circle, which designated the metal in the writings of the alchemists and chemists.

Not until the eighteenth century was this ancient sun symbol for gold replaced by the Au that scientists use today. Au is the abbrevia-

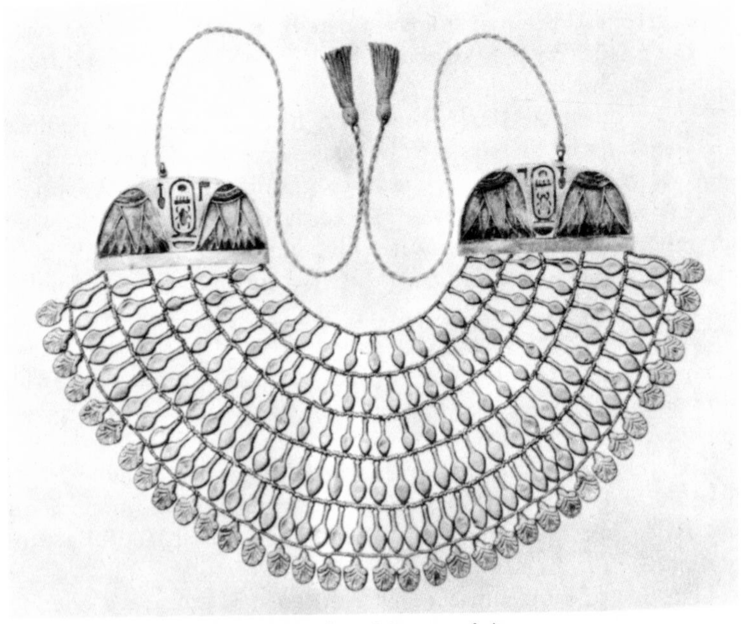

The Metropolitan Museum of Art

Ancient Egyptians used gold to represent the sun, which they worshiped. The first hieroglyph for gold was a stylized necklace, as shown in the drawing. The ornate gold collar, worn by an Egyptian lady of court, had religious as well as ornamental value.

tion of the Latin word for gold, *aurum,* which was in turn derived from Aurora, goddess of the dawn.

The Greeks felt that the deities who blessed men with gold had been more generous with the world's first inhabitants than with those who came later. In the beginning, the stories went, the sands of the river beds had been solely of the precious metal. Whole islands were made of it. Forest fires melted the gold in mountains and sent molten streams pouring over the earth.

That was man's golden age, wrote the Greek poet Hesiod eight hundred years before Christ. After it came a less prosperous silver age, then a bronze age of weapons and war, and finally an iron age

Overlaying a necklace.

Blowing up a fire for refining gold.

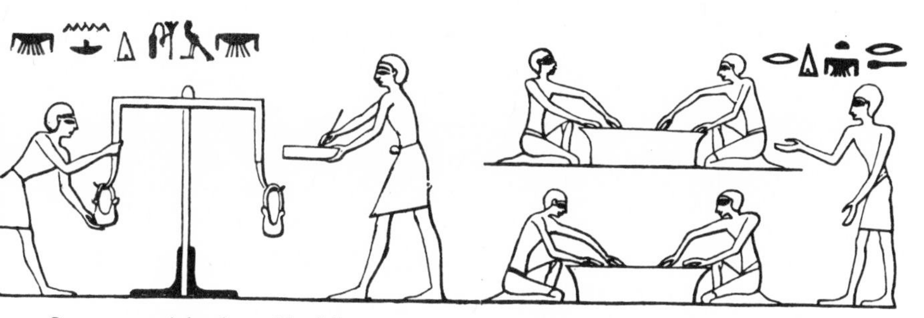

One man weighs the gold while the other records the amount.

Four men overlay two halves of a door.

Giving gold to the overlayers.

Two men work on a shrine mounted on a sledge.

On top, one man gives gold to the other. Underneath two men are overlaying.

Overlaying with gold.

J. G. Wilkinson, *Manners and Customs of the Ancient Egyptians*

This drawing, copied from ancient Egyptian art, shows goldsmiths at work. The necklace symbol for gold appears in each group of hieroglyphs, which describe what the goldsmiths are doing. English captions are rough translations of the hieroglyphs.

of poverty and toil into which, Hesiod regretted, he had been born.

Four centuries later, Plato wrote of the lost continent of Atlantis, whose golden spires once lighted the whole world and fixed Apollo's course as he drove the chariot of the sun across the sky each day to this earthly paradise. Atlantis lay just west of the Pillars of Hercules. There the first mortals lived with the gods in golden luxury.

According to Plato, the interbreeding of gods and mortals produced beings so inferior that the great Zeus lost all patience. Deeming these creatures unworthy of anything as precious as gold, Zeus sank the land, its luckless population, and all their wealth beneath the sea. Since then, as a punishment for his sins, man has been forced to scratch in the ground for grains of gold that the gods once gave generously.

It is true that before there was life on earth nature had been mining gold for thousands of millions of years, but the first harvest was too small to make a golden age or even to furnish one golden continent. Most of the gold found by the world's first humans, plus a large part of that collected in the eons after, belonged to the men who inhabited the world when Hesiod complained about a lack of the metal. Much of it is still with us.

For gold endures. It does not rust like iron nor tarnish like copper and silver. Chemically inactive, it is not corroded by air, or water, or common acids. The gold that one civilization buries is dug up by another, centuries later, in mint condition, usually to be buried again.

In this way gold accumulates. A part of the gold now in Fort Knox was undoubtedly buried by our ancestors many thousand years ago to keep evil spirits from their graves.

Men learned to count and write in order to keep track of the gold in temple treasuries. This long record stretches back five thousand years and includes stones and baked clay tablets marked in cuneiform and hieroglyphs. These accounts, plus the fact that gold survives, make it possible to estimate the total amount of gold man has gathered from the earth during his history.

If you were to take it all to the ball park and melt it together you could fashion a square brick that would fit neatly within the baselines of the baseball diamond. Your brick would be ninety feet in each direction.

Because gold is one of the heavier elements, with an atomic weight of 197.2, your gleaming brick, containing all the gold man has ever known, would weigh 100,000 tons. This is an impressive amount of weight for such a small block, but it is rather a skimpy reward for a hundred thousand years of effort. Three times that tonnage of pig iron is produced every twelve months.

Your imaginary gold brick makes up in value what it lacks in size. In dollars today it is worth $112 billion. Of that amount, $50 billion worth is held by governments and banks in monetary reserves. The next biggest chunk is believed to be in private hoards, and not a little lies in treasure ships at the bottom of the sea.

Man's small output of gold through the ages does not imply lack of industry. He has spent the better part of his days on earth searching for the precious metal. Though he wishes it were more plentiful, he considers it precious in large part because it is scarce.

Astronomers tell us that the shortage of gold was predestined long before our sun was formed and that in other planetary systems gold is also in short supply. Gold's extreme weight makes it universally scarce.

According to the new cosmology, the interstellar gas of outer space is composed mainly of light hydrogen atoms. Atoms of heavier elements are created through nuclear reactions occurring in the interior of existing stars, such as our sun.

As a star uses up its supply of hydrogen, it is forced to ever more strenuous and complicated atomic transmutations until, exhausted, it dies. Whether it sputters to death over a long period of time or explodes dramatically, it leaves behind, in the interstellar gas, a sprinkling of the heavy atoms it has created. From this gas new stars are formed.

Gold is one of the heaviest of these atomic by-products of the energy produced in nature's celestial cyclotrons. A star in the prime of life produces helium continuously and abundantly from a storehouse of hydrogen atoms. Only in its dying spasms is a star compelled to produce energy by also creating heavy atoms such as gold.

Gold, then, is a frugal gift from dying stars to others not yet born. But if gold's weight has made it scarce in the universe, it is also the reason we have any at all on earth.

For gold was not evenly distributed among the planets when they were created. As our sun spun itself into being from a cumulus of interstellar gas, it pushed away a part of the vapor. As this cloud rushed outward, the heavy elements of low volatility condensed like rain to form the small rock-and-metal planets that orbit closest to the sun—Mercury, Venus, Earth, and Mars.

A future space-age prospector would be ill-advised to go searching for gold on the larger, more distant planets, such as Jupiter or Saturn. By the time those planets took shape, the heavy elements, even the common silica of rocks, were all but gone.

The segregation of elements according to weight did not stop as the planets condensed from the cloud of interplanetary gas. According to a geological theory originally advanced by the Russian geophysicist A. I. Oparin and recently substantiated by the Canadian Robert J. Uffen, the heavier elements continued to fall toward the center of the earth as the planet cooled. When this idea was first announced it brought forth a flurry of speculation that the interior of our globe might consist entirely of molten gold.

So far, men's drills have explored the crust of the earth to a depth of less than five miles. They will have to increase this to four thousand miles to reach the center of the world. What they will find there no one knows for certain. The evidence to date suggests that there will be more iron than precious metals. Even where it is presumed to be most plentiful, gold is still scarce.

Fortunately for gold-greedy men, the heavy elements embraced by the earth's hard cover keep seeking—and finding—release. Driven outward by the enormous pressure of a weighty crust, the molten material in the globe's core oozes and explodes its way into every fault and fissure of the surrounding shell. These invasions cause far-flung mechanical and chemical reactions by means of which the intruding substances advance and spread.

Far above this continuous scramble, we rarely know anything about it. Seismographs record it as a faint and frequent trembling of the earth's surface, and all around us, slowly, imperceptibly, but inevitably, coastlines rise and fall and the geography of the world changes.

Sometimes the change is violent. A destructive tidal wave heralds a disturbance of an ocean floor. An erupting volcano buries landmarks. Mountain ranges are heaved upward from the beds of seas, carrying their fossil deposits with them. Continents sag and are covered with water. An incidental part of this geological restlessness is the distribution of gold through the surface rocks of the earth's crust—not generously, but generally.

Gold is not only where you find it—gold is everywhere. It is usually so sparsely dispersed, however, that it can't be seen by the naked eye and trying to gather it would be humanly impossible.

Nature can do what man cannot, and so man depends on nature for a larger part of his mining effort. The same processes that bring gold from the core of the earth concentrate it in mountain ranges.

As the surface of the earth heaves and buckles, lifting mountains, rock is shifted, twisted, broken, tumbled. The resulting strains and stresses produce heat and faulted areas. Sometimes the heat melts the rock, altering its composition and concentrating its gold content. Or the heat may vaporize moisture that leaches gold from the rock and redeposits it in cracks and fissures.

In this way gold is stockpiled in hilly fortresses. But this is not the end of nature's mining activity. The surface of the world wears out. As it does, gold is eroded from the mountains by wind and rain and freeze and thaw. With vegetation, soil, and rock itself, the precious metal is carried from the peaks into the streams the mountains feed.

Again gold's weight and chemical snobbishness play a large part in its fate. The rock that held it is dissolved or worn away by the water. Some of the gold is swept off too, in solution or in particles so small they float. But most of it lags heavily behind and sinks eventually to bedrock. There it gathers, sometimes for millennia after millennia. When at last it is discovered, the mountains that first knew it may have disappeared and the stream that harbored it may have left no other trace in a sandy desert.

Nature had been mining gold for thousands of millions of years when the first man saw the first gold nugget. He made the discovery a little late. Some eight to ten billion tons of the precious metal had already found their way into the oceans' waters.

This is 100,000 times more gold than the 100,000 tons man has managed to scrape from the earth. For this reason the wealth of the oceans has always enticed him. In the 1920's when Germany was in dire need of gold to pay her war debt and replenish the treasury, the noted German scientist Fritz Haber attempted to extract the metal from sea water.

In a super-secret expedition he set out on a ship named the

Meteor to mine gold from the Atlantic. For four years the *Meteor* crossed and recrossed the ocean, filtering gold through a specially designed filtration plant. It proved necessary to treat a thousand tons of water to get a single gram of gold, a process that cost more than it paid.

Since nature does not have to worry about costs, she mines gold from the sea as she does from mountains, precipitating the metal to the oceans' floors, replacing it with colloidal gold from the world's rivers. As miners today dig gold from mountains whose fossils tell a history of a long life beneath the sea, so the children of our children in a distant future may mine the gold accumulating on ocean beds right now.

Or they may find the way to sift it from the oceans' waters or to manufacture it as needed. The desire for gold has inspired many of men's accomplishments and a fair share of his transgressions.

He has not always wanted gold for the same reasons, but he has always wanted it enough to strain his physical endurance and his ingenuity to get it. In search of gold, man explored the earth beneath him and the land and seas around him. To capture gold he perfected weapons and the art of war. To mine it, he developed slavery.

Architecture advanced to meet the need for guarding gold. Treasure hunters prowling through the ruins of the past became the archaeologists of the present. Trying to turn lead into gold, the alchemists discarded magic formulas for the methods of science and planted the seeds of nuclear physics. Traders turned man's religious regard for gold into an economic asset.

Throughout his history, man has searched for gold and found so little that this, his most continuous occupation, might also be called his most spectacular failure. But the long search has not been in vain. For better—and for worse—it has played a large part in shaping the world in which we live today.

IN HOMAGE

THE WORLD'S FIRST PROSPECTORS were Stone Age men who found their gold in the streams which were their source of water and their highways. "The first metal to attract the attention of man was gold because it is one of the few metals that are found in the elemental or free state in nature."

This was the opinion of Dr. T. A. Rickhard, who devoted his experience with metals to a study of man's historical relationship with them. It is an opinion shared by many experts but not by all. Nuggets of copper and meteoric iron were also lying around, as stones, to be picked up by the world's first humans, and copper is more plentiful in prehistoric cult sites.

But a study of man's beginnings through the inspection of his leavings can be misleading as well as informative. There is reason to believe that Paleolithic, or Stone Age, men used meteoric iron where it was available, yet no iron has been found in their rubbish heaps.

Through thousands of years the iron rusted away. The gold they took with them or, when they left it behind, it was carted off by those who came later.

Dr. Rickard believed that man was first attracted by nuggets of gold because "only gold exhibited luster. The other native metals were tarnished by weathering." Chunks of copper and iron looked much like ordinary rocks and without fire they behaved like rocks. Indestructible gold shone like the sun and was immediately useful.

Gold, though heavy, is extremely soft. Modern man can cut it with a knife. Primitive man could cut it with a piece of flint. With the same flint he could pound it back together again. When he continued pounding, the gold flowed like water beneath his stone, into thin sheets and new shapes. He could pull it into wire for use as pins and fishhooks.

Today an ounce of gold can be stretched into a wire fifty miles long, and goldbeaters cold-hammer the metal into sheets as thin as tissue paper, so that one ounce can be made to cover an area of one hundred square feet. Modern architects say that the Babylonians, who topped their ziggurats and temples with gold, were using the ideal roofing material—thin, light, weather and time resistant. Gold pipes and fixtures, impervious to rust and acids, could also solve present-day plumbing maintenance problems.

Men of the ancient world and primitive men of the modern world have used gold for just such practical purposes. It has been hammered into bowls and basins, sharpened into knives and scrapers and razors, pointed for daggers and digging sticks.

Columbus found the natives of the West Indies fishing with gold hooks in 1492, and twentieth-century adventurers have reported gold fishooks still in service in Colombia. In the interior of Africa the gold that was once shaped as daggers is now molded into bullets, for which purpose it was also used in eighteenth-century North Carolina.

But gold's working life has been spasmodic. The very qualities that made it useful, made it magic. When men had to choose, they fished with hooks of bone and hammered their gold into sun images, idols, and magic charms.

Our oldest gold artifacts are of this type. They came from caves in Spain which were used by Paleolithic men for thousands of years, sometimes as homes, more often as places of worship. In these mountain caverns man's ancestors performed their magic and religious rites. On the walls they left the world's first paintings and in a stratum formed during the fourth glacial age, about 40,000 B.C., they left simple cold-hammered amulets of gold.

It was this early in man's history that gold's magic became more important than its utility, a fact not insignificant in its later economic role. Even more important, this happened wherever and whenever gold was found.

The Stone Age was more than half a million years old when the cave men of Europe hammered out and decorated their religious charms. It would be another thirty thousand years before men began to live in cities and develop trade. By that time gold's divinity was firmly established in many widely separated parts of the world.

To prehistoric men who valued gold as the metal of the sun, today's concern over which metal they discovered first would sound like nonsense. Gold is rarely found without impurities, and in its natural state it is usually alloyed with silver, or copper, or both. This changes both color and properties, so prehistoric men had many different kinds of gold which they differentiated according to hue. Like these alloys, other metals were considered different kinds of gold. The conception persists in the Chinese word *chin,* which means both gold and metal.

Purple gold from Egyptian tombs contains so much iron that it responds to a magnet. In some of the gold from the same source, flecks of platinum are so large they can be seen with the naked eye.

Gold alloyed with copper is harder and more brittle than pure gold and has a brassy sheen. The green gold that Queen Hatshepsut's ships brought back from Punt contained small amounts of silver. Gold alloyed with larger proportions of silver was called pale gold, or electrum. Silver itself was known as white gold.

The finest gold was reserved for religious purposes. It was not only raised on towers to the sun but also buried with the dead to serve them and keep them safe in the afterworld. This took immense amounts of gold. To furnish the graves of one generation, older tombs were often robbed of their treasure.

Still, some of the gold has survived to tell a part of the story of men and women who lived five thousand and more years ago. In the valleys of the Tigris and Euphrates rivers, time and the dampness of the soil destroyed perishable relics of the ancient civilization of Sumeria, but the gold which was dug up by the archaeologist Sir Leonard Woolley was as bright and gleaming when it was found as it was when it was buried.

The gold found by Sir Leonard in the temple cemetery at Ur of the Chaldees shows that the Sumerians of about 2700 B.C. were already accomplished goldsmiths. In one grave there was a beaten helmet which had been buried with the warrior Mes-kalam-dug. It was made from a single nugget and might be called a wig of gold. A diadem, the ears, and locks of hair were hammered up so that they stood out from the main body of the helmet in a technique still used, called repoussé. Then each strand of hair was incised, in waves and curls.

The rulers of the city states of Sumeria were patesi, or priest-kings. When they died, their tombs were furnished with gold and with the bodies of those who had served them in life, sometimes numbering as many as seventy-four.

One of these graves, in which Queen Shub-ad was buried with her royal attendants, had not been robbed of its gold. On the queen's skull was her beautiful diadem of golden rings, leaves, and flowers. Around her were golden god figures, her golden goblet, bowl, and beaker, and a dagger of gold, fourteen and a half inches long, encased in a delicately patterned gold sheath. Each of her ladies in waiting wore gold diadems and jewelry, and among the bones of the court musicians lay a golden harp.

At about the time that Queen Shub-ad was buried at Ur, the pharaohs of Egypt began building their great stone pyramids to protect their mummies and their gold from thieves. This was important to the divine sons of the sun, for without a body and an eternal home the ka, or spirit of the dead, would perish.

The pyramids are numbered among the wonders of the world but they did not deter the grave robbers. In both Babylonia and Egypt, raiding tombs for treasure became a profession, and it was largely through these looters of the cemeteries that gold appeared as a commodity in the barter markets. Gold from other sources was monopolized by the gods, the priests, and the dead.

When the pharaoh Thutmose returned to Egypt with the gold he had captured from the Near East, about 1520 B.C., the Egyptian sons of the sun had been building pyramids for twelve hundred years and nearly all of them had been stripped of their gold. Thutmose decided that instead of marking the site of his grave with a pyramid of stone, he would hide it. So he had slaves hollow out his burial chambers in the limestone cliffs near Thebes. The slaves were killed when their work was done, and when Thutmose died his mummy and gold were concealed behind a narrow opening in the face of the bluff, carefully sealed to resemble the natural rock.

Thutmose's innovation was followed by succeeding pharaohs. Soon the cliffs on the west wide of the Nile, in what has since been known as the Valley of the Kings, were riddled with secret burial chambers and filled with gold and sacred mummies.

The sandswept bluffs looked starkly white and peaceful by moonlight. Actually, for centuries, their quiet was disturbed by a cops-and-robbers drama enacted each night as thieves searched for gold in the secret chambers of the dead and priests tried to save the sacred mummies of the pharaohs.

To do this the priests were forced to rob graves too. With armies of slaves they entered the tombs and moved the heavy sarcophagi to new hiding places, which were promptly found and plundered by the bandits.

Often, priests and robbers met in the same tomb, and pitched battles disturbed the hallowed dead. Spies for each side watched and reported the nocturnal activities of the enemy.

To protect the deceased, the priests found it necessary to pile sarcophagi together in strategic caves and stand guard over them. To protect themselves from the determined thieves, who were more adept at killing, the holy men moved their collection of mummies from place to place, night after night. It was an arduous and dangerous task.

At last the priests managed to transport the kings of the eighteenth to twentieth dynasties out of the valley of the tombs to a mass grave at Deir el-Bahri, near the temple built by Queen Hatshepsut. Before the robbers found the site, the sand had covered it.

Thieves were still digging in the Valley of the Kings in the nineteenth century when the archaeologists began their investigations of the ancient graves. Many a carefully planned archaeological expedition came to naught after years of study, preparation, and careful digging because pillagers had emptied the burial chambers thousands of years before. Contemporary robbers let the scientists lead them to new treasure troves and then made off with the spoils.

In the case of the mass grave of the lost kings, however, thieves proved a help rather than a hindrance. Archaeologists had found no trace of the missing kings. Then, in 1875, antiquities from this period appeared mysteriously in the black market at Luxor.

Disguised, and armed with a profusion of gold coins, an expert from the Egyptian Museum in Cairo moved to Luxor and let it be known that he was in the market for stolen relics of the past. He was finally offered objects that could have come only from the mass grave of the missing kings. Modern thieves had succeeded where archaeologists had failed. This time, unwittingly, robbers led the scientists to the grave at Deir el-Bahri.

It was logical that it should happen this way. Archaeology was still in its infancy. The thieves who had found the lost kings could trace their trade back to the thirteenth century. They had learned it from their fathers and their grandfathers and they were experts. They were also leaders of the village of Kurna, which specialized in pillaging ancient tombs, forging antiquities, and similar shady practices.

The mass grave at Deir el-Bahri served the village of professional thieves as a bank. Treasure was withdrawn only as it was needed. The villagers had expected their buried gold to support them and their descendants comfortably for generations.

By 1922 the Valley of the Kings had been searched for so many years by robbers and archaeologists that it seemed unlikely that any graves had been missed. Neither had any graves been discovered that had not been violated by thieves.

In the hopes of finding one, two Englishmen had worked for six long, fruitless years. In the fall of 1922, Lord Carnarvon had returned to England while his partner, Howard Carter, tried one last excavation. The site was not very promising. The face of the bluff had been covered by the sand that had blown against it for centuries, and rock from other tombs had been allowed to fall into the sand.

Measurements proved that there wasn't room at this spot for impressive burial chambers. Even if a grave was found it would probably be one of little importance. Still the determined Howard Carter dug carefully through the rubble and the sand. In the solid rock he found a passageway, narrow and dark and winding. It was blocked periodically with rubble and stone barriers. One of these was exceedingly thick and carefully sealed. The workmen broke an opening in the rock wall, and Howard Carter thrust a candle through it.

"At first I could see nothing," he wrote later, "the hot air escaping from the chamber causing the candle flame to flicker. But presently, as my eyes grew accustomed to the light, details of the room within emerged slowly from the mist: strange animals, statues, and gold —everywhere the glint of gold."

Photograph by Harry Burton, The Metropolitan Museum of Art

The richest treasure store ever found by archaeologists belonged to an unimportant boy pharaoh named Tutankhamen. His carefully hidden tomb was discovered, after many centuries, by Howard Carter, an Englishman. In this picture, Mr. Carter is bending over the coffin, brushing away sand.

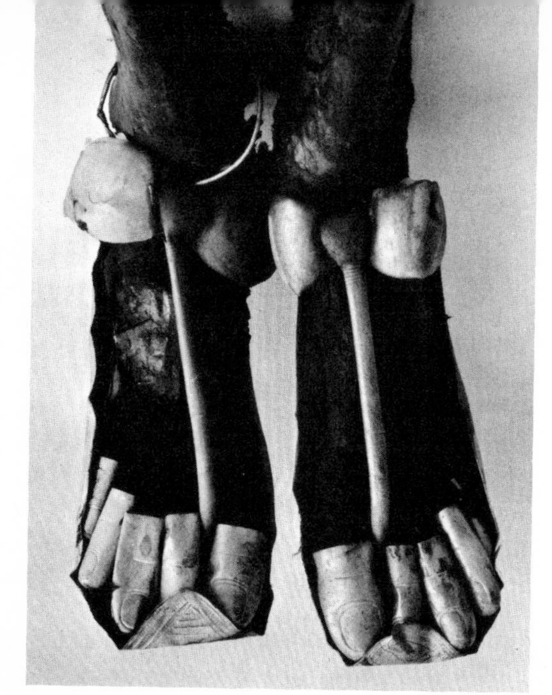

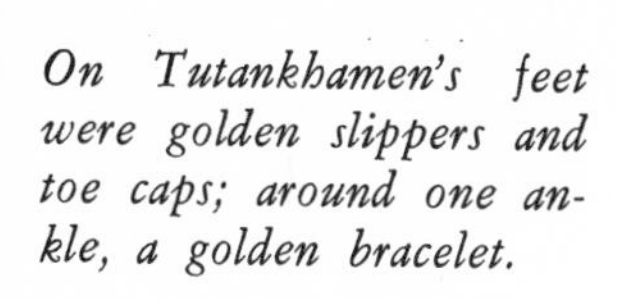

On Tutankhamen's feet were golden slippers and toe caps; around one ankle, a golden bracelet.

Photograph by Harry Burton, The Metropolitan Museum of Art

In one of the smallest of the Egyptian tombs, he had found the richest treasure of gold ever unearthed by archaeologists. The tomb was Tutankhamen's. Though it had been visited by thieves three thousand years before, the trespassers had reached only the first chamber when they were caught or frightened away. Even there, though the room had obviously been disturbed, gold was plentiful.

There were chariots of pale gold, a golden throne, golden scepters, and idols. Three golden couches were decorated with animal gods and charms. Jewelry and amulets of gold and precious stones were scattered everywhere. One wall of the room was guarded by life-sized statues dressed in gold from their sandals to their crowns.

Again a thick stone wall had to be removed to find out what the statues were protecting. It turned out to be a wall of gold, which was just one wall of a golden enclosure, nine feet high and seventeen feet by eleven feet. The sheets of gold were paneled with brilliant blue opaque glazes, decorated with magic symbols, and topped with a cornice of sacred cobras.

Within this room of gold were three smaller ones, each walled with heavy gold plate. The last was a shrine which resembled a golden tabernacle. It surrounded a stone sarcophagus that was

ılden image of King Tutankhamen forms the lid of his coffin. crossed hands he is holding the royal emblems: a crook and a

Photograph by Harry Burton, The Metropolitan Museum of Art

covered with a granite slab which weighed a ton. As the block and tackle lifted this sheet of rock, Carter and his helpers saw a golden image of the boy pharaoh who had been buried in the tomb. This likeness formed the lid of the outer coffin. It was seven feet long.

The effigy was held by two winged goddesses, also of gold "as brilliant as the day the coffin was made," wrote Carter. "The head and the hands of the king were 'in the round,' in massive gold of the finest sculpture. The hands, crossed over the breast, held the royal emblems—the Crook and the Flail—encrusted with deep blue faience. The face and the features were wonderfully wrought in sheet-gold."

This is the coffin you see today when you visit the tomb of Tutankhamen in the Valley of the Kings. The gold glows softly in the dim light, modeling the delicate, handsome features of a boy, not yet twenty, who died about 1350 B.C.

Within this coffin, the archaeologists found another, made of oak and plated with heavy gold. On this too, Tutankhamen had been immortalized in the magic metal. Inside this coffin was a third, so heavy it took eight men to lift it. It was made of solid gold and held the mummy.

On the mummy itself was a mask of gold, slippers covered with golden sequins, and a dozen bracelets. In his right hand, the preserved ruler held a golden dagger.

The linen wrappings were removed with difficulty because of the unguents that had been applied to preserve the body. They had, instead, eaten away some of the features. Not the ointments used, but the dry Egyptian air preserved the dead in the land of the Nile.

As the cloths were unwound they revealed one hundred and forty-three amulets and charms of gold and jewels. In an adjoining chamber was the golden jewelry the pharaoh had apparently worn in life—anklets, bracelets, rings, crowns, and collars. And with them, a sling shot and pebbles and a number of mechanical toys.

Much of the gold from the tomb is displayed at the Cairo Museum where those who see it react as did the discoverer. "One is impressed," wrote Carter, "by the extreme care and enormous costliness lavished by this ancient people on the enshrinement of their dead. Everywhere there is evidence of the accomplished artist and skilful craftsman. The modern observer must be astounded at the enormous labor and expense bestowed on these royal burials, at the precious metal so generously devoted to the princely dead!"

Photograph by Harry Burton, The Metropolitan Museum of Art

The king's golden throne was buried with him. This close-up view of the backrest shows Tutankhamen with his loving wife Ankhesenamen against a background of pale electrum. On them shine the rays of the divine sun.

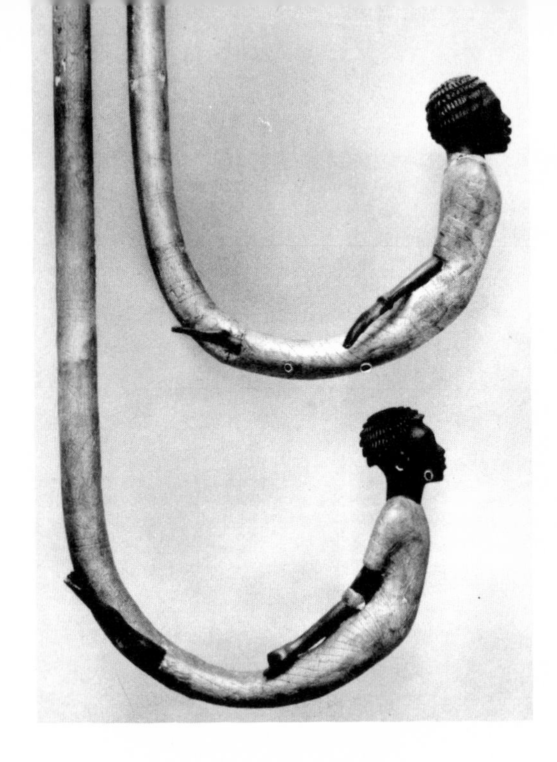

Ceremonial walking sticks, covered with gold leaf, were among the magnificent treasures heaped in Tutankhamen's tomb. Ebony Negro slaves form the handles.

Photograph by Harry Burton, The Metropolitan Museum of Art

With the excavation of the tomb, the work had just begun and it is still going on. Reading history from graves is a slow and arduous task. With the information they gleaned about the early Egyptians, the historians learned much about the boy who had been buried in three golden caskets.

Though the quantity of gold in the grave seemed to belie it, Tutankhamen lived in an impoverished Egypt. About the time of his birth, the pharaoh Ikhnaton deserted the capital city of Thebes and the god Amen-Ra and built a new capital, Akhetaton, whose temple honored a new god, Aton, "sphere of the sun."

While Ikhnaton worshiped Aton, an old priest, Ay, devoted himself to attaining power. Neglected, Egypt's eastern dependencies fell to her enemies. Gold no longer came from subject nations. No slaves were captured to work the mines. What gold there was went to the temple of Aton at the new capital of Akhetaton. The temples of Amen-Ra, at Thebes, were poor, their priests threatening revolt.

The boy who was to become a pharaoh was known then as Tutankhaton, in honor of the new god, but he lived in Thebes and received his education from the priests of Amen-Ra, with whom he was a favorite. He was also welcomed in Akhetaton for he was closely related to the pharaoh Ikhnaton, possibly a half-brother or a son by a lesser wife.

Egyptologists now believe that when Ikhnaton died, about 1362 B.C., he left his third daughter, Ankhesenaton, a widow. She was also a mother and possibly thirteen years old. Tutankhaton was younger, and the old priest Ay hoped to make him the next pharaoh by marrying him to the widowed Ankhesenaton. He managed the marriage, but the husband of Ikhnaton's oldest daughter grabbed the throne and ruled without Ay's help.

Within two years the new pharaoh disappeared and it is doubtful if he accomplished that without the old priest's aid. Tutankhaton was proclaimed king. Ay became his mentor. Thebes again became the capital, and the royal bride and groom changed their names to honor Amen-Ra.

While Ay governed, the boy pharaoh, now called Tutankhamen, played at his games and led the many religious processions that diverted the citizens of the ancient city. In these parades he rode in a golden chariot, wore an elaborate golden headdress with a golden serpent leaping from his brow, and carried the royal scepter tipped with the falcon head of the sun god Horus.

When his official duties palled, the little pharaoh amused himself by striking at his servants with the graceful scepter. He used human targets when he practiced shooting and had the sculptors carve pictures in bas-relief that showed him kicking prisoners of war. The carvings reveal much about his character and his relationship with his young wife.

He could be thoughtlessly cruel, as boys can be cruel. He could also be playful, and gay, and affectionate. Ankhesenamen loved him. He was at once husband, sweetheart, playmate, and child. When he was well, she joined him in his games. When he was ill, she mothered him. And then he died.

Ay, who took care of everything, had prepared for this too. Slaves had dug a tomb in the limestone bluffs that streaked the Valley of the Kings. Goldsmiths had worked ceaselessly on the amulets and charms, the masks and effigies, coffins and shrines that would grant the young pharaoh life after death. All had been made to fit the spacious chambers of a tomb whose size made it worthy to receive the mummy of a sacred son of the sun.

At the last minute Ay had the golden furnishings placed in a smaller tomb. Possibly the larger excavation had not been completed. Perhaps Ay feared that its location had been discovered by grave robbers. Or he may have wanted to save the greater tomb for his own sacred mummy. For the old priest expected to become the next pharaoh by marrying the young widow, Ankhesenamen.

The grieving girl had one hundred days to escape her fate. This was the length of time needed to purify and mummify the dead.

Hastily and secretly she sent a message to the Hittite king, Shubbiluliuma, whose armies had been conquering the lands of the Near East that had once belonged to Egypt. The message, recorded by Hittite scribes on clay tablets, was as urgent when discovered by archaeologists in our own time as it was when sent by the frantic Queen Ankhesenamen. "My husband is dead. Your sons are said to be grown; so send me one of your sons, and he shall be my husband and king of Egypt. I send bridal gifts."

Shubbiluliuma accepted the proposal. He dispatched generous gifts of gold to the young widow and a message that he was readying a ship to carry his son to Egypt.

From the palace Ankhesenamen watched the river below for sight of the royal Hittite vessel. The old priest Ay was busy preparing the tomb and the mummy of the young pharaoh, but not too busy to protect his future bride from a rival. It is presumed that Ay knew definitely, before Ankhesenamen suspected, that the Hittite prince would never arrive.

It was a common belief that Ay, who became Egypt's next pharaoh, had a magic talent for making people disappear. If the unhappy Ankhesenamen suffered because of Ay's forbidding power, history is indebted to the ambitious priest for hiding Tutankhamen's grave and gold so well that they escaped discovery for more than three thousand years.

FOR TRIBUTE

EVEN AS QUEEN HATSHEPSUT was building her mountains of gold to the god Amen-Ra, smoke billowed over the island of Crete in the northwest. For centuries the kings of Crete and the kings of Mycenae, on the Greek Peloponnesus, had sent out pirate ships to rob each other of gold.

These kings did not rule because they were divine but because they were strong. Gold was to them a royal metal. It was the reason for war and the prize of battle. To gain gold everything was risked and anything was fair.

So the pirates from the city kingdom that Homer called "golden Mycenae" burned the palaces of Cnossus, on Crete, to the ground. Rid of this rival, the king of Mycenae looked greedily across the Aegean Sea to the wealthy city of Troy.

Repeatedly looted and destroyed by enemies, as Cnossus had been, Troy had risen again and again, with ever higher and stronger walls. Like a cat, Troy had nine lives and was rebuilt that many times on the hill that guarded the riches of Anatolia and overlooked the narrow strait of the Dardanelles.

Caravans traveling between Europe and Asia Minor, ships leaving and entering the Black Sea, passed the mighty fortress that was Troy and paid tribute for the privilege. There was not a king on the shores or islands of the Mediterranean who had not been forced to contribute to Troy's wealth.

The stories of the golden treasure mounting behind the forbidding walls grew through the years. Envy compounded resentment. Finally, around the beginning of the twelfth century B.C. (the exact date is disputed) the kings of Greece stopped fighting each other and united against Troy.

History has been shaped by wars fought for gold, but avarice has never been a favorite of poets. So Homer sang of the beauty of Helen, wife of Menelaus, stolen by Paris, prince of Troy, and of the gold that belonged to the city's ruler, King Priam, father of Paris.

To retrieve the faithless Helen, according to the poet, the Greek kings left their own wives and homes to fight for ten long years against the forces of King Priam of Troy. They were led by Agamemnon, ruler of Mycenae and brother of the cuckold Menelaus.

The story of their heroic battle was often repeated and much loved, as all Greek myths were loved. But only credulous little boys believed that there had really been a Troy and a Trojan War in which the gods participated. One such boy was Heinrich Schliemann, born in Germany in 1822.

Son of a poor pastor, he read over and over the stories of Helen's beauty, King Priam's wealth, and the adventures of Homer's heroes. But he was not one to be satisfied with reading and dreaming. Before he was thirty, he had traveled over most of the world, taught himself half a dozen languages, including ancient and modern Greek, and amassed a private fortune through his commercial enterprises. He proposed to use his knowledge and his fortune to search for Homer's Troy, which most sensible people knew had existed only in the blind poet's imagination.

Before he was well started on the project, gold was discovered in California. Heinrich Schliemann joined the rush. He didn't need more wealth. He had enough. But he could not resist the lure of gold.

He loved gold for its beauty, its durability, its texture, its glowing color. He enjoyed looking at it and feeling it. Even while he increased his fortune in California, he envied King Priam of ancient Troy who had lived intimately with the royal metal, wrapped in golden armor on the battlefield and in golden luxury within the palace walls. He pictured Helen in his mind, breathtakingly beautiful in glittering golden jewelry fashioned by the goldsmiths of Priam's court. He could not turn back the clock and live in those golden days but he could, he hoped, recover them.

Heinrich Schliemann, *Ilios*

Obsessed with gold and with the idea that mythical Troy had really existed, Schliemann went to Greece and found both—gold and ancient Troy. This drawing shows his young wife, Sophia, wearing the most beautiful golden diadem he found, made of 16,353 pieces.

Leaving California, he prepared to do just that. In Greece he advertised for a wife. From among the young girls who responded, he chose the one who resembled Helen of Troy, as Homer had described her, as he himself had imagined her. By this time

Schliemann was almost fifty. His bride was less than twenty. She brought to her marriage not only her beauty but an unexpected enthusiasm for the project her husband had set for himself.

With his wife beside him and the *Iliad* in his hand, Schliemann followed the trail of Homer's clues to the possible site of ancient Troy. It was an intricate bit of detective work and it led him to the right place. But when the workers began to dig they found that there had been many Troys, built through centuries, one upon the ruins of another. Schliemann selected the second city as the one the Greeks had conquered.

Carefully the spades exposed the ruins. Anxiously Schliemann watched the earth as it was turned up. On a June morning in 1873, he spied that for which he had been searching—gold.

According to his own account, he ordered the workmen to go home. Armed with his knife and his wife's red shawl in which to collect the bounty, he dug out the gold, dangerously hacking away at the foundations of a wall of massive rock that towered above him. He was, he explained later, too excited by the sight of the treasure to worry about the risks he was taking.

This find, he wrote, "crowned my labors with a golden splendor." He took the gold to a wooden hut at the site of the digging, where he sorted and examined it. There were cups of gold and electrum, a gold bottle and sauceboat, gold diadems and necklaces, sixty earrings and almost nine thousand gold rings and buttons.

Not since he had bought gold dust from the California prospectors had Schliemann handled so much gold. He enjoyed it, but it also made him nervous. When he had gold he was always afraid that someone would take it from him. In California he had guarded his safe night and day. He inventoried the gold of Troy behind a locked door with a gun beside him.

The diadems were particularly ornate. They consisted of interlocked gold rings which were made to surround the head in a wide band. Long tassels hung from either side.

Lifting the most beautiful of the headdresses, he placed it over the thick black curls of his wife, Sophia. This was the moment he had anticipated when he advertised for a bride. He dressed her in the golden jewelry that had been worn by Helen of Troy and imagined them both in Priam's rich court.

The gold Sophia wore had been worn before by people, probably

This silver cow's head with its gold horns was one of Schliemann's finds in the ancient tombs of Mycenae. The cow was a symbol of Hera, patron goddess of the city.

Heinrich Schliemann,
Mycenae

male rather than female, who lived and died a thousand years before Helen. Schliemann had dug the treasure from the second city of Troy. Helen had lived in the seventh.

But there had been a Troy, nine of them, in fact. Schliemann had proved that Homer's tales were history as well as art. His excavations at Troy brought him fame—and trouble.

He had begun digging without the permission of the Turkish government. When the Turks heard about the treasure, they insisted that it was theirs. Schliemann refused to part with his gold. He smuggled it into Greece where it was hid by Sophia's relatives.

The Turks sued and won the battle in court. Schliemann was ordered to pay the Turkish government fifty thousand francs. He was so overjoyed he sent them five times the amount. The treasure he had unearthed at Troy was easily worth a million francs and once the orders of the court had been carried out the gold was his.

He was invited to display his golden find in every capital in Europe. Nations vied for the honor of keeping the treasure on permanent display. Schliemann decided, finally, to give it to the Germans who housed it in a museum in Berlin named for its discoverer. There it remained until World War II, when it became the prize of victory and disappeared behind the Russian lines.

Following Homer's clues once more, Schliemann began to dig on the Greek Peloponnesus. He was searching for the grave of Agamemnon in ancient Mycenae.

About this leader of the Greeks, Homer told a tragic story. Returning from the Trojan War, Agamemnon had been murdered, along with many of his guests, at his own homecoming banquet. Both the feast and the deaths had been arranged by Agamemnon's wife Clytemnestra and her lover, Aegisthus.

Again at Mycenae, the spades of Schliemann's workers struck gold. In shaft graves just within the gates of the buried city they found sixteen skeletons. Little was left of them but the gold with which they had been buried. Golden masks provided portraits of these rulers of antiquity. Golden crowns and armor, vessels and statuary, jewelry and utensils told the story of their wealth and their lives.

But this time, too, Schliemann had dug deeper than he knew. These were not the graves of Agamemnon and his guests, killed at Clytemnestra's bloody banquet. These were the graves of men and women who had ruled the Peloponnesus five hundred years before the return of the Greek warrior. The death masks they wore may be seen today at the Greek National Museum of Archaeology in Athens.

Heinrich Schliemann, their discoverer, collapsed and died in the Piazza della Santa Carita, in Naples, on Christmas day, 1890. Those who came to his aid, looking for identification, found his pockets filled with gold. He clung to gold in death as he had followed it in life, around the world and into the depths of history.

South of Troy, on the eastern shore of the Mediterranean, the wealthy Sidonian kings lived many centuries ago. The Greeks called these men Phoenicians, and credited them with the invention of the alphabet.

They were a remarkable people, expert shipbuilders and sailors, miners and metalworkers, but they did not invent the alphabet. They merely borrowed it and scattered it about the world as they searched for gold. In like manner they spread products and inventions, customs and ideas, foods and plants and people.

At the time of the Trojan War, these restless pirate traders were bringing gold to their cities of Sidon and Tyre from as far away as Ireland and the western coast of Africa. Tyre, built on a rock in the sea, was described by Biblical authors as a place in which silver was heaped up as dust and fine gold as the mire of the streets.

But no king ever had enough gold. Hiram, in wealthy Tyre, needed more. South of Canaan, in divided, destitute Israel, King Soloman had no gold at all. Together, about 1000 B.C., the two kings conceived of a remarkable way to acquire the gold they needed.

It involved neither theft nor war, the traditional methods of gaining gold. It was built on a premise of continuing, voluntary cooperation between two independent nations—an idea that has more often been an ideal than an actuality. Hiram and David made their vision real.

With Hiram's help, Soloman united his kingdom and drove off his enemies. This opened a route south from Canaan to the Red Sea. Over it, gangs of Israelite porters carried ore from Hiram's copper mines and logs from his cedar forests. On the shore of the Red Sea, at Ezion-gebre, where a constant wind increased the heat of furnace fires, the ore was smelted and the logs made into ships.

Loaded with copper, the ships set sail on the Red Sea to trade their cargo for gold in distant Ophir, whose exact location has never been known. Copper from the great smelters also crossed the Mediterranean to fetch gold from Tarshish, which lay just beyond the Pillars of Hercules, in Spain. The trip to Tarshish took three years. The trip to Ophir took even longer.

When Solomon inherited the kingdom of Israel the gold that trade brought him in one year was "six hundred three score and six talents of gold," as reported in the Bible. The historian Will Durant suggests that one talent of gold in King Solomon's time might be considered the equivalent of ten thousand dollars today.

With a part of the gold King Solomon built a temple in Jerusalem. "The whole house he overlaid with gold. And the floor of the house he overlaid with gold, within and without," according to the Bible.

Jehovah's house was completed in seven years. Then the king began a house for the women in his family. The Old Testament numbers them as "seven hundred wives and three hundred concubines."

It took thirteen years to complete the palace. Each of the wings of this house of the king was four times the size of the House of the Lord. The palace was lavishly decorated and furnished with gold, from the throne to the drinking vessels. None of these were of silver, says the Bible: "For silver was nothing accounted of in the days of Solomon."

Israel's prosperity lasted for three quarters of a century. Then the pharaoh Shishak marched on the copper smelter at Ezion-geber and kept right on marching, capturing one Israelite city after another. In Jerusalem he stripped the House of the Lord and the house of Solomon of the gold that the people of Canaan and Israel had gathered for their kings from the far corners of the world.

Nebuchadnezzar gave the Israelites three hundred years to replace the gold that had been stolen by Shishak. Then he looted Jerusalem, leveled it, and marched the Israelites off to Babylon to help make that sinful city the most beautiful in the world.

King Cyrus of Persia, marching triumphantly into Babylon less than fifty years later, praised its wonders extravagantly and left them intact. While he was having himself proclaimed the son of Bel-Marduk, with a divine right to rule Babylonia, he freed the captive Israelites, returned the gold that was left from the robbery of their temple, and permitted them to go back to their homeland and rebuild Jehovah's house.

The Persian king's munificence was unexpected and unusual. The art of war—nourished by the greed for gold—had changed in the twenty-five centuries of Babylon's tortured history.

The city's first conquerors had devoured the flesh of their foes and carried off their heads as battle prizes. Later victors had taken their captives alive, to work or sell as slaves. Both had destroyed the city as they plundered its wealth.

Now Cyrus saved the metropolis, spared its gods and its gold, and sent its slaves back to rebuild their own capital. He was not prompted by generosity alone. He was farseeing. The slavery he imposed was economic rather than physical. The cities he saved, the cities he rebuilt, would yield golden tribute throughout many, many years.

It was not a new idea. Cyrus understood that to get he must also give. The warrior king was learning to govern.

He had learned some of his lessons, half a dozen years before, from Croesus, King of Lydia, in Asia Minor. Croesus was renowned for his wisdom and his wealth. His wealth came from the pale gold in the River Pactolus.

By the time Croesus gathered gold from the Pactolus, the river was already famous for its abundant treasure. Prospectors and conquerors had been harvesting its riches for centuries.

No other river known in the ancient or modern world has ever mined and milled gold for men so generously over such a long period of time. But even the fabulous Pactolus, like all gold sources, was doomed to eventual exhaustion. Roman historians reported it barren in the days of the Roman Empire. Today its very location is in doubt.

Some authorities believe that the river itself dried up and disappeared. Others identify it with the Sarabat that flows near Izmir and believe that the gold it tumbled toward the sea came from Mt. Tmolus.

The Greeks were so impressed with the wealth of the Pactolus that they felt compelled to explain how the river had been favored by the golds. The result was the story of Midas.

Long before the time of Croesus, according to the legend, a simple peasant people, the Phrygians, settled in western Asia Minor. So poor were the Phrygians that their first king, Gordius, owned nothing but a pair of oxen. His son, Midas, was a glutton and a drunkard. He had a heart of gold, but little else of value.

Despite his poverty, Midas shared what he had, even with strangers. One recipient of his hospitality turned out to be the foster father of the god Bacchus. In gratitude, Bacchus granted Midas a wish. Midas asked that everything he touched might turn to gold.

And so it did. To celebrate his wondrous new power, the joyful king ordered a banquet. But when he tried to eat, the food turned to gold as he touched it and the wine hardened in his throat. His blessing had become a curse.

Frantically, the strangling king prayed to Bacchus to take back his awful gift. The god ordered him to wash in the River Pactolus, which took his power into its own waters that then turned the rocks and sands over which they flowed to gold.

With the Greek account of the ill-fated Midas, passed on to us through the Roman poet Ovid, gold changed character. Reserved originally for gods, and then for kings, it became a lure for fools. As if to typify the kind of man who would wish for gold, the deities of Mount Olympus blessed Midas with a pair of ass's ears which he was forced to keep hidden under a cap.

Long thought to be a purely mythical character, Midas has been identified by prehistorians as the last king of the Phrygians, one of a band of European tribes who swept through the Near and Middle East at the beginning of the first millennium B.C. Defeating the Hittites who controlled the riches of the Pactolus, the Phrygians settled down in western Anatolia, now Turkey, to harvest the pale gold of the Pactolus.

For from three to five hundred years they shared this wealth, unwillingly, with the Lydians, and both nations grew rich, so rich that they attracted the wandering Cimmerians from Crimea who squatted on their eastern frontiers. The intruders maintained themselves for decades by looting their wealthy neighbors.

When Phrygia fell to the foe, never to rise again, Midas, then king, committed suicide. The persistent Cimmerians were responsible, too, for the death of the Lydian king Gyges, about whose riches the Greeks also spun elaborate tales.

Unlike the Phrygians, the Lydians made a comeback. Within a hundred years the Pactolus once more poured forth gold for their king. This king was Croesus, who used the gold to conquer much of Greece and to buy the allegiance of the Mediterranean islands he could not defeat. He won the loyalty of the subject Greeks by contributing generously to their gods. His golden offerings to Apollo, in the shrine at Delphi, included a bowl which weighed 875 pounds, a golden lion of 1000 pounds, and a four and one-half foot statue of a woman.

While Croesus was building an empire in the west, Cyrus was defeating the Medes in Persia and looking for new golden lands to conquer. It was inevitable that the two kings should meet in battle. According to Herodotus it was not the superior strength of the Persians that defeated Croesus. It was the smell of their camels, which panicked the horses of the famed Lydian cavalry.

Croesus' fate is still debated. According to one version of the story the vanquished king prepared his funeral pyre and mounted it with other prisoners. His farewell speech was so eloquent and wise that Cyrus rescued him from the flames and took him back to Persia as a trusted counselor.

Cyrus also took back some of the golden coins Croesus had minted for use in trade. Before the Persian king could start a coinage system of his own, he was killed in battle. Impartially the River Pactolus continued to pour forth gold for other kings.

The gold in the river was of generous quantity but inferior quality. Actually it was an alloy which contained varying proportions of silver, sometimes almost half. This gave it such a pale color that the ancients called it by a special name—electrum.

Despite its pallor, electrum was highly valued. Kings refused to drink from goblets made of anything else. The reason, explained Pliny, was that goblets of electrum could detect poison. They warned of its presence by hissing fiercely and flashing a bright rainbow in their bowls.

For reporting this unlikely phenomenon as fact, Pliny is still accused of gullibility. The truth is, however, that many electrum goblets behaved in exactly the manner Pliny described. When the common poison, arsenic, was poured into them, they hissed, or spit, and separated themselves from the deadly liquid with a rosy film.

The film was iron oxide. Peeled from the goblet, it came away colorless and the gold retained its original appearance to the unaided eye. Under a microscope, however, it is possible to see today that the surface of the metal was affected. It is covered with tiny beads, exuded as gas escaped with a hissing noise.

The iron, responsible for the iron-oxide film, and the sulphides and arsenates which produced the escaping gases came from the gold. Along with other impurities they had been trapped in the metal when it was concentrated under pressure in the earth during nature's mining process.

All native gold contains adulterants, most of which are driven off when the metal is fused or refined in a furnace. But gold in the ancient world was often worked cold. Heat might be applied with a primitive blowtorch to points that needed welding or annealing, but it was not enough to rid the metal of extraneous matter. The impurities that had been imprisoned in the gold when it was formed remained captive in the finished product.

Some of these can still be seen in golden objects retrieved from the Egyptian tombs. Silver alloyed with gold makes it pale, or sometimes green. Other metals, in varying proportions, produce a wide range of colors. Flecks of free platinum can be distinguished in museum pieces. Occasionally there is enough iron to attract a magnet. The sulphides and arsenates are not visible, but they are there if the gold is the kind the Greeks called *apuron*—"without fire." Moreover these compounds can be made to reveal their presence by releasing gases.

Arsenic liberates them. Making contact with the apuron gold it sets off a dramatic chain of chemical reactions by means of which the confined arsenates and sulphides escape as hissing gases and the iron forms an oxide skin on the surface of the gold. This happened not only in the goblets of the kings but also in Egyptian tombs when embalming unguents containing arsenic oozed over gold that harbored the reactive impurities.

On Tutankhamen's mummy some of the sequins that decorated his slippers had been microscopically beaded and, when they were found, bore an iron-oxide film colored from red to violet. They were intermixed with sequins which had not been changed in any way, though all of them had been exposed to ointments which contained arsenic.

The same thing happened with the goblets of the kings. Some reacted to arsenic. Some did not. The monarchs tried to assure protection against poisoning by insisting on goblets of electrum, which they considered an impure gold. It was that, since it was alloyed with silver. But it didn't necessarily contain iron and it had often been fused in a furnace, the heat of which was not enough to affect the alloy but had driven off the volatile impurities.

So in many instances electrum goblets did not protect against poison. Neither did their unlucky owners live to tell of the betrayal. Kings who owed their lives to the timely warning of a hissing, flashing goblet spread the tale of the death-defying magic of pale gold. As the stories multiplied, goblets of pale gold ceased to be an extravagance. Their possession became imperative, a matter of life or death.

FROM HADES

THE FIRST GOLD RUSH of record was started by the Phoenician Cadmus, who left his native Canaan sometime in the fourteenth century B.C. to look for gold in the north. He found it in Greece and, wrote Strabo, "carried thither the alphabet and other germs of civilization."

In a similar way gold seekers have ever blazed the trail into new lands, building cities where none were before, spreading and mixing religions, cultures, and technology. Sometimes the cities died when the gold was gone. Sometimes they lived on, supported by the by-products of the search for gold—other metals, lumber, new agricultural products.

Miners and metallurgists were among the world's first specialists, explains V. Gordon Childe, a leading authority on the development of civilization. "The operations of mining and smelting and casting are too elaborate and demand too continuous attention to be normally conducted in the intervals of tilling fields or minding cattle. Metallurgy is a full-time job."

Miners, therefore, had to carry civilization with them when they searched for gold. With priests and magicians they were dependent on others for the food they ate and the clothes they wore. With these specialists began the division of labor that characterizes today's world.

Because their work was unique it was considered mysterious by their neighbors. Miners who could turn river sands into gold, metallurgists who could melt rock into the coveted metal, goldsmiths who could turn the metal into magic charms or likenesses of the gods were thought to possess supernatural powers.

Their exploits were much admired but little understood. Mythology dressed up accounts of early gold rushes with magic, gods, and dragons. One of the more famous of these tales was that of Jason and the Golden Fleece.

The patriotic Greeks who told the story insisted that the gold mine Cadmus had found on Greek soil was the first mine in the world. And the world's first ship was built by Argo to carry Jason and the Argonauts to the eastern shore of the Black Sea in search of the Golden Fleece.

Jason and the Argonauts were descendants of Cadmus. Once in their kingdom there had been a ram with a golden fleece. The color of his coat gave him magic powers. He could fly. And for this reason the Thessalians lost him.

Fearing her faithless husband might kill their children, Nephele, the queen of Thessaly, placed her son and daughter on the back of the ram and bid him fly with them to the end of the Black Sea. The daughter fell into the water, but the ram carried the boy, Phryxus, safely to the kingdom of the Colchis, in the region of the Caucasus.

Phryxus sacrificed the ram to the gods in gratitude for a safe journey and assured himself a welcome in a strange land by presenting the golden fleece to the king. The king valued it so highly that he placed it in a sacred grove under the protection of a dragon who never slept.

It was this fleece that Jason and the Argonauts set out to retrieve. Like many more recent gold seekers they endured incredible hardships. But with the help of the Colchian princess, Medea, Jason slew the dragon and made off with the fleece and Medea as well.

This was the popular version of the story. In truth, Jason and the Argonauts built their ship and undertook their hazardous journey for the same reason that the conquistadores set out across the Atlantic, because they heard that there was gold to be had at the end of the journey.

They may well have brought back some of the gold in glittering fleece, for sheepskins were the sluice boxes of the ancient world. The skins were placed on the bottom of gold-bearing streams. The force of the water pushed light sand over the pelts. The heavier particles of gold were trapped in the tangled, greasy wool. The oilier the wool, the more effectively it clung to the gold, which has an affinity for oil. This characteristic, exploited by gold washers at the dawn of history, is still used by modern metallurgists in the flotation process.

The early Persian kings, trying to cheat the Persian Gulf of the gold that tumbled down the Tigris and Euphrates during the annual floods, kept armies of naked slaves tending sheepskins in the rivers day and night during the period of rapid flow. By the time of Darius I, whose thirty-six year reign began about 521 B.C., this placer-mining operation was so well organized that the riverbeds were lined with wool continuously for hundreds of feet.

Even the float gold, carried in suspension in the water, was caught by the slaves who held the skins stretched taut against the current between them. Long caravans of camels carried bales of fresh hides to the gold washers and bales of golden fleece to the king in his wealthy capital of Persepolis.

When the sheepskins were taken from the water, the coarser gold was collected and the pelts hung to dry in the sun. The curly wool, coated with minute particles of glittering gold, as if the metal had snowed from the sky, presented a sight every bit as breathtaking as Bel-Marduk's ziggurat in Babylon. Dried, the skins were shaken and the nap beaten with sticks to thresh the specks of metal from the wool.

The gold that men found in rivers was eroded from the mountains through which the gushing streams cut their paths. The metal was tumbled downhill to settle heavily in depressions in the riverbed. These pockets of wealth are called placer deposits. Washing them from their hiding places is called placer mining. It is a comparatively easy way to get gold, for the original digging is done by water.

But nature's methods are slow and man is impatient. Early in his history he learned to follow gold-laden rivers upstream to find the original home of the metal and dig it out himself.

Deeper and deeper he followed the auriferous ore into the dark underground world he had formerly reserved for the dead, surprised to find in this kingdom of Hades a storehouse of treasure for the living. Not only gold but silver, copper, iron, and lead were to be had for the digging.

To locate gold hidden in the earth, men employed the golden

bough. Originally this was a branch of the mistletoe, which grew mysteriously, without roots, planted in the air and nourished and cared for by the sun. As gold was a child of the sun, so was this strange vine, with fruit the color of pale gold.

The magic and kinship of the two was employed to find buried gold, and the divining rod was born. It is still used today, made of a variety of woods and even of metal, to search for gold, water, oil —anything men wish to find beneath the earth.

It is a forked stick, which no longer has to be a branch of mistletoe. The tines are grasped firmly by the diviner who moves slowly over the ground, holding the rod out straight before him.

It was thought by those who first used branches of mistletoe above the ground to search for gold below, that one child of the sun would pull the other to it. If there was gold in the earth the branch would bend toward it. Restrained, it would writhe and wriggle in the diviner's hands, trying to answer the call of its divine brother.

If gold was later found where the rod had failed to indicate its presence, the answer was obvious. The wood of the rod was of the wrong sort or, if of mistletoe, it had been cut at the wrong time or in the wrong way. It was quite possible that the diviner himself, through a flaw in his nature, had prevented the transmission of vibrations from the treasure in the ground to the rod above. Miners themselves who live in hope of the lucky strike have never been immune to magic.

More dependable than the divining rod, then and now, is dirt scratched from the earth by burrowing animals. These busy little diggers have been credited, quite properly, with many important gold discoveries. The first gold of the famous Comstock lode, for instance, was dug by a ground squirrel.

Animals burrowing in gold country are prone to find gold because they dig in the softest earth. This is often the weathered outcrop of a gold-bearing vein, exactly the kind of easily extracted treasure for which prospectors are searching.

Many early historians felt that if animals found gold they must have been searching for it. Hearsay stories were passed on as fact. In distant lands noted for their wealth in the precious metals, it was believed that animals not only found gold but mined it. Men merely had to take it from them.

The ease of acquisition in this case contrasted sharply with the difficulties of underground mining. In "Happy Arabia," it was reported erroneously that ants dug the gold. In "Miserable Kush," gold was taken from the earth by men.

In Arabia, according to Agatharchides of Cnidus, writing about 200 B.C., gold was found in chunks, "the smallest pieces not less than an olive stone and the biggest a walnut." The happy Arabians wore these nuggets in strings around their wrists and necks, and even the poorest people of the land used nothing but gold for tableware.

Several ancient writers attested to the industry with which the ants dug holes in the sand and drew forth the gold. The only problem the Arabians had was getting the gold from the ants. It was a problem they shared with the people of India, Tibet, and Siberia, where insects and animals were also reported to be zealous miners.

Gold-digging ants were somewhat oversized. The historian Herodotus described them as slightly smaller than gods but larger than foxes. They were as ferocious as lions. They dug gold in the cool of the day and rested during the heat. This gave men a chance to steal the gold while the ants were sleeping. But the thieves had to be swift and stealthy or the ants would awake and give chase, "and not a man of them could be saved," Herodotus reported.

The courageous Persians captured the dangerous creatures and took them home to perform at the court of the king. The geographer Strabo's human robbers were less sporting. Rather than take their chances with watchful insects, they scattered poisoned grain for the ants who did their mining.

Pliny the Elder had the ants digging in India, a country famous for the pure gold and silver islands which were supposed to lie within the mouth of the Indus River. The Indian ants were the color of cats, the size of wolves, and could, when angry, outrun any other animal. When their gold was stolen they chased the camels that bore it away and tore apart both the beasts and their riders. "Such is the speed and savagery the love of gold awakens in them," Pliny explained.

The ants who dug gold on the Red Sea islands that lay between Happy Arabia and Ethiopia had to contend with thieves from both shores. The Ethiopians were particularly adept at making off with the gold. Each morning they fitted brood mares with open, empty saddlebags and rowed them in boats to the islands, keeping their foals confined on shore. While the mares grazed through the day, the ants dug gold and, having nowhere else to store it, stuffed it in the gaping saddlebags. When the bags were plump with treasure, the robbers on the mainland led the foals to the edge of the water. Seeing their mothers in the distance, the hungry babies cried. The mares answered their call by plunging into the sea and swimming to shore, carrying milk for their offspring and gold for their masters, and leaving the deceived ants with nothing to show for their hard day's labor.

Not ants, but foxes dug gold in Siberia, mounding it in hills for men to collect. In Tibet, griffons scratched gold from the barren rocks on which they nested, but no one dared to take it from them. The sharp claws that tore apart rocks with ease made short work of flesh and bones.

In Miserable Kush, Egypt's eastern desert, also called Akita, there were no birds, or animals, or insects to do the mining. Nor was there any food or water. An expedition to take gold from this desert wasteland could be more perilous than a military campaign against the strongest enemy.

In 524 B.C., the Persian king, Cambyses, son of Cyrus, had little trouble conquering the kingdom along the Nile, but when he tried to capture the gold-rich deserts east and south he found his army of 50,000 men unequal to the task. They ran out of food and water, ate all their pack animals, and were finally forced to draw lots, sacrificing every tenth man to nourish the others.

Cambyses got back to Persepolis alive, but insane. Four years later, in his beautiful golden palace, he committed suicide.

Despite the treachery of the deserts and the high, barren mountains that had to be crossed to get to gold, the Egyptians found the metal and mined it long before they settled down to plant crops and build cities in the fertile valley of the Nile. They marked the way to the mines by drawing pictures on rocks—perhaps the world's first maps. Centuries later these rock carvings led the pharaohs to gold. The trails became royal roads and the signs on the rocks were transcribed to papyrus.

Eventually, roads leading to gold mines branched out from the Nile in all directions. The Egyptian pharaohs sent gold-mining expeditions east to Miserable Kush and the Sinai peninsula, west to Libya, and south to the Sudan and Ethiopia.

All the roads led through deserts. Over them armies of soldiers marched armies of slave "gold washers" to distant mines to bring back gold for the sons of the sun. Or the soldiers compelled the natives in the gold fields to produce the metal.

On a commemorative stele, Sa-Hathor, an assistant treasurer under the pharaoh Amenemhet II, boasted: "I visited the minelands as a youth and I forced the chiefs to wash gold."

Sa-Hathor was named after Hathor, the goddess of the mines, often called The Golden One. For some reason she was also the goddess of love and had the body of a cow. In the temple of Redesieh, the goddess is quoted as saying to the pharaoh Seti I: "I have given to thee the gold countries."

Seti had always had the gold countries. He raised the temple with its inscription to thank the gods for water, without which the gold countries were useless to him.

His attempts to drill wells along the roads that led to Miserable Kush had failed repeatedly. At that time the Egyptians had no camels. The donkeys and men sent to "wash" gold could not carry enough water for the journey in their gourds. By the time they reached the mines all the donkeys and half the slaves had died of thirst. Seti drilled many dry holes more than two hundred feet deep before he finally reached water at Redesieh, thirty-seven miles from the Nile, and built the temple to celebrate his achievement.

Before this he had been able to get gold only in Nubia, in the northern Sudan. The name Nubia comes from the Egyptian word *nub,* which means gold. In this Gold Country, the metal had been mined before the memory of man. The ruins of cisterns which stored water, and the sloping stone tables on which the gold was separated from the sand are still to be found on the Nubian desert. Along with gold from Nubia, the Egyptians brought back slaves to work the mines in Miserable Kush.

Ramses II (*ca.* 1315 to 1225 B.C.) was more successful at finding water than his father, Seti, had been. On his stelae he explained that his ability to make water flow in the desert was a gift from Hopi, the god of the Nile, with whom he was a special favorite.

He was apparently a favorite of all the gods. He lived ninety years. His income from the gold mines has been estimated at almost

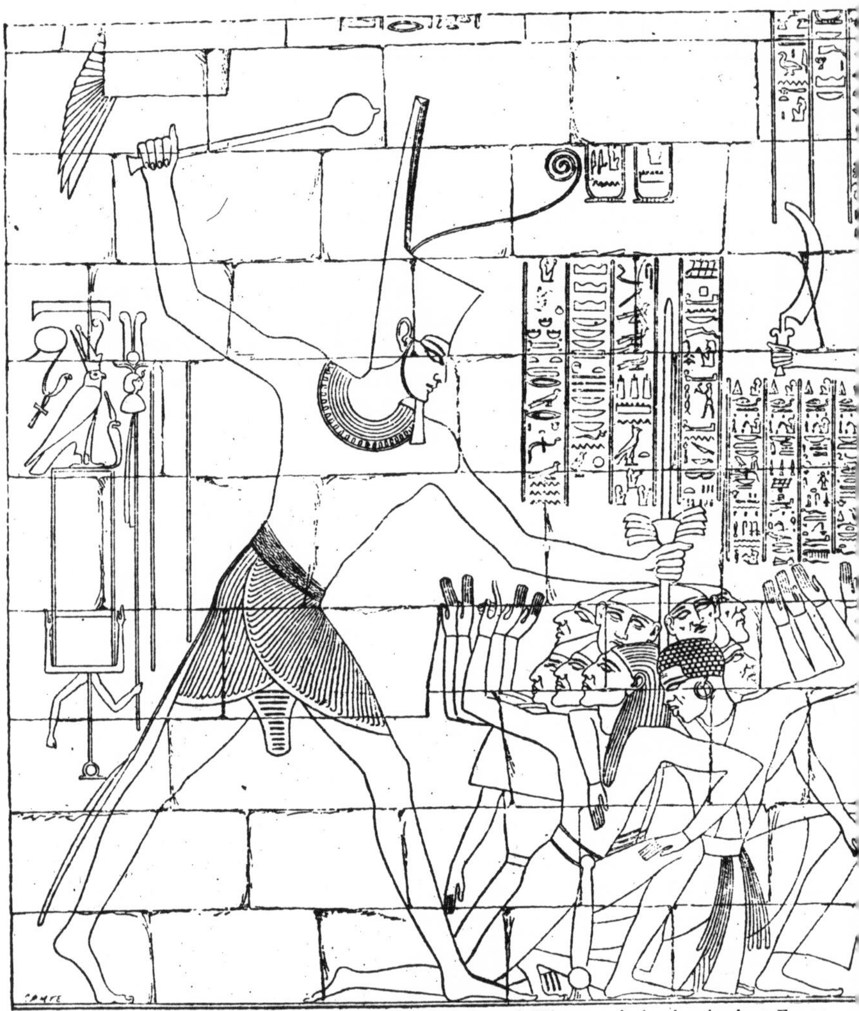

Georges Perrot and Charles Chipiez, *A History of Art in Ancient Egypt*

Egyptian pharaoh Seti I put war prisoners to work in the gold mines of Miserable Kush, where they died in great numbers. Since slaves were plentiful, it was more economical to replace them than to provide food and water. In this frieze from the great temple at Karnak, Seti is shown striking prisoners with his mace.

half a billion dollars annually. But he used gold faster than his slaves could dig it.

He supported a hundred wives and all their children. Every year he ordered more than five hundred pounds of gold made into idols, statues, shrines, and temple spires for the gods. When the mines didn't supply enough gold for his many needs he stripped the memorials of his ancestors to make memorials of his own.

About fifty years before Christ, Lucretius wrote: "What malignant breath is exhaled by gold mines! How it acts upon men's features and complexions! Have you not seen or heard how speedily men die and how their vital forces fail when they are driven by necessity to endure such work?"

At the same time, Diodorus Siculus set down his impressions of the Egyptian gold mines which he had visited. They had been seen and similarly described a century before by Agatharchides. They were, even then, thousands of years old, and unchanged.

They were worked by droves of slaves sent out under military escort whenever gold was needed. Even after water wells were dug near the mines and along the roads, the marches took their toll of human lives. In a land of burning sun and blowing sand, whole caravans lost their way, to wander aimlessly in the hostile desert until all died of thirst and hunger.

Desert gods resented intruders. Powerful spells and many sacrifices were necessary to get the gold washers safely to the mines. To get them back again, alert and well-armed guards were needed, for bands of nomadic desert bandits lay in wait for the gold-laden travelers.

For the soldiers who escorted the slaves to the mines, the assignment was difficult and unpopular. The remains of the stone huts that sheltered them and the guards and overseers who worked the vast number of slaves can still be seen near the ancient mine shafts. It took as many as two thousand of the crude stone hovels to house these supervisors. Men who could successfully command these gigantic undertakings were rewarded by burial in tombs recording their accomplishments.

A man named Ameni, "Superintendent of the Expeditions to the Mines," was laid to rest in one such tomb. On the walls, the story of an excursion to Nubia, about 2000 B.C., was inscribed: "I went to fetch gold for his Majesty, may he live forever. I went with a company of four hundred men of the choicest of my soldiers who by good fortune arrived safely without loss of any of their number. I brought the gold I was ordered to bring and the king's son honored me."

Diodorus described Miserable Kush as a black land streaked with bands of remarkable whiteness. These streaks were the quartz veins which contained the gold. The earliest mines were trenches, or open cuts, sliced into the gold-bearing quartz. But even before they had tools more efficient than stone hammers, the Egyptians were digging tunnels which followed the veins of ore deep into the earth.

The dark, narrow passages wriggled underground, wherever the quartzite ore led. Rarely were the adits large enough for a miner to stand upright. Often he had to crawl on his belly like a snake.

Diodorus couldn't count the slaves working at the mines. They were of "infinite" number—criminals, prisoners of war, or merely the families, relatives, and friends of men the pharaoh disliked. They were bound in fetters and closely guarded so that there was no possibility of escape.

Slaves were relatively cheap and plentiful. Transporting provisions to the inaccessible gold mines was an expensive and arduous undertaking. So the pharaohs found it economically expedient to replace the slaves rather than to feed and clothe them.

They were worked naked, without food, water, or rest, driven to their tasks by the blows of their guards and overseers. "Until," wrote Diodorus, "they fall dead in the midst of their insufferable labors."

Burning torches flickered feebly in the underground darkness of the mine's galleries. The solid rock at the end of an adit was broken by setting great fires against the face. The fire cracked the rock, a process that was further facilitated by splashing the hot wall with water, to cool it quickly. Scarce water was denied the miners that it might be used in the mining process itself.

This method of breaking ground was expensive in terms of human life. The fires robbed the air of oxygen and filled it with deadly fumes. The miners who were not overcome by lack of air were in constant danger of being crushed by falling rock or scalded by the steam that filled the narrow working as they doused the heated ore with water.

Besides cracking the rock, the fire volatilized its impurities. The more dangerous of these was arsenical oxide. To quote Agricola, men who inhaled this fallout "swelled immediately and lost all movement and feeling and died without pain."

Death was slower and more agonizing for those who came after the poison had settled to the ground. If they disturbed and inhaled the sediment, Agricola noted, their hands and feet swelled and became spherical and useless. Their lungs rotted slowly and they lost their sight. When they had walked or crawled on the infected ground the poison ate away the flesh, leaving deep, ulcerous wounds.

Everybody worked at getting the gold—the aged, the lame, the sick, the women, the children. Only death brought rest.

The stronger men broke the rock beneath the ground. Children carried the heavy chunks of ore in great baskets through the winding galleries to the outside mill. There the older men and women hammered and ground the rock until it was like flour.

On an inclined bed of stone, enfeebled workers poured the precious water they were not allowed to drink over sheets of the rock flour, rubbing the muddy mixture with their hands to aid the separation process. The gold clung to the rough bed while the water washed the rock dust away.

The grains of metal were gathered from the slab with sponges and placed in earthen pots. A little salt was added, along with barley bran and a lump of lead. The salt acted as a flux which helped the grains of metal fuse together. The barley bran was a reducing agent used to remove oxidizable impurities. The lead acted as a scorifier, uniting with nonoxidizable adulterants to form a slag. Sometimes tin was placed in the pots also, to harden the gold.

The pots were sealed with clay and baked in an oven for five days and nights. The clay of the crucible absorbed everything but the tin which was alloyed with the gold during the baking process. When the pot was cooled and broken open, the gold emerged in a brilliant, solid lump.

When enough of these gleaming yellow briquettes had been formed, or when the soldiers ran out of provisions or there weren't enough living slaves to continue the mining, the precious gold was carried back over the long road through the desert to the capital city on the Nile. There it was made into glittering memorials to the gods or buried again, with the mummies of the kings, in the underground kingdom of Hades from which it had come.

Wrote Diodorus: "The working of gold is done with all this toil, for nature makes it clear that gold has a laborious begetting, a hard guarding, the greatest covetousness, and its use lies between pleasure and pain."

The mines of Miserable Kush yielded gold to the Egyptian pharaohs for more than three thousand years. Nineteenth-century prospectors looking for the metal tried to find it in the heaps of tailings outside the ancient mines. They found instead that the extraction methods of Sa-Hathor and Ameni had been as thorough as those of any modern mining company.

They turned their attention to the old, caved galleries, some of which curved and twisted beneath the ground from a desert entry, six miles inland, to the shore of the Red Sea. Though the mines had been worked for centuries, there were still shoots and pockets of unexploited ore. In 1899, several English mining companies reopened the ancient diggings. Before they closed them again, in 1921, they took out three million dollars in gold and an incredible number of human bones.

Royal Metal *classical times to the Renaissance*

ENSHRINED

IN THE SEVENTH CENTURY B.C., Periander, dictator of Corinth, faced an economic crisis. There was no gold in the city's treasury.

Even today a government without a gold reserve to back its currency is in trouble. In Periander's day gold *was* currency. It performed all the duties we now expect of paper francs and dollars, bank checks, charge accounts, deferred payments, and a multitude of complicated credit arrangements which were then nonexistent.

The only substitute for gold available to Periander was another metal, and other metals had the disadvantage of deteriorating in value as gold grew scarcer and silver and copper proportionately more abundant. This had been happening throughout Greece for several generations.

The mines and placer deposits that had yielded gold for former kings were no longer productive. Gold from foreign lands was acquired not by rulers but by traders. Long before Periander's time the merchants had used their gold to depose kings and set up their own governments presided over by elected councils which were sometimes controlled, in turn, by dictators. The wealthy merchants could eliminate Periander in the same way, by offering gold to his armies, his governmental servants, his friendly allies, his subjects, and his gods.

The gold of the merchants was always in sight. Without banks in which to keep it these pioneers of commerce used their dwellings and their women as treasuries. Profits, capital assets, and savings were stockpiled in the form of golden jewelry, statues, vases, tableware, and even as cloth and chamber pots.

In public, wives and daughters advertised the wealth of the men who owned them. Gold was interwoven in the fabric of their clothes. It bordered hems and flounces and was attached to the surface of the cloth as spangles. Jewelry was heavy, elaborate, and abundant, dangling from ears and throats, circling heads, arms, and ankles. Social standing was measured by the quality and quantity of a woman's golden adornments. Vanity would not allow a lady to display herself without also displaying her master's wealth.

Periander counted on this custom to solve his financial troubles. He invited the women of Corinth to a huge civic festival. When they were assembled in their glittering gold, the dictator gave a signal to his army. The soldiers swooped down on the gathering and stripped the ladies of their treasure, including their gowns. Modesty impelled them to take cover instead of revenge. The contribution they unwillingly made to the city's finances allowed the wily Periander to rule for forty prosperous years.

Periander was not the first ruler, nor the last, forced to take extreme measures to alleviate a crippling shortage of gold. Women have often been denied the right to wear gold jewelry. Plato advocated the restriction in the *Laws.* Today India is trying to limit the amount of gold jewelry each woman may possess.

In other countries of the modern world gold jewelry is permitted citizens who are not allowed to use gold as currency either in the form of coins or bullion. This, too, is an ancient method of conserving gold. It was part of the code of laws which Lycurgus introduced in Sparta.

These laws forebade citizens of the city to own either gold or silver and made iron the official currency. As a result, men were forced to exchange their purses for wagons and ox teams to get their money to the marketplace. Lycurgus insisted that the new laws had been dictated to him by the oracle at Delphi, an explanation which did not save him from the wrath of the outraged Alcander who struck out one of the legislator's eyes.

A more popular method of dealing with a gold shortage was to look for gold in other lands. The Greeks did this too. Following the example of Jason and his Argonauts, Greek colonists searched for gold from the eastern edge of the Black Sea to the western end of the Mediterranean, spreading their people and their culture and expanding their trade frontiers.

Then as now, finding gold was only a small part of establishing and maintaining a continuous supply. Many of the gold mines the Greeks opened on the island of Sicily had to be abandoned when they were flooded by underground water.

Archimedes, perhaps the greatest of ancient scientists, applied himself to the problem of draining these mines. He improved old methods and developed new pumps and the famous Archimedean screw. His inventions not only saved mines in Sicily but are still used today in primitive parts of the world in both mining and irrigation. According to Vitruvius, the Roman architect and engineer who made himself an authority on Greek technology, Archimedes discovered the principles of hydrostatics by devoting himself to the practical problems of mining and testing gold.

The Greeks were successful in their search for gold not only in Sicily and Italy but also in Macedonia and Thrace, north of the Greek peninsula, and on the eastern shores of the Mediterranean. These rich sources of gold extended Greek frontiers beyond the little independent nations' abilities to defend them. Greek settlements along the eastern shore of the Mediterranean found themselves subject first to Croesus of Lydia and then to Cyrus of Persia. The gold the Greeks had found enriched not Greece but Persia.

Not fifty years after Cyrus had captured these Greek colonies the Persians controlled every major source of gold from the Nile to the Indus. From the conquered countries, known as satrapies, gold flowed to the ancient Persian City of Susa at the rate of an estimated $200 million a year.

Each satrapy was assigned an annual donation. Egypt contributed 700 talents a year. Babylon's quota was 1000 talents. Asia Minor's was almost twice that. India was taxed 4600 talents annually.

In the days of the Persian king, Darius I, the old capital of Susa grew so busy and noisy as a gold collection center that Darius moved his court to Persepolis. There he built what many called the most beautiful city in the world.

It was known as Paradise, which it seemed to be. Magnificent palaces housed the loveliest women on earth, brought with gold from Persia's subject countries. The king's harem was necessarily large, for no woman was allowed to share the royal couch twice. For the diversion of the monarch and his ladies there were artificial lakes and well-stocked hunting preserves. Everything else that surrounded the king was of gold, including the canopy that shaded him from the sun and the chariot in which he rode.

The wealth and grandeur of Persepolis impressed the emissaries from the satrapies, as it was meant to do. They carried back to the subject countries stories of fabulous riches displayed at the capital and buried, as golden bullion, in both Persepolis and Susa.

These tales were the most effective kind of propaganda, for all who heard them knew that the gold could be turned into invincible military power. Not only would it buy troops and arms to fight for Persia—it could be expected to lure away the armies fighting for less wealthy kings. The display of gold at Persepolis kept subject nations loyal and caused smaller states to seek the protection of their wealthy neighbor.

Persian gold also brought trade advantages. For purposes of trade, the metal was minted into darics, or "pieces of gold." Against these golden coins Greek drachmas, made of silver, bid at a disadvantage for rare luxuries and even for the grain Greece had to import to adequately feed her population.

The Greeks minted gold into the coins they called staters only when silver would not buy needed troops, allies, or food for import. Gold was saved for these emergencies in Greek temples. There it glorified the gods, courting their favor, and they in turn were expected to protect it from thieves and enemies.

According to legend, Apollo did just that when the Persians marched on the gold that had been dedicated to him in his shrine at Delphi. This collection of gold was the largest in Greece and represented at least a part of the gold reserve of every Greek city-state. Some of the metal was in the form of bullion. More of it had been fashioned into shapes that might be pleasing to the deity.

Marching westward, the Persians had already captured the rich gold mines owned by Athens in Thrace and Macedonia. This was their main objective. Only soldiers looking for loot ventured into the mountain vastness that hid the treasure of Delphi. Though this was but a small part of the mighty Persian army, it was a larger contingent than the Greeks could defeat without divine help.

Through the oracle at the shrine, Apollo told the Greeks to

leave the defense of the sacred Delphi gold to him. The Greek warriors retreated. In their place Apollo sent forth the ghosts of long dead heroes equipped with their arms which had been consecrated at the shrine.

Attacked by these brave and invisible warriors the Persians fell back in fright, but the Greek god did not let them escape. He pelted them with bolts of lightning and crushed them by rolling down great crags from Mount Parnassus.

To recapture the mines of Thrace and Macedonia and drive the Persians from Greek soil many Greek city-states joined Athens in the Confederacy of Delos, so named because the gold each contributed to the cause was stored in a temple on the sacred island of Delos. The confederacy collected less gold, it was charged by Greece's defenders, than some Greek states collected from the Persians for the aid they gave the enemy.

Still the Persians did not buy victory. When they retreated at last there was gold left in the war fund at Delos, and Athens, though burned to the ground, was strong enough to appropriate it for herself. With this stolen treasure and the gold that poured again from the mines in the north, the dictator Pericles rebuilt and beautified the city.

To design the new capital, the ruins of which still grace the Acropolis, Pericles called on the most famous architects, artists, and engineers in Greece.

Among them was Pheidias, the renowned sculptor, who labored for years on three statues of Athene, the city's patron goddess, who would guard the city's gold reserve as Apollo guarded the gold at Delphi. Pheidias also designed and executed the bas-relief sculptures that decorated Athene's temples, the Hegatompedon and Parthenon, which also served as Athens' capitol and mint.

In these sacred and busy buildings, silver was made into drachmas and gold into staters. Both were impressed with the Athenian owl, which became as dependable a guarantee of the weight and metal content of the coins as the stamp of Croesus had once been. Traders flocked to Athens to trade gold, to deposit it, to borrow it. For a brief period the gold shortage that had crippled Greek trade was overcome, and Athens became the commercial center of the Mediterranean world.

In 438 B.C., Pheidias unveiled the thirty-eight-foot ivory-and-gold

Fratelli Alinari

Pheidias' towering gold-and-ivory statue of Athene no longer adorns the Parthenon, but this small Roman copy gives us an idea of its grandeur. The goddess wore 2,500 pounds of gold, which was fastened on so that it could be removed in an emergency.

statue of Athene which he had created for the Parthenon temple. It was so placed that throughout the day the sun shone on the ivory face of the virgin goddess of wisdom and chastity and was reflected with a blinding intensity from the gold of her crown and robes.

The statue was a religious memorial, a work of art, and a gold reserve. The twenty-five hundred pounds of gold that adorned the goddess were fastened to her figure so that they could be quickly removed in case of an emergency.

In arranging this with the sculptor, Pericles had been thinking of war. As it turned out, Pheidias was forced to strip the goddess of her golden raiment almost as soon as he had completed his work to protect himself against a charge of theft. Unfortunately, when the gold was weighed there was less than the sculptor had been issued. He was convicted of theft and fined forty talents of gold.

The people of Olympia refused to believe him guilty. They offered to pay his fine if he would make a chryselephantine likeness of Zeus for their city. For them, Pheidias created his masterpiece.

His Olympian Zeus, seated on a throne of ivory, ebony, and gold, was sixty feet high. The god wore a crown of golden olive branches and leaves, held a gold-and-ivory statue of Victory in his right hand and a golden scepter inlaid with precious stones in his left. He wore golden sandals, and his golden robe was engraved with flowers.

So magnificent was the statue that when it was completed the god Zeus himself struck the pavement before it with a bolt of lightning to show his approval. The man the Athenians had accused of theft proved himself an artist beloved of the gods.

Athens' years of glory came to an end in the Peloponnesian war. Shortly after Pericles' death, in 429 B.C., the gold from the statue of Athene in the Parthenon was removed once more to finance this campaign against Sparta.

As the Greeks fought one another, the Persians struck again, capturing the gold mines of Macedonia and Thrace and sending back to Susa the four thousand pounds of gold the mines produced each year. The Greek city-states were too weak and war weary to resist the new invasion. It fell to the Hellenized Macedonians to free the world's gold from the grip of the Persians.

King Philip of Macedonia battled a decade to recapture the mines that had produced gold for Athens during her golden years. The conquest he started was completed by his son Alexander.

In 334 B.C. the young warrior king set forth on his mission. With 5000 horses and 30,000 foot soldiers he invaded Egypt, had himself crowned pharaoh, and laid out a new capital city, Alexandria, at the mouth of the Nile. Then he marched on through Palestine toward Babylon. At Arbela the king of Persia, Darius III, met him with an army of 600,000 soldiers.

To pay his mercenaries, Darius had loaded six hundred mules and three hundred camels with eight thousand talents of gold. He himself rode on a golden throne on a gold-pillared phaeton shaded by a golden canopy and drawn by gold-caparisoned horses. Since he did not expect his encounter with the little Greek army to be much of a battle he also took with him his wife, his daughter, and several hundred concubines. Five days were required for this mighty contingent to cross the Euphrates on a bridge of boats.

As Darius had predicted, the encounter at Arbela was not much of a battle. The small, cohesive fighting machine led by Alexander quickly routed the confused hordes assembled by the Persians. Darius didn't wait for the end of the contest. Fearing he had lost his army and possibly his empire, he chose to save his gold.

By the time his generals found him, the gold was gone and so were the slaves that had been part of his retinue. The generals assumed that both had been buried. Before they could find out where, one of their number had killed the king.

Turning detective, the defeated Persians traced the lost gold to Ecbatana, now Hamadan, in northwestern Iran. There, fortune hunters have been digging for the buried treasure for centuries, with no more luck than Darius' generals had in 331 B.C.

In Babylon, Alexander's soldiers fared better. The people welcomed them, gave food, wine, women, and gold. But the king would not tarry. Susa waited—that city which had been collecting the world's gold for a century and a half. There Alexander helped himself to 50,000 talents in gold, roughly equivalent to $300 million.

Still he didn't stop. He rushed his troops over the mountains to Persepolis and gave them the Persian capital to do with as they would. They looted the palaces and the royal treasury, raped the women, killed the men, and burned what may have been the world's most beautiful city.

Carrying their spoils over mountains and through deserts, the

Macedonians marched on. They captured gold-rich Bactria and the wealth of fabled India. For almost nine years they trudged and fought their way farther and father from their homeland.

Alexander was a generous general. The least of his soldiers dragged behind him the assorted booty of the lands he had helped win and spoil—gold and silver in the strange forms of foreign gods, bullion and coins, royal scepters and diadems, jewelry and rare gems, slaves of many colors, and women of many tongues.

But with all their wealth, the campaigners were also tired, footsore, ragged, maimed, diseased, almost always hungry and often without water for days at a time. In the Indian desert, ten thousand died of heat and thirst. The survivors, defying their general's orders, turned toward home. In the face of more hardships, gold had lost its allure.

The empire Alexander won lasted little longer than his campaign of conquest, but his contribution to the western world was none the less significant. Marching through the East he released the gold the Persians had monopolized and immobilized for the greater part of two centuries. No longer did most of the world's gold flow into the vaults at Susa. Instead, from East and West, it poured into the world's markets.

As gold began to circulate, it stimulated trade. Since in its new abundance it was readily available in exchange, substitutes became acceptable in its place. Silver was no longer discriminated against. Merchants were not forced to restrict their commercial activities to the markets where one metal was available or the other acceptable. They were free to roam the world. As they did, commerce expanded and grew and the merchant nations of the West prospered.

The man who had given Persia's gold to the world did not live to help reap the harvest. In 323 B.C., at the age of thirty-three, he died in Babylon from the bite of a malarial mosquito. A part of the gold he had won was made into a golden sarcophagus in which his remains rested in Alexandria. But even that memento of his conquest was destined to be taken from him by Egypt's ruler, Ptolemy Cocces, who melted down the gold for his own purposes.

CONQUERED

WHEN ROME CONQUERED SPAIN, in the middle of the second century B.C., that El Dorado of the ancient world had been pouring out gold for foreign masters for many hundreds of years, and still the rich placer deposits were not exhausted. Strabo described Rome's new acquisition with enthusiasm:

"The gold is not got by mining alone, but is also washed down. Rivers and torrents carry down the golden sand: it is also to be found in waterless districts, though there it is invisible . . . . . They lead water to the arid spots and so make the gold dust glitter. Nuggets of up to half a pound in weight are said to be found sometimes in the gold dust and these need little refining: they say, too, that when stones are split, little nuggets like nipples are found. In the river beds the sand is carried along in the stream and then washed in troughs by the river." From Spain, Rome took ten thousand pounds of gold a year.

Today when we rarely see or handle gold it is difficult to realize the importance of the metal to the Romans. At the time of the Roman Republic, both the political structure and the trading economy were much like our own except that both required large amounts of gold, not as a reserve for currency but as currency itself. Gold bought political power at home and imports from abroad.

Rome was a trading nation which had neither agricultural surpluses nor manufactured goods to exchange for the imports on which the people depended for their very existence. The city's main export was gold. This was true even after the Romans developed a complicated and sophisticated system of credit finance which included mints and coinage, banks and bank notes, money lenders and money changers, letters of credit and promissory notes.

These innovations were useful in business dealings within the city and with merchants of other advanced nations, but such negotiations formed the lesser part of the extensive commercial activities in which the Romans engaged. In most of the world, and even among the ordinary citizens of Rome, banks were suspect or unknown and Roman paper was worthless. The merchants themselves who used paper substitutes for gold in their commercial dealings continued to save and display their personal wealth as they had always done in the form of golden furnishings and jewelry.

Rome's dependence on gold was reflected in the growth of the empire. First one gold-producing country and then another was annexed until, at its peak, the empire included every source of gold then known to the western world.

Not all the gold Rome conquered found its way back to the temple treasuries in the capital city. It was accepted practice for conquering generals and governing praetors to serve without salary in the provinces, paying themselves and their armies with a share of the gold that came from the mines they captured or supervised. The proportion of gold they took was often much larger than the amount they sent back to Rome.

When Julius Caesar was sent to Spain as praetor in the seventh century B.C., his debts totaled $7,500,000. When he returned, a year later, he paid off everything he owed with Spanish gold and had enough left over to buy his way into the First Triumvirate, formed in 60 B.C.

Rome was then a republic and votes were bought with gold. The voters would accept no substitute. Each returning general or territorial governor seeking political power distributed gold among the citizens. Since the most generous could expect to gain office, competition was keen. The demand for gold for political purposes continually raised the interest rates charged by the temple bankers and money changers.

Buying votes became such an expensive proposition that many candidates for office considered it cheaper, if more dangerous, to eliminate rivals. The price for this service rose also and was payable only in gold. In 82 B.C., when one of Rome's first dictators, Sulla, decorated the Forum with the heads of his slain enemies, each head represented an investment of gold equivalent to ten thousand dollars. By the time of the Second Triumvirate, less than forty years later, murderers were charging fifteen thousand dollars in gold for each severed head.

To keep from being slain, candidates and office holders were forced to maintain large standing armies, which they rewarded with loot from captured territories. By the time of the empire, a select three hundred of these soldiers, called the Praetorian Guard, were buying and selling the throne, increasing their own gold holdings and their power.

In A.D. 193, Julianus offered gold equivalent to five thousand dollars to each member of the guard for the privilege of ruling the empire. To oblige him, the guard killed the Emperor Pertinax and allowed Julianus to rule for two months before they beheaded him to place the crown on Septimius Severus.

"Make your soldiers rich and don't bother about anything else," Septimius advised his son, Caracalla, but the advice did not save the new ruler. In A.D. 217 at Carrhae, in Mesopotamia, he was stabbed to death as he advanced on the rich gold land of Parthia, as Persia was then known.

This gold country had lured the Romans for centuries. Two hundred and seventy years before, in 53 B.C., another Roman general on the same mission met death at the same spot.

His name was Crassus. With Caesar and Pompey, he had formed the First Triumvirate seven years earlier. To keep themselves in power the mighty trio needed gold. Leaving Pompey to administer Rome, Caesar marched into Gaul and Crassus led his army east toward Parthia.

At Carrhae, his troops, numbering forty thousand, were defeated by the forerunner of the modern tank. This was the armored horse and mounted archer, completely mobile and impervious to Roman arrows and lances. Legend has it that though Crassus lost the battle, the Parthians gave him what he wanted by pouring molten gold down his throat.

Caesar acquired his gold in a more orthodox fashion. He conquered western Europe, or Gaul, which became one of the richest sources of gold in the empire. Then he invaded the British Isles and later tried to take the gold of Egypt, which Cleopatra protected not with armies but with her charms.

When Caesar returned to Rome, in 46 B.C., his triumphal procession was the greatest the city had ever seen. The purses of his soldiers were bulging with the gold of Gaul and so was his own. He had taken millions in gold from the conquered territory. Generously he bestowed some of it on Rome's citizens and gave each of his soldiers a three-thousand-dollar gold reward. Just as generously, the Romans made him dictator.

Caesar used his powers and Rome's gold to guarantee an army for the future. Centuries of warfare had dangerously reduced the population. In an attempt to increase the birthrate, Caesar offered golden rewards for large families and forbade childless women to wear gold jewelry. He drafted young men into his army and retired veterans to plots of land in Tuscany, where they were encouraged to take wives and raise future soldiers.

The soldiers were inexperienced farmers, but scratching the ground they found a source of wealth that was more to their liking and seemed inexhaustible. It was gold from the graves of the Etruscans who had lived on the Italian peninsula long before the Romans arrived.

Who the Etruscans were, and where they came from, no one knows. There is some evidence that they emigrated from Lydia and, as they had once washed gold from the River Pactolus, began to wash it from the River Po and to mine it in the western Alps. They were expert goldsmiths, but the largest part of their goldwork was melted down by the Romans who took over their land.

To bring in the gold of Gaul, Caesar pierced the land to the north with thousands of miles of stone-paved turnpikes. Over the roads the bullion traveled to Rome, carried by tribute collectors from the provinces in sealed baskets, called *fisci,* and gathered in a temple called the *fiscus*. Both are memorialized in our word *fiscal*. Coins, called *aurei*, were minted in the Temple of Juno Moneta, from which came the word *money*.

The older coins of Babylonia, Lydia, and Greece had been impressed with the seal of the monarch, merchant, or city that minted them. Caesar had the aureus stamped with his own portrait that people throughout the empire might know their governor. This

The Metropolitan Museum of Art

The Etruscans were expert goldsmiths, as shown by this gold funeral wreath from a third century B.C. grave.

made the medium of exchange a medium of communication as well.

In a land without newspapers, or even a common language, people made the acquaintance of the head of their government by seeing his head on their coins. A change in the face that appeared on the money meant a new ruler. Or the old emperor might add his family to his likeness to announce the birth of an heir.

On the back of the coin the emperor's achievements were pictured—a public building, a larger harbor, or an abundant crop. Often his virtues were lauded. The goddess Fortune was shown as subservient to his wishes, or his honesty was attested by the goddess Aequitas, or Fairness.

Aequitas was most apt to appear on a coin in which the gold content had been dishonestly reduced. But even a debased coin was valuable for propaganda purposes. New issues, with new designs, made their appearance more rapidly than the seasons.

Caesar's aureus was an honest coin, but by the time it carried his portrait to the far corners of the empire Caesar himself was dead. In the struggle for power that followed his assassination, Octavian, later given the title Augustus, emerged triumphant, but Mark Antony took Caesar's gold, valued at thirty million dollars. He also took the rich, tribute-paying dependencies of the Near East, marching through them compelling the payment of ten years' taxes in advance.

When the island of Rhodes could gather together only ten million dollars worth of the precious metal, its cities were destroyed. To escape this fate, the other subject lands melted down the golden art work that had decorated temples and public buildings for centuries. Defecting, Antony took the gold to Alexandria and presented the eastern lands from which he had gathered it to Cleopatra.

In 31 B.C., Octavian won back all that Antony had taken, plus the gold of Egypt. As trade flourished, men of commerce began to live as kings had lived in the past. Their homes rivaled palaces and temples. Their chairs resembled golden thrones, and their tables were set with gold.

Both men and women wore gold jewelry lavishly, though it was considered in good taste to leave one finger on each hand ringless. Pliny, the historian, regretted that "many hands are worn down that one little joint may be adorned."

Pliny knew with what difficulty the gold was obtained. Even at that time the rich placer deposits of Spain and Gaul were showing signs of exhaustion. Under Octavian, gold was mined from the mountains in northwestern Spain, from which, according to Pliny, about seven tons of gold were obtained each year.

"It is dug out by sinking shafts, or gained by the destruction of mountains," he wrote. He described the destruction of mountains as a feat that "may seem to surpass the achievements of the Giants."

"By the light of lanterns, mountains are hollowed out by galleries driven deeply into them. Lamps are also used to measure the length of the miners' shifts, for many of them do not see daylight in months together.

"Arches are left at frequent intervals to hold the mountain up. They break the hard rock with iron rams of 150 pound weight. The pieces are carried out, night and day, on their shoulders in the darkness along a human chain: only the last in the chain see daylight. When all is ready, they cut the keystones of the arches, beginning with the innermost. The earth on top subsides, and gives a signal, and a solitary lookout on a peak of the hill observes it. With shouts and gestures he orders the mine to be evacuated, and he himself speeds down as well. The mountain then breaks and falls apart with a roar that the mind can hardly conceive, and with an equally incredible blast of air."

These were the "golden prisons" in which, Diodorus stated, generations of Spanish slaves had been forced to work by their conquerors. The shouts and gestures of the lookout on the hill did not guarantee the escape of the miners before the mountain collapsed. As the mines grew more numerous, and the Spaniards less so, slaves were imported from Africa and other parts of the empire to hollow out the mountains. Many unsung Christian martyrs lived out their years of captivity in the darkness of the Roman mines.

After the mountains were collapsed, rivers were channeled to fall on the debris from great heights. The force of the water crushed and freed the gold. The water and rock were then run through sluice boxes lined with shrubs in which the heavy gold was trapped.

Years later, in California, the forty-niners used a similar technique, called hydraulicking, to wash away mountains. It is a swift but destructive method of getting gold from the ground.

Tons of sand from which the metal has been removed clog streams and wash over fertile lands as tailings are released from the sluice boxes. Even in Pliny's day the refuse-filled rivers were building up the coastline where they emptied into the sea, filling harbors and turning once-prosperous ports into inland towns.

Octavian, the first Roman emperor, devoted himself to getting gold. Succeeding emperors seemed more interested in spending it. Among these was Nero who fancied himself a musician, poet, and architect. Rome's ugliness offended him. He was often heard to complain that the capital city didn't match the grandeur of subject cities such as Alexandria and Antioch.

Nero was not in Rome when the fire that destroyed it started in the summer of A.D. 64. The fire burned for nine days. The rumors linking Nero to the disaster have persisted ever since.

It was said that he watched the flames from a nearby tower, singing songs of his own composition and accompanying himself on the lyre. People suspected that his incendiaries had started the conflagration and that they continued to feed it until it reduced to ashes the structures that offended Nero's sensitive eye. Once the fire was out, the emperor returned to the capital and began to restore it with enthusiasm.

The vast rebuilding program depleted the royal treasury, leaving so little gold for currency that Nero was forced to reduce drastically the amount of gold in the aureus. Still he continued building, and topped his public works with a palace that glittered so grandly it was called the Golden House. He built the magnificent residence for his third wife.

All his life the emperor had been plagued by woman trouble. At the age of twenty-two he had found it necessary to kill his mother. Later he had been forced to use the same method to rid himself of his first wife, Octavia, in order to marry his true love, Poppaea.

Nero adored Poppaea and was delighted when it became evident that she would present him with an heir. Unfortunately both she and the unborn child died after a lovers' tiff in which her devoted husband happened to kick her in the stomach.

The widower was heartbroken. He searched all of Rome for someone who resembled the wife he mourned. He found a young boy who met his qualifications, had him castrated, and married him in a great public ceremony. Then he built him the Golden House.

For the brief time it stood, it was one of the wonders of the world. A statue of the emperor, complete with golden curls, rose one hundred and twenty feet high at the entrance. The pillared arcade stretched beyond it for a mile.

The grounds contained an enormous pool. "More like the sea," Suetonius described it. The pool was surrounded by gardens and woodlands filled with exotic plants and trees and animals.

Whole sections of the house were overlaid with gold and studded with precious stones. Ivory-and-gold ceilings revolved or opened that guests might be showered from above with perfumes and flowers. Various kinds of curative waters ran from golden taps in the bathrooms.

Suetonius reports that when the palace was completed Nero said, with some relief, "At last I can begin to live like a human being."

To cheat the Senate of the pleasure of his execution, Nero was forced to take his own life. Yet he gained a certain immortality, despite his wickedness, and lives today in the Bible as the villain of John's Book of Revelation.

Though John condemned Nero and Nero persecuted the Christians, they shared the same dream of a paradise that glittered with gold. The Christians desired their gold in the next world. Nero the Roman wanted his in this.

Even as his Golden House crumbled, Rome became the magnificent city Nero has envisioned. On the ruins of Nero's palace, Vespasian built the Colosseum, and Trajan constructed an enormous public bath.

The remains of the once-glorious city that we see today are misleading. They are really the cores of the buildings and were never meant for display. Originally they were covered with marble and alabaster and trimmed with gold-tiled roofs and doors.

As Rome declined, the emperors themselves melted down part of the city's golden splendor to pay the troops that fought the Vandals. Though Rome was sacked repeatedly, there was still gold left to be peeled and scraped away by the occupants of the city in the Middle Ages.

Some of the most beautiful of Rome's monuments were erected by the emperor Trajan in the first century of our era. These included a forum, the Triumphal Arch of Trajan, which still stands, and a column of marble twelve feet in diameter which rises more than eighty feet in the air. On this column is carved the story of Trajan's military conquest of the gold country of Dacia, roughly approximate to present-day Romania.

The bas-relief story, from which the original gilding has disappeared, reads upward in panels as though a scroll had been unwound on the column. The Roman military expedition is pictured, then the battle scenes, and the burning villages of Dacia. Mothers and children are shown begging Trajan for mercy. Soldiers parade around the column, proudly carrying the heads of slain enemies on spears. Conquered Dacian princes ceremoniously drink from their goblet of poison. Then the long lines of prisoners trudge away from their homeland, to Rome and slavery.

Dacia brought new wealth to Rome and fattened Trajan's fortune by half a million pounds of gold. From Dacia, Trajan marched south into Arabia, north into Siberia, and east into Parthia, capturing new gold lands.

At the top of his triumphal column he placed, symbolically, a likeness of himself holding a globe of the world in his hands, as Rome had held the world for four hundred years. But for Rome the golden era was almost over. The gold was slipping away, to the provinces, the peasants, and the slaves. They were using it as the Romans had, to buy political power.

Trajan was from the province of Spain. The Emperor Aurelian was the son of an Illyrian peasant. In A.D. 284, Diocletian, taking over the government, moved his palace from the old capital city of Rome to Nicomedia, just south of Constantinople in Asia Minor.

There he surrounded himself with gold and dressed in silk and gold. Visitors kissed the hem of his robe, and Diocletian received them seated on a throne of gold and wearing his golden crown.

He was, he said, the earthly embodiment of Jupiter.

CONJURED

SHORTLY AFTER THE YEAR A.D. 1000 the old quarter of a village named Kufa, in Iraq, was torn down in an early slum-clearance program. Beneath one of the buildings a chemical laboratory was discovered. Though it was then more than two centuries old, a chemist of today might have stepped into it and proceeded with his work.

It contained more furnaces than a modern laboratory. The furnaces, of many kinds and sizes, were for the smelting and refining of ores and metals. There were athanors for the sublimation, or purification, of chemicals, and a variety of stills, heated from above and below, and including the still-familiar water bath. There were leather bellows to increase the heat of the fires, balances, beakers, flasks, phials, glass crystallizing dishes, ladles, shears, tongs, forceps, rolling and crushing equipment, moulds, crucibles, and double crucibles.

There were also laboratory notebooks that had been kept by the owner of the laboratory and textbooks that had been translated from several different languages. The one thing a modern chemist would have missed was a thermometer. There was none. The textbooks called for temperatures as hot as a broody hen, a manure heap, or June sunshine.

Legend has it that a great lump of gold was also found. It had, presumably, been made by the alchemist who worked in the laboratory. It was appropriated, according to the story, by the king's chamberlain.

The laboratory belonged to Abu Musa Jabir ibn-Hayyan, more commonly known as Jabir, or, in Europe, as Geber. The most celebrated of medieval chemists, he was, as all chemists were then, an alchemist. With the metallurgists and the healers, the alchemists were the forefathers of modern scientists. Geber was one of the most dedicated and influential in both the East and the West.

His father was a druggist who, shortly after his son's birth about 722, fell into disfavor with the Umayyad rulers in Baghdad and was beheaded. The child was whisked into Arabia where his education included astrology, magic, and the art of turning base metals into gold.

When Harun al-Rashid, caliph of the *Thousand and One Nights,* ruled in Baghdad, Geber became his alchemist. Many rulers employed court alchemists, and though it is not recorded that any one of these experimenters ever enriched his patron many of them did enrich man's knowledge of the world in which he lived.

In their trial and error attempts to create gold, they advanced metallurgy, discovered new elements, created many chemical compounds, and learned the laws that govern heat and gravity and motion. Most important of all, they took the contemplation of nature away from those who were content to theorize, and put the theories to test in their laboratories.

Some of them were charlatans, seeking only to produce something that would "pass for gold" and fool the public. Some were mystics and magicians, cluttering their minds and work with occult theories and hocus-pocus. But the dedicated alchemists were the world's first scientists, faced with the forbidding task of separating demonstrable truth from fanciful theory and accepted superstitions.

The Baghdad in which Geber found himself in the eighth century was an ideal place for a man interested in science. Though we think of it as wealthy and wicked, it was rapidly becoming a leading center of learning. In the Arabia where Geber had grown up, science was smothered in the occult. In the West it was often discouraged by a narrow interpretation of Christianity.

The maligned Bluebeard, Harun al-Rashid, made Baghdad a haven for purged books, persecuted scientists, and dedicated teachers. He and his son, Mamun, built laboratories, set up observatories, and filled the court library with the works of Arab and Egyptian alchemists and Greek and Roman philosophers and mathematicians.

As a result Geber did not have to work alone, as many of his fellow alchemists did. He was surrounded by other experimenters and had access to most of the work that had been written previously in the field.

As his laboratory resembled a modern laboratory, so his days were not unlike those of a modern research chemist connected with a university. He seems not to have been required to produce gold.

Geber, or Jabir, was the most celebrated alchemist in the Middle Ages. From his book comes this drawing of an alchemist heating a liquid in a water bath.

Geber ibn-Hayyan, *De Alchemia*
The New York Public Library, Rare Book Division

Michael Maier, *Secretioris Naturae*
The New York Public Library, Rare Book Division

The shortage of gold in the Middle Ages drove alchemists to far-fetched attempts at creating it—as above, in a fire. Although their experiments were based on superstition, they made discoveries that advanced metallurgy.

Rather he was allowed to pursue his experiments in freedom and to publish his results.

He wrote voluminously, and one hundred manuscripts and lithographs bearing his name exist in European, Indian, and North African libraries. Not all of them were written by Geber. So famous did he become that many later alchemists signed their own work with his name to draw attention to it. As a result, scholars have spent centuries weeding forgeries from authentic Geber treatises and deleting the additions made by translators.

At the age of eighty-one, Geber retired from his Baghdad position and returned to his father's village of Kufa to work another ten years in the laboratory that was unearthed two centuries later. At the age of ninety-one, it is said, he returned to Baghdad to accept honors from the court.

The word *alchemy* is Arabic in origin. The Greeks called goldmaking *chemeia,* or "black," and referred to it as the black art. The Chinese called it *kem-mai* which means "gone astray in search of gold."

The original goldmakers were miners and metallurgists who could turn sand and rock into precious metal. Able to do more than they understood, they themselves believed that they transmuted rock into metal—sometimes dull lead, sometimes red copper, sometimes white silver, sometimes yellow gold.

Trying to explain the phenomena, they decided that metals grew in the earth, changing color as they ripened. The idea persists today in places like the Philippines where native miners insist on leaving seeds of gold in the mine, from which more gold will grow.

As late as the sixteenth century, Calbus of Freiberg described the growth and *witterung* of metals. Generated by exhalations from their respective planets, the metals ripened through continued exhalations, to "perfect gold." But if the gold was not harvested, like fruit, at the peak of perfection, further planetary influences caused it to wither into a reddish earthy residue. This was the reason that gold was scarce.

In the laboratory the metallurgists, turned alchemists, tried to imitate the transmutation of metals that they felt sure was taking place within the earth. It was generally assumed that this could be accomplished through a *lapis philosophorum,* or philosopher's stone.

Some thought the stone would be a solid, others an elixir. There was disagreement as to its composition and its powers. Many insisted that a white elixir would be less potent than one of a red color. Others maintained that the elixir, when found, would not only transmute base metals into gold but would also restore youth and prolong life.

The fact that sulphur was often found with gold in mines and that mercury would extract gold from crushed ore led many alchemists, including Geber, to believe that metals were a combination of these two substances. Wrote Geber: "Metals are all, in essence, composed of mercury combined and solidified with sulphur.

They differ from one another only because of the difference of their accidental qualities, and this difference is due to the difference of their varieties of sulphur, which again is caused by a variation in the soils and in their situations with respect to the heat of the Sun."

Geber also wrote, "He who makes no experiments will attain nothing." If he did not create gold from his own experiments Geber did discover nitric acid and combined it with hydrochloric acid to make aqua regia. With this royal water he could dissolve the royal metal he could not create.

The origins of alchemy are lost in the mists of antiquity. Hermes Trismegistos, of Egypt, is often called the Father of Alchemy which was, in turn, called the Hermetic Art. Little is known of Hermes.

Medieval miners thought that seeds of gold sowed in the ground would grow and ripen into more gold.

Michael Maier, *Secretioris Naturae*
The New York Public Library, Rare Book Division

After his death he may have been worshiped as the Egyptian god Thoth and he is generally credited with having developed the air-tight, or hermetic, seal while trying to cement together the separate halves of his philosopher's egg that it might hatch gold.

The Israelites believed that the science of metal working was brought to earth by fallen angels who taught it to the women with whom they cohabited, who in turn instructed their daughters. One of the more famous of these female alchemists was Maria the Jewess who has been identified by some as Moses' sister, Miriam.

Maria is thought to have invented that useful piece of chemical equipment, the water bath, which is still known in France as the *bain-marie*. The alchemists also used her *kerotakis*, a closed apparatus which, when heated, allowed a volatile substance to vaporize, react on an enclosed metal, and condense again in a continuous reflux action.

In the Middle Ages the search for the common denominator of all metals led Kanada, a Hindu, to a conclusion first reached by the Greek philosophers Leucippus and Democritus, working independently, in 500 B.C.—the building blocks of the universe were atoms. Instead of accepting this theory, his fellow alchemists nicknamed Kanada "the atom eater." They were no more receptive in the fourteenth century when the alchemist Jildaki, of Cairo, proposed that when atoms of elements combined to form compounds they united in definite proportions according to weight. The atomic age was predicted but not achieved by the goldmakers.

The list of notable alchemists is long and their achievements were many. We know most about those who lived and worked in Europe during and after the Middle Ages. The monk Albertus Magnus wrote a history of metals in the thirteenth century. Another monk, the English Roger Bacon, was a famous teacher of science at Oxford and in Paris, known by his pupils as Doctor Mirabilis, "the Admirable Doctor." His experiments advanced the science of optics and in his writings he predicted the steamship and the airplane. Unfortunately both were interrupted by long jail sentences during which he was denied material for either writing or research.

The sixteenth-century Swiss alchemist and physician Paracelsus was persecuted because he railed against the medical practices of the day, "designed to make the apothecaries rich and the patients poor." Experimenting with quicksilver in his laboratory Paracelsus discovered a remedy for syphilis.

Trying to make gold, Basil Valentine learned the secret of producing crystalline antimony. Libavius was the first to prepare stannic chloride and ammonium sulphate, and he invented various wet and dry methods of chemical analysis.

As late as the eighteenth century, Isaac Newton experimented with transmutation and consulted books on alchemy. The poet Goethe was also a dabbler in alchemy and imitated the style of alchemical authors in his "Witch's Multiplication Table," a part of his masterpiece, *Faust*:

> "This must thou know:
> "Of one make ten,
> "And let two go,
> "Make even three
> "And rich thou't be."

It was for this kind of riddle writing that the Englishman Robert Boyle, often called the father of chemistry, criticized his fellow alchemists in *The Sceptical Chymist.* But he did not resign from the brotherhood and his laboratory contained the large variety of furnaces the alchemists used for their transmutation experiments. In the seventeenth century the distinction between alchemy and chemistry had not yet been made.

It was not entirely the fault of the alchemists that they camouflaged their work by reporting it in picture puzzles, riddles, hieroglyphs, and occult signs. In Europe in the Middle Ages they were often persecuted by church authorities for impiety and exiled or imprisoned by rulers who feared their success would debase the currency. Even when their work was encouraged they knew that they could be punished tomorrow for yesterday's experiments.

If there were charlatans among the alchemists—and there were many—they were as often conned as they were cunning. They were hired, kidnaped, and imprisoned by rulers who wanted to use their magic talents. When they failed to create gold they were killed, sometimes with ironic ceremony.

Duke Frederick of Württemberg, in the late sixteenth century, disposed of any number of unsuccessful goldmakers. He hanged them from a gallows made of the iron they had failed to convert into gold and watched the proceedings, with his friends, from a grandstand covered with gold leaf.

Sometimes monarchs did not care that their protégés could not

Lazarus Ercker, *Aula Subterranea*
The New York Public Library, Rare Book Division

Alchemy, practiced in laboratories like the one above, was a dangerous pursuit. Many an alchemist who failed to make gold was hanged by his royal patron.

make gold as long as they made something that would pass as gold. In 1461, Henry VI of England rescinded the law that made the practice of alchemy a crime and called for goldmakers to produce coins to pay his soldiers fighting on the continent.

At the same time Charles VII of France, caught in similar financial difficulties, named Jacques le Cor, the richest man in the country, his financial minister. When Le Cor's fortune was gone and the war not yet won, the minister rounded up the French alchemists to manufacture gold to pay the French army.

Neither the French nor the English technicians made gold coins that would fool the troops. Men on both sides exchanged their ersatz currency for the enemy's money only to find they were no better off than before. The coins were a brass-colored alloy of copper and silver, color-treated with cinnabar.

Thanks to Joan of Arc, the French won the war, but the English won the gold. Retreating, they abandoned their own counterfeit coins and those of French origin and took with them all the genuine gold they could scavenge. France was left denuded of gold and overflowing with bogus coins.

Soldiers and citizenry alike screamed for the execution of Jacques le Cor, whose personal resources had not been large enough to support the war. In consideration of his finance minister's past generosity, however, King Charles spared the unlucky man the usual sentence of death and transmuted his punishment to exile.

The child prodigy Johann Böttger suffered most of his life for a reputation as an alchemical genius achieved before he was sixteen years old. He had been apprenticed to an apothecary in Berlin and was allowed to use the druggist's equipment for his own experiments in the evening.

As proof that he was not wasting his time he kept a few bits of gold in his pocket which he displayed on request. His fame spread. It was rumored that he was one of the reasons for the war between Prussia and Poland that opened the eighteenth century.

Whether or not he precipitated the conflict, he was thrown into prison for safekeeping at the start of the hostilities. Captured and imprisoned repeatedly, first by one army and then the other, young Johann was to know nothing but confinement for most of the days of his life. Even when the fighting ceased it seemed prudent to keep the valuable goldmaker carefully guarded.

Augustus the Strong, King of Poland, did just that. Johann Böttger was locked up in the Gold House in Dresden with all the equipment he might need to manufacture gold. He worked desperately at the project, worrying himself into ill health and premature old age. For if his life as a successful goldmaker was no more than that of an imprisoned criminal he knew that for failure he could be hanged. Still he couldn't make gold.

Among the few visitors the lonely alchemist received in his closely guarded quarters was a man named Walter von Tschirnhaus. At a time when people were setting their tables with porcelain imported from China, Von Tschirnhaus was manufacturing glassware. If he could find the secret of making fine china he could turn it into a fortune. Otherwise he faced bankruptcy.

Böttger couldn't transmute base metals into gold but his reputation as an alchemist was not undeserved. In his laboratory at the Gold House he succeeded in making a porcelain so fine that it produced a fortune for himself and Von Tschirnhaus and brought fame to Dresden. As a reward for this achievement he was allowed to spend his last years in freedom. Two centuries later, in 1923, the product of his laboratory actually passed for gold when the Germans, short of metal, made coins of Dresden china.

Wrote the English essayist, Francis Bacon: "Alchemy may be likened to the man who told his sons that he had buried gold in the vineyard; where they by digging found no gold, but by turning up the mould about the roots of the vines procured a plentiful vintage."

A fruit of the vineyard the alchemists tilled for so many thousands of years was nuclear physics, born of their belief in the oneness of matter, founded on their faith in transmutability and advanced through the experiments in their laboratories.

Nuclear reaction proved at last to be their philosopher's stone. In 1936, in a cyclotron at the University of California, gold was transmuted from another metal.

The other metal was not one the alchemists knew nor one they would have predicted. It was rarer and more costly than the king of metals they coveted. It was platinum.

Nevertheless, man's most persistent dream had come true. Transmutation of one element into another is now an everyday occurrence, but nobody turns the switch to make up a batch of gold from Geber's sulphur and mercury. Instead gold is transmuted into the special mercury (Hg198) that is needed for ultra-precise length measuring. The vines the alchemists cultivated in their vineyard have indeed grown strange fruit.

DISPLAYED

IT WAS AFTER DARK and the man walked alone, hemmed in by a wall on one side and the River Seine on the other. He was not a young man, having passed his fortieth birthday three years before, in 1540. But he was lithe and agile and stepped briskly, his dark cape flowing behind him.

Beneath the cape he wore a shirt of mail and, handy to his right hand, a long sword in a scabbard. His left arm was burdened with a heavy, covered basket which he had carried all the way from the house of the king's treasurer. Though he was an Italian, Benvenuto Cellini was going home to his castle in Paris.

As he hurried along the narrow walk, he heard quick footsteps behind him. Turning, he faced four swordsmen, weapons drawn, the blades shining cold and sharp in the pale night. Pulling his own sword, Cellini kept them at bay while he dropped the basket from his arm and let his cape fall over it.

Then, shouting in Italian, he thrust and slashed so violently that he narrowly missed killing one or another, according to his own description of the fight. "My skill in using the sword made them think I was a soldier rather than a fellow of some other calling," he explained with pride in his *Autobiography*.

The attackers fell back. Picking up his heavy basket, Cellini rushed to the safety of his castle. Once there, he couldn't resist calling after his assailants, this time in French so they would be sure to understand. The four of them were of such cowardly stuff, he screamed into the night, that they had failed to steal from him the basket filled with a thousand golden crowns, so heavy it had almost broken his arm to carry it.

Such adventures were to be expected if one was a goldsmith in sixteenth-century Europe. On their persons, or in their workshops, goldsmiths were known to have jewels and precious metals and were, therefore, favorite targets for robbers. Benvenuto Cellini found this out in Rome early in his career.

Pope Clement VII had invited the leading goldsmiths of the city to submit designs for a new button for his cope. The medallion was to be of solid gold, about the size of a man's palm, featuring a large diamond and adorned with numerous rubies, sapphires, and emeralds. Young Cellini won the competition, and the pope's treasures, with the exception of the diamond, were moved to his workshop.

The goldsmith was extremely careful with the valuables placed in his trust. Every night he hid the gold and jewels in a special chest. He and his assistants slept in rooms off the workshop, and a loyal dog slept in the shop itself.

He did not even keep a woman model, as he usually did, for purposes of sketching the female body and for his own pleasures. Nor did he allow his assistants to bring women to the premises for fear the guests might discover where he hid the precious materials with which he was working.

One night, feeling the need of female companionship, he stole to the kitchen quarters to crawl into bed with the maid. While he was gone, thieves visited the workshop. Thanks to the dog, the pope's gold and jewels were saved—and with them Cellini's reputation.

A goldsmith could be forgiven for any crime, including murder —and Cellini was not innocent on that score. But he could not afford a reputation for dishonesty or even for laxity in guarding the gold placed in his custody. The slightest doubt about his reliability might leave him without the gold he needed to earn his living.

The pope's button was probably Cellini's masterpiece, according to C. R. Ashbee, who translated the famous goldsmith's "treatises." The treatises were written, Cellini explained, to instruct "all those many youths always springing up and eager to learn the beautiful art of the goldsmith."

Cellini was eager to teach them. He urged them to be imaginative as he had been in designing the papal medallion. All his competitors for the privilege had placed the magnificent diamond in the breast of the Lord, who was the central figure. Cellini seated his God on the diamond, a conception so unusual that he was allowed to execute the work. He described it as "God the Father giving the benediction . . . surrounded by a number of jolly little angels."

In his treatises Cellini lauded gold as the material most worthy of an artist's best effort, since it was everlasting and would not tarnish. Unfortunately the artist's best efforts were often sacrificed by those who valued the material more than the design. This happened to Cellini's papal medallion in the nineteenth century. He himself was guilty of melting down some of the finest examples of the goldsmiths' craft during the sack of Rome, in 1526.

At that time, as enemy troops stormed the city, Cellini was hiding with Pope Clement in the Castle of St. Angelo. Fearing capture, the pope asked the goldsmith to strip the jewels from his regalia and sew them in the hems, cuffs, and linings of his apparel.

This done, Cellini took the golden settings and a brazier to a castle tower and melted down the gold while shooting at the enemy from a window. The result: two enemy leaders killed and two hundred pounds of golden art pieces melted into uniform bars for easy burial or transport. For himself, Cellini kept the sweepings from the room which yielded about a pound and a half of the precious metal.

In Italy, Cellini had two patrons, Pope Clement VII and the Duke of Florence. He made their jewelry and metal artwork and stamped their coins. He had every reason to believe that he would continue in their service for the rest of a peaceful and profitable life.

In 1534, Pope Clement died, and three years later the Duke of Florence was murdered. The political enemies who destroyed the duke sent Cellini back to the Castle of St. Angelo, but by this time the castle had been turned into a prison.

After more than a year of confinement, Cellini tried to escape. In the attempt he broke his leg, was recaptured, and thrown into a dungeon. There he might have stayed indefinitely had it not been for the King of France, Francis I.

Many an artist in the strife-torn Europe of the sixteenth century found a haven at the court of King Francis. The king was a

The Metropolitan Museum of Art, Bequest of Benjamin Altman, 1913

Benvenuto Cellini was famous for his sculpture and goldwork. Although the salt cellar made for his patron, King Francis I of France, is better known, this gold-and-enamel bowl, called the Rospigliosi cup, is thought by many to be even more beautiful.

connoisseur and patron of the arts. He had befriended Leonardo da Vinci and wished to do the same for Benvenuto Cellini, whose work he had seen and liked.

King Francis succeeded in obtaining Cellini's release from his dungeon cell and brought him to Paris. There the king gave the goldsmith a retainer, work to do, and a castle, called the Little Nello, which was supposed to be haunted. Cellini was returning to the castle with his basket of gold when he was attacked by the four swordsmen.

With the gold he rescued that evening he created the famous salt cellar for the king's table. The salt cellar with its two golden figures, representing the earth and the sea, may still be seen at the Museum of Vienna. Cellini's golden bowl, thought by many critics to surpass the salt cellar, is displayed at the Metropolitan Museum of Art in New York.

Said King Francis when the goldsmith presented the completed salt cellar: "Of a truth I hardly think the ancients can have seen a piece so beautiful as this."

Of a truth no words could have pleased Cellini more. The art he practiced was older than recorded history and the works of many anonymous goldsmiths, retrieved from ancient tombs and buried cities, were so perfect in design and execution that to be compared with these ancient masters was to receive high praise indeed.

Many of the techniques Cellini used and taught to his eager young goldsmiths had been developed by the highly civilized Etruscans who occupied the Italian peninsula and built a wall around the seven hills of Rome centuries before the arrival of the people we call the Romans. The granulated gold pieces retrieved from Etruscan graves remain today among the finest examples of this rare and difficult art.

They proved that the Etruscans were expert craftsmen—and that they suffered from a shortage of gold. For like most of the techniques perfected by goldsmiths, granulation was more than an artistic treatment of the metal. It was also an ingenious economy measure.

Granulation simulated the effect of a great mass and weight of gold by covering a thin sheet of the metal with minuscule globules, so light they would float. Arranging the globules so that each tiny sphere reflected a maximum amount of light took both skill and artistry. Producing the grains and welding them to their backing demanded patience and long training. So difficult was the technique that several different times in history it was lost and had to be rediscovered through trial and error and close study of the ancient masters by new generations of goldsmiths.

The granules were formed by pouring molten gold from a height of several feet into a water bath. As the hot metal fell through the air it separated into liquid drops. The water cooled and preserved the tiny, hollow spheres.

The goldsmith arranged the globules with painstaking care on a thin sheet of gold which he had painted with a copper salt flux. When heated, all visible trace of the flux disappeared and each small globe of gold was welded to the background with a strong, though microscopic, speck of copper.

The necessity for economy in the use of his material shaped the art of the goldsmith from the beginning. It is evident in the strings of simple gold beads found in early prehistoric tombs, which were interspersed, to save gold, with beads of semiprecious stone.

Even after goldsmiths learned to fashion and stretch gold in more artistic ways, they were called on to create the strands of plain gold beads. Losing their religious significance, the beads became important as articles of barter. One solid gold bead could be offered for an item of small merit or a whole string exchanged for something of great worth. The beads were accepted in a market without testing, since color and weight were evidence of their value—at least at first. Eventually the goldsmiths learned to shape shells of gold around stone centers so that the unwary could not distinguish them from beads of solid gold.

Coating stones with gold, or even entire buildings, was not always done with fraudulent intent. The practice grew out of the craftsman's familiarity with the elastic possibilities of his material. Gold could be spun into a wire as fine as the finest thread and beaten into a sheet of gold leaf as thin as tissue paper.

Such delicate leaves of gold have been used by bookbinders to edge pages and adorn backs and covers since the days when books were copied by hand on parchment and vellum. Medieval artists used thin sheets of gold as backgrounds for their religious paintings. Monks employed it to illuminate their manuscripts.

This in itself was an exacting art. The glue had to be just right. One recipe called for simmering the skin of an eel with the dried bones of the head of a wolf fish and an egg dipped in the milk of a fig tree.

The Metropolitan Museum of Art, Rogers Fund, 1912

Gold is so flexible that it can be spun into a fine thread or beaten into a tissue-thin leaf. This decoration from a fifteenth-century Italian manuscript displays delicate gold tracery in the letter S, set against a background of gold leaf.

If all went well in the preparation and application of glue and gold, the illuminated letter could be polished with a hound's tooth until it glowed brightly. If something went wrong, as it very often did, the golden letter refused to shine and it was all to do over again.

Gold used on buildings is usually of a thicker leaf, though even in the days when it shown from King Solomon's temple, Cleopatra's palace, and Nero's Golden House, an ounce of gold could be spread over forty-seven square feet at a cost, figured in today's prices, of seventy-five cents a square foot.

Gold gleams now on the Taj Mahal, Buckingham Palace, and the dome of the Arkansas state capitol, to mention only a few of its prominent habitats. Though it varies in thickness and in purity, an ounce of gold ordinarily covers an area of 100 square feet at a cost of thirty-five cents per square foot.

Originally every goldsmith was expected to master the art of beating gold into thin leaves, an exacting and time-consuming process finally taken over by specialists. Besides its Worshipful Company of Goldsmiths, London has had a Guild of Gold Beaters since the twelfth century. The gold beater's art is still practiced, its techniques similar to those used by the craftsmen of whom Homer wrote.

Beating gold requires strength, rhythm, and infinite care. Today the workman starts with a cutch of about seventy-five one-inch-square sheets of gold which have been rolled out by steel rollers. Once he started with a nugget. The cutch of gold weighs an ounce and, if it is of pure gold, it is worth thirty-five dollars. The beater separates the squares of gold with sheets of vellum and parchment on which he drops a seventeen-pound hammer, turning the cutch deftly as he strikes it with paced, rhythmic blows numbering about fifty per minute.

The hammer thins and spreads the gold until it covers an area four times its original size. Then the sheets of metal are cut into smaller squares again, each leaf dusted with the hind foot of a hare and placed between tough membranes taken from the intestines of cattle. The pounding and cutting usually continue until the layers of gold are so thin and fragile the worker can move them only with his breath. At this point the original seventy-five one-inch squares of gold have multiplied to twelve hundred leaves, each 3¼ inches square.

As the gold beaters sprang from the shops of the goldsmiths, so did the specialists of many other fields. Artists of all kinds, metallurgists, smiths, engineers, architects, chemists, apothecaries, physicians, dentists, watchmakers, jewelers, and bankers learned their fundamentals in this ancient craft, called *oreficeria,* which demanded many different skills from its practitioners.

Anonymous goldsmiths engineered the world's first skyscrapers, the ziggurats of Sumeria and Babylon; built the gold-and-silver war chariots of the Egyptian pharaohs; designed Jerusalem's first temple. Following in their footsteps, the versatile goldsmith Pheidias created the architectural wonders of ancient Athens. The designs of the former goldsmith's apprentice, Filippo Brunelleschi, brought Florence to her Renaissance glory.

Every goldsmith was, of necessity, a metallurgist, and many extended their metallurgical laboratory techniques and the tools of their art to the fields of science, pharmacy, and medicine. Moses was said to have cured the wandering Israelites of idolatry by giving them aurum potable, liquid gold.

Throughout history the demand for this magic potion lured many a goldsmith into the fields of medicine and pharmacy. Aurum potable was supposed to prolong youth, grant strength, dispel fever, cure warts and epilepsy. The recipes for this remarkable elixir varied, and were often a closely guarded secret. Usually the gold

Renaissance artists and scientists of all kinds often began their careers in a goldsmith shop. This drawing shows apprentices applying a few of the many skills demanded by their craft.

Henry Havard, *Histoire de l'Orfevrèrie Française*

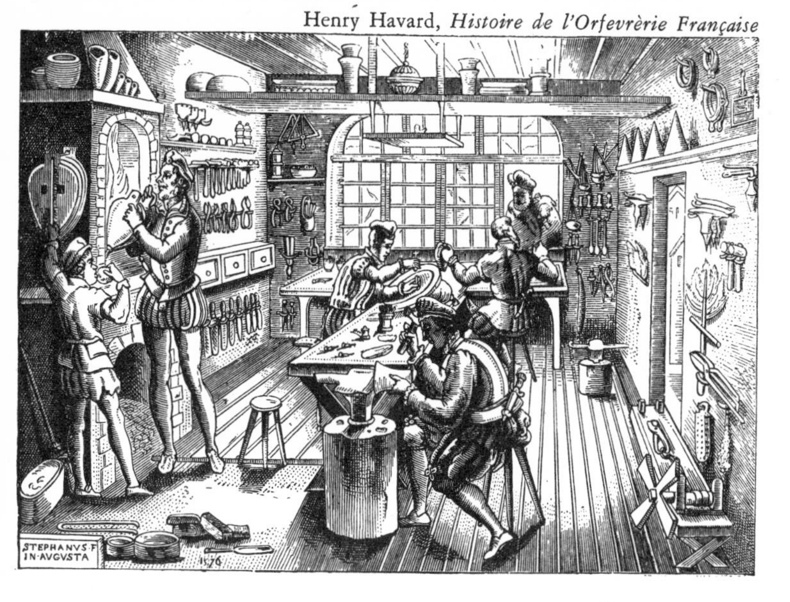

was dissolved in an acid. Gold bromide is still sold in many parts of the world as an aphrodisiac. Sometimes gold in powder form was added to a liquid in which it did not dissolve, and was swallowed in minute quantities in this form.

As late as the eighteenth century, gold leaf was applied to the faces of European ladies suffering from smallpox. Supposed to prevent disfiguration from the disease, its removal by needles often left scars as ugly and numerous as those suffered by commoners who could not afford the gold treatment.

So comprehensive was the education of a goldsmith that in the days of Benvenuto Cellini an apprenticeship in a shop of *oreficeria* was considered ideal training for all the arts and crafts. The famous Renaissance sculptors Donatello and Ghiberti began their careers apprenticed to goldsmiths, as did the versatile artists Michelangelo and Leonardo da Vinci.

Cellini remained primarily a goldsmith but he also made knives and scalpels for physicians, sometimes as the patient waited on the operating table, and he created the beautiful bronze statue of Perseus for the Piazza of Florence. At a later date, in another land, a goldsmith who used his craft to create dentures gained fame as the American horseman and patriot, Paul Revere.

Wrote John Ruskin, in honor of an art to which civilization owed much: "True goldsmith's work, when it exists, is generally the means of education of the greatest painters and sculptors of the day."

When Ruskin lived, in the nineteenth century, true goldsmith's work was mostly a memory. The busy age of mass production and specialization had little patience with handcrafts or with men trained to be Jacks-of-all-trades.

The goldsmiths of Ruskin's day devoted themselves to the ornamentation of persons and buildings and to the ever more pressing problem of stretching a supply of gold which grew scarcer and dearer as the world's expanding trade made greater demands on the rare metal. So successfully did the goldsmiths learn to economize that they almost eliminated their craft completely.

For gold tableware, they substituted gold plate and created such beautiful pieces of silver that this metal eventually surpassed gold in popularity. The less gold they could afford to use, the more they had to depend on art. They developed some of their most beautiful

In an effort to economize on gold, goldsmiths made tiny cells of gold wire, soldered them to a gold-sheet backing, and filled them with enamel or semiprecious stones. An example of this art, called cloisonné, is this eleventh-century Byzantine medallion of St. George.

The Metropolitan Museum of Art, Gift of J. Pierpont Morgan, 1917

techniques simply because they could not afford to use gold lavishly.

One of these was cloisonné. For cloisonné work the gold was pounded into thin sheets and stretched into wire. The wire was bent to form cells and soldered to the gold sheet backing. Then the tiny cells, or *cloisons,* were filled with enamel or with precious or semiprecious stones which were ground even with the gold wire. The gold backing shone through the filling and the gold wires patterned it. The effect was of a great amount of gold enhanced by the color of the enamel or stones.

As people learned to accept and admire cloisonné, the gold was stretched even farther by eliminating the backing. This was called *plique-à-jour.* The cells that held the enamel or the stones were open on both sides. Only the gold wire remained, surrounding the colored gems or enamel. To make *plique-à-jour* acceptable, the goldsmiths spent more and more effort on increasing the beauty of the enamel and stones.

In the middle of the fifteenth century they learned to cut gems to reveal their hidden brilliance. Soon the precious stones that had been a substitute for gold became more valuable than the metal.

The goldsmith was transmuted to a jeweler whose important work was cutting and mounting gems. He used gold merely as the setting for the jewels. One day platinum replaced it in that capacity.

Gold, the metal once reserved for royalty, became the simple wedding band of the servant girl whose true love couldn't afford to ring her finger with diamonds. In the eighteenth century a Mr. Christopher Pinchbeck, English goldsmith and watchmaker, offered even the servant girl a glittering jewelry she quickly preferred to gold.

For long years alchemists had been making a copper and zinc alloy which counterfeiters stamped into coins and hopefully passed for gold. The English goldsmith gave the alloy a new name, his own—Pinchbeck—and a new use. He made it into frankly fake gold jewelry and liberally sprinkled his glittering creations with gems of glass and paste.

Russian-born Carl Faberge was a goldsmith in the days when mass production of costume jewelry had put many other goldsmiths out of business. Each year he created an intricate golden egg and presented it to the tsarinas. This one, made in 1897, opens out to display four scenes.

The Collections of the Virginia Museum of Fine Arts,
The Lillian Thomas Pratt Collection, 1947

He charged a fair price and sold his jewelry to servant girls who wanted to look like ladies and to ladies who were afraid of thieves. He made a fortune and started the costume-jewelry business which has been growing ever since.

The mass production of costume jewelry was hard on goldsmiths and jewelers alike. Many—but not all—turned to other trades. Among those who refused to give up the traditional family calling was Peter Carl Faberge who learned the art of the goldsmith in his father's shop in St. Petersburg. Masters in the ancient trade were scattered and scarce in the late nineteenth century, but after he left his father's establishment Carl Faberge found them and studied under them in Germany and in Florence, where Cellini had learned his art almost four centuries before.

Returning to the House of Faberge in St. Petersburg, young Carl started making the exquisite and intricate Easter eggs which were presented each year to the Russian Tsarinas. Their artistry and delicacy delighted visitors to the International Exposition in Paris in 1900. They hailed Faberge as "the new Cellini." His work was in demand all over the world.

Besides displaying Faberge's art, the Easter eggs reveal the changing world in which he practiced it. The first one, made in 1884, was an exact model of a hen's egg created of enameled gold. Opened, it revealed a golden yolk which, opening in turn, held a miniature hen. Within the hen was a diamond reproduction of the Imperial crown, and inside this a tiny ruby pendant.

Like the coins of the ancient Roman emperors, Faberge's Easter eggs celebrated achievements of the government. In 1901 the egg contained a platinum locomotive which could be wound up to pull a golden streamer of railroad cars.

The miniature train commemorated the completion of the Trans-Siberian Express which had followed the gold strikes across the vast wastes of Siberia as similar railroads had trailed the prospectors over the plains and mountains of western America and the great deserts of Australia.

As World War I approached, the Easter eggs lost their gaiety and much of their gold. They became austere in theme and in materials until at last the House of Faberge was converted to the manufacture of small arms, never to know again the art of "the new Cellini."

As the railroads followed the prospectors to far places, so did the goldsmiths. In the latter part of the nineteenth century they found a new prosperity in the tent or log-cabin shops where they celebrated the discovery of new claims for lucky finders by turning gold dust and nuggets into rings, watch fobs, cane handles, and studs.

Some of them linger still in ghost towns whose only remaining source of gold is an annual stream of tourists. The goldsmith plying his ancient craft is one of the attractions. The tourist, buying the golden trinket, helps keep the fading art alive.

In the 1890's Paul Farnham, of New York's Tiffany and Company, was commissioned by the American Cottonoil Company to create a gold vase for Edward Dean Adams, chairman of the board. Farnham wanted the vase to be completely American in both material and design, so he hammered it out of nuggets from the mine of the Ruby Gold and Gravel Mining Company of Sierra County, California. The Ruby mine produced gold of a green cast which Farnham felt would be an ideal background for his design featuring cotton plants and a figure of husbandry.

The creation of the vase, almost twenty inches high, was a tremendous job. After it was shaped, the figures were "chased," or hammered, out of the body of the vessel. Twenty-one chasers worked eighteen months on this delicate task.

Then one night the unfinished vase disappeared from the Tiffany workshop and was never found again. Presumably, thieves melted down the months of labor into the 472 ounces of gold, worth about ten thousand dollars, from which the vase had been fashioned. Paul Farnham and his workmen started the project all over again. Eventually the completed vase joined Cellini's gold bowl in the New York Metropolitan Museum of Art.

There, in 1963, visitors could see the Adams gold vase, the Cellini bowl, and a special exhibition of the work of Carl Faberge. While children clapped their hands over the Easter eggs that had delighted the Russian Tsarinas, the economists in the world outside wrote darkly of dwindling gold stocks. And the Titan, sheathed in gold, streaked majestically into the stratosphere.

In the same city, on the same avenue, goldsmiths worked in Tiffany's top floor workshop, some of them faithfully following the

The Metropolitan Museum of Art, Gift of Edward D. Adams, 1904

In the 1890's, Tiffany's Paul Farnham and his twenty-one assistants labored a year and a half to make an elaborate gold vase. It disappeared and was never found. The work had to begin again, and the result was the vase in this photograph.

designs of Jean Schlumberger who, in the past quarter of a century, has been repeatedly hailed as "the new Faberge."

Their equipment was modern. Blow torches could be adjusted with proper mixtures of oxygen and air to produce a needlepoint flame of precise temperature. Hammers and grinding and polishing pieces were electric. But on the workbenches, close to each of the thirty-five goldsmiths and jewelers, were the personal kits of tools they had used as apprentices, most of them in Europe, and which they still used frequently, ignoring the modern equipment at their disposal.

As the worn hammers tapped the gold, as the workmen coaxed their flames with blowpipes like those pictured on the walls of Egyptian tombs, the centuries slipped away. Yet, even here, there was change. Missing were Cellini's "many youths always springing up and eager to learn the beautiful art of the goldsmith."

The beautiful art of the goldsmith has existed in almost all countries in all ages. Examples of this art are shown on the following pages.

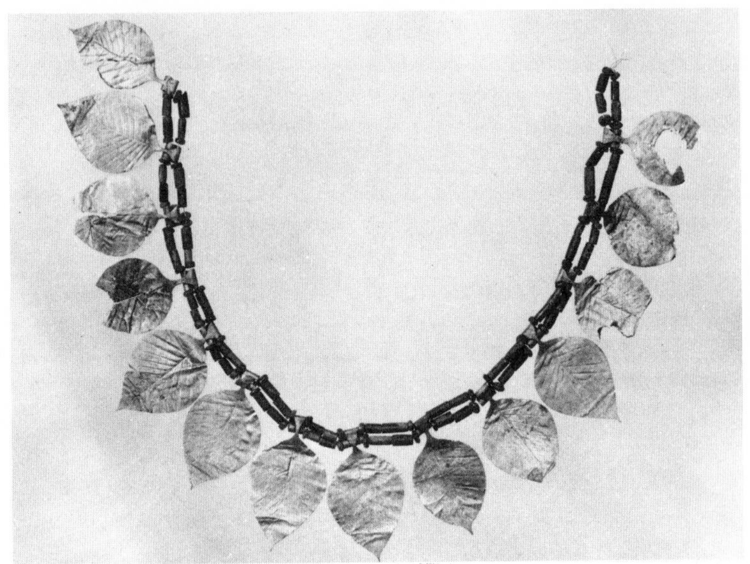

The Metropolitan Museum of Art, Excavations of the University of Pennsylvania Museum and the British Museum, 1927–1928; Dodge Fund, 1933

Wreath of gold beech leaves from ancient Sumeria, strung on beads of carnelian and lapis lazuli.

Ancient Egyptian ornament made of gold inlaid with carnelian, lapis lazuli, turquoise, and garnet.

The Metropolitan Museum of Art, Rogers Fund and contribution from Henry Walters, 1916

The Metropolitan Museum of Art, Gift of J. Pierpont Morgan, 1917

Byzantine gold cup from Albania.

Gold staff head from Colombia.

Museum of the American Indian, Heye Foundation

Museum of the American Indian, Heye Foundation

Gold crown from Peru, 10 3/4 inches high.

The Metropolitan Museum of Art, Gift of J. Pierpont Morgan, 1916

Italian chasuble embroidered in gold, sixteenth century.

Seventeenth-century German chalice of gold, enamel, and jewels.

The Metropolitan Museum of Art, Gift of J. Pierpont Morgan, 1917

Sixteenth-century Spanish shrine of gold, gems, and enamel, set against rock crystal.

The Metropolitan Museum of Art, Gift of J. Pierpont Morgan, 1917

Gold-and-agate jewel box from England, eighteenth century.

The Metropolitan Museum of Art, Gift of Admiral F. R. Harris, 1946, in memory of his wife, Dena Sperry Harris

Gold-and-diamond perfume bottle from France, eighteenth century.

The Metropolitan Museum of Art, Bequest of Catherine D. Wentworth, 1948

The Metropolitan Museum of Art, Gift of Samuel P. Avery, 1906

An Imperial Decree of early-nineteenth-century China, engraved on four leaves of a gold book.

Nineteenth-century gold necklace from India, filled with enamel and gems.

The Metropolitan Museum of Art, Gift of Henry L. de Forest and family, 1945

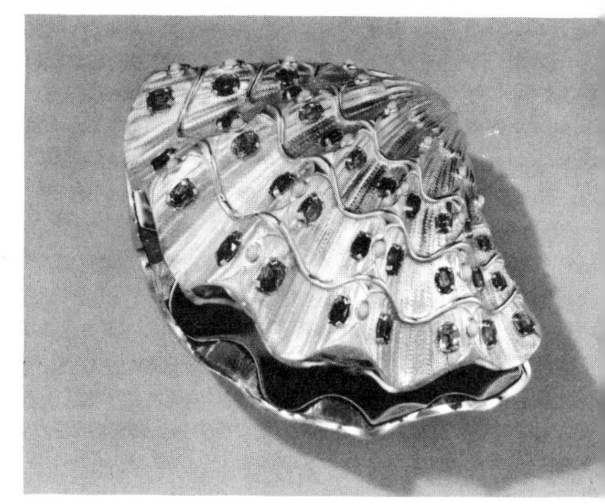

Compact of sapphires, emeralds, and turquoises set in gold; designed by Jean Schlumberger in 1958.

Tiffany & Co., New York

TRADED

WHILE SEARCHING FOR GOLD in New Guinea after World War I not a few prospectors lost their heads to tribesmen who needed them for money. It was no consolation to the victims that the severed heads would not be spent frivolously. To their new owners the heads represented the highest form of wealth, to be displayed proudly and protected by life itself, if necessary.

A man who had captured a head would part with it only to buy a bride, a purchase that could be made with no other commodity but a substitute daughter to compensate a father for the loss of a member of the family's labor force. A warrior without the head of a foe to prove his bravery was not considered man enough to own a wife. The hunter who had severed fifty heads could, if he wished, exchange them for fifty wives.

The prized heads came from strangers and enemies. The penalty for murder within the community was a life for a life. The death sentence could be avoided only by offering something equal to a life—in this case a captured head. In New Guinea in the twentieth century shrunken heads were still performing the oldest duties of money.

Man's first economic need, long before he had goods to barter in a market, was for "bride price" and "blood price." At different times in different parts of the world almost everything on earth has been used in this capacity—human heads, metals, cattle, grain, rice, tools, weapons, salt, cocoa beans, shells, whale teeth, feathers, animal skins, red ochre, rugs, logs, silk, spices, and stones so heavy they can't be moved. The latter are still prized on the island of Yap.

Economists list a great many requirements for money. It must not be so abundant that it is rendered worthless, nor so scarce that it is unattainable. The supply should be steady so that the value remains constant. Its worth must be easily recognizable. It should be durable, portable, and divisible.

Obviously, using these standards, the economists would have rejected many kinds of primitive money. But then they were not buying or selling brides. The one thing that all these early forms of money had in common was acceptability. This is, as Stuart Chase has pointed out, the only absolutely essential requirement of money.

Some primitive money shared with our present paper francs and marks and pesos a grave limitation—its acceptability was limited to the clan, or tribe, or nation. Just as money was born in "bride price" and "blood price," so were international relations.

The life that had to be paid for might well belong to a tribe that had a taboo against collecting human heads. The man who had spent his best years hoarding red ochre could not use it to purchase a bride from a tribe that did not paint their bodies with it. Peace and procreation, both essential to the continuation of the community, depended on finding something that could be gathered and saved with some certainty that it would be acceptable in place of a life everywhere and under any circumstances.

For the New Guinea headhunters the solution never came. Perhaps the problem was not pressing. In other places, where the domestic bride price was gold, it became the international bride price. Unlike human heads, gold was acceptable everywhere.

This had little to do with the virtues that are usually accorded gold as money. It was as acceptable in Spain and Ireland, where it was plentiful, as it was in Canaan where it was scarce. It was as coveted in Lydia, where it was picked easily out of the Pactolus River, as in Egypt where mining was hazardous and costly.

It was valuable, but so were amber and jade, and they were less easily adulterated or imitated than was gold. These stones, and others, were also durable and portable. In fact, throughout his history man has had metals and gems that equaled and in some cases surpassed gold's alleged qualifications as an ideal medium of exchange. Yet nothing has ever replaced gold as the universal standard and store of monetary value. It is, and always has been, acceptable everywhere.

Economists attribute this acceptability to gold's mystique, and some of them wish that the metal's grip on the economic system rested in some attribute more easily duplicated or argued away. Gold's mystique is older than its use as money. It is rooted in its divine relationship to the sun. This conception appears as part of man's early religious history in widely separated places all around the globe, from the Orient to South America.

Gods were represented in gold, and the metal was first used as blood price on religious altars where it took the place of a human sacrifice. There, too, it became a standard of value. That is, a certain amount of gold was considered equivalent to a life. This evaluation became a part of the moral code of the community, first administered by the priests. A man who had killed could pay for his crime with gold instead of blood. The amount of gold needed depended on the social status of both the victim and the convicted.

If the murderer was of noble birth, the lives he took were not expensive. If he was a commoner who had slain a nobleman, he probably couldn't beg, borrow, or steal enough gold in his lifetime to pay for the offense. If he had killed a slave, a gold ring would take care of the matter.

Gold was also demanded as bride price and in this case too it took the place of a life. Originally, in most societies, when a man took a woman from her home to his he was expected to replace her with one of his sisters. Like slaves and donkeys, women were economically valuable as cheap labor and beasts of burden. When a daughter left home, her family suffered an economic loss for which compensation was expected, first by replacement and then by gold.

The father, in turn, provided his daughter with a dowry that she might not walk empty-handed into the home of her husband. Legally the dowry belonged to the bride, and she took it back with her again in case of divorce or annulment—unless her husband could talk her out of it before the separation.

The terms and the amounts involved in both the bride price and the dowry were open to negotiation. As with the blood price, the bride price was inevitably greater for the man who was poorer. Since the poor man rarely had the asking price in one lump sum of gold, he bought his bride on the installment plan, a credit arrangement we usually associate with our industrial age.

Many a man spent his lifetime paying for his wife and, like modern refrigerators, the women sometimes wore out before the payments were completed. Other men, like the prophet Hosea, who paid fifty shekels for his helpmate, spent a lifetime deploring the extravagance. In Hebrew the word for wife was *beulah,* which meant "owned."

Besides compensating the bride's family for the loss of her services, the bride price legitimized the marriage. Without it, the maiden was presumed to be stolen and the couple living in sin.

The ring which still symbolizes the legality of a marriage was originally part of the gold that paid for the bride. It was placed on the third finger of the left hand because an artery was believed to run from this finger to the heart, the source of love. A golden ring thus strategically placed would keep the heart of the wearer true to the man who had paid for her with his precious gold.

In paying for human life, whether as blood price or bride price, gold was performing several of the duties we demand of money. It was a medium of exchange in these particular and very important transactions. Since it had been equated with human life, it could be used as a standard to measure the value of other things. Acceptable in place of life itself, it could be trusted to maintain its own worth.

This, combined with its scarcity, durability, and portability, made it an excellent store of value. It was scarce among common folk even when kings and priests had an abundance, so it was always in demand. It could be buried as a hoard just as it was buried with the dead. Dug up years later, it was unchanged in quality or quantity.

Or gold could be worn on the person, adding the prestige that comes with displayed wealth, and adding beauty and magic as well. In any form, gold savings could be carried off in an emergency to find a welcome everywhere.

While gold was hoarded, markets grew around the temples as people brought their surpluses to exchange for the surpluses of others. These were the homely products of the area—the familiar grains grown in the fields, the leather goods, the homespun fabrics, the native fowl and domesticated animals. Some of these commodities also took on the duties of currency, for gold was rare in the marketplace, more often saved than spent.

Certain people couldn't save their gold. These were the non-agricultural specialists—the priests and magicians, the miners and metalworkers, the professional soldiers, and finally the traders.

They had to spend their gold for the food and clothing they did not produce. Mercenary soldiers were in large part responsible for bringing gold to the markets. They also distributed the new luxuries for which gold could be exchanged. Both arrived as booty from their campaigns.

The exotic products from foreign lands enticed men to part with their hoarded gold. Traders could carry the gold to distant cities, as they could not carry cattle or bags of grain, to exchange it for more of the coveted goods. International trade was founded on gold's portability and universal acceptability.

Though the gold served as money, it was not coined. It came in many forms and was valued by purity and weight. The talent, so often mentioned in the Bible, was not a coin but a weight, of approximately 8.5 grams.

When the gold reached the marketplace it was weighed and tested for purity by the goldsmiths. The testing was often done on a touchstone. This was a smooth black stone, called coticula, and found, according to Theophrastus, only in the River Tmolus. The mark made on the stone by rubbing it with the golden object being tested was matched by a mark made by one of the goldsmith's touch needles.

The needles came in sets of twenty-four, suspended from wire rings. Three sets were needed to properly test gold. The needles of one set were made of varying proportions of gold and silver alloy. Another set contained needles of gold and copper, and a third combined all three metals.

The first needle on the ring contained only one part gold to twenty-three parts of the metal with which it was alloyed. The proportion of gold in each needle increased until the twenty-fourth was of pure gold.

"This method is so accurate," wrote Pliny, "that they do not mistake it to a scruple." From it came our division of the fineness of gold into twenty-four parts, or karats. Twenty-four karat gold, like the twenty-fourth touch needle, is pure, unadulterated gold.

The touchstone method was an accurate test for the surface of the gold. Men who doubted the uniform quality of the metal they were offered often demanded a test by fire. In this test a sample of the gold was heated to drive off impurities. If the gold weighed as much after it was heated as it had before, it was considered pure gold. It was downgraded in value in proportion to the weight lost.

A sample of the gold was easily obtained if the product was flour gold, sifted from the sands of a river and brought to market in purses made of the horns or bladders of animals. Solid objects had to be nicked to obtain gold for testing.

The constant sampling, evaluating, and weighing of gold was wasteful and time-consuming. In their effort to speed and ease the process, the professional merchants invented coins.

It happened at different times in different places and the coins took various forms. It is generally believed that coins had been used, and misused, in China for at least a thousand years before Croesus minted his. The first Chinese coins, made indiscriminately of *chin,* the word that designated both gold and metal, were simply called red, white, and yellow, deriving their value from weight and color.

Everywhere, early coinage was extremely simple. The goldsmith melted down the variety of gold the trader had collected and reshaped it in the form the traveler found most convenient to carry.

The pieces of gold were of more or less regular weights, and sometimes both the weight and the merchant's seal were stamped on them. If the merchant had a reputation for honesty his seal was accepted as a guarantee of his gold. Many merchants annulled the convenience their new coins were supposed to achieve by adulterating their gold and exaggerating its weight.

The form the money took depended on the preference of the merchant who had it minted. Men traveling by boat preferred beads and bars of gold that could be dumped into sacks for loading and unloading. Overland traders used hooks and rings that could be worn. The hooks were inserted in clothing. The rings were dangled from larger rings, called purses, which were worn on the neck, waist, and arms.

Bead and ring money proved popular with everybody. Women became walking banks.

When gold was valued for its magic powers alone, men wore it themselves. Unless they possessed the riches of royalty, their wives went without. When gold became money, women were given the task of carrying and guarding it.

Wives of prosperous men were so loaded with strands of heavy golden beads and dangled so many rings from their fingers, arms, and legs that movement was seriously impaired and they were forced to shuffle slowly and awkwardly from home to market. This manner of walking was carefully and enviously imitated by women less heavily encumbered.

Many merchants found bar money convenient. A *taleis,* meaning "something cut off," could be hacked from the bar to pay for a purchase, no matter how small. Clippers found the bars convenient too. These thieves shaved off a bit of every bar that came their way, industriously gathering enough tallies to make bars of their own.

The characteristic round coin, edged with a design, was developed to discourage clippers. In Asia the designs were first made by dropping ants on the rims of the molten metal discs. As the ants struggled to escape they marked the outer edges of the coins so that clipping could be detected.

The goldsmiths who had once worked inside the temples fashioning gold for religious purposes now worked outside, in the busy marketplace, minting and changing money for merchants. But though gold had taken on new economic duties, its old magic and religious significance was not forgotten.

Many people brought their golden coins to the goldsmiths to have them changed back to idols or amulets, preferring to have gold in a form that would do double duty as hoarded wealth and magic protector. The coins themselves began to take on magic properties and special functions in the public mind.

Some were bad-luck coins, which goldsmiths exchanged for those associated with good fortune. Others were considered unworthy of offering to the gods. Certain coins, placed in the nostrils of the dead, had the power to prevent the entrance of evil spirits disguised as insects.

The use of gold in trade added to the goldsmith's duties and greatly increased the amount of gold entrusted to him for conversion into coins, jewelry, charms, and images. Since he stayed in one place he could afford to protect his gold with strong buildings, vaults, locks, and guards.

The merchant traveling roads where robbers lay in ambush, or venturing in seas infested with pirates, had greater difficulty guarding his treasure. The gold that found acceptance everywhere could as readily be traded by thieves. And thieves could carry it as easily.

In one unguarded moment a trader could lose the profits from a long expedition or even of a lifetime.

Reluctantly and slowly traders abandoned gold for the very reasons they had first begun to use it. According to Sulayman, an Arab merchant of the ninth century, the Chinese dealt only in copper, refusing to accept either gold or silver. Their reason, he explained, was that a thief could not carry off more copper than his victim could afford to lose.

More generally merchants gave their gold to the goldsmiths for safekeeping, receiving in its stead a paper receipt for the amount of gold left on deposit. The paper was lighter to carry than the metal and it was robbery-proof. By leaving gold with goldsmiths in markets wherever they traveled, merchants found that a receipt signed by a known and trusted goldsmith of the community was as readily negotiable as gold itself.

The receipts became the first bank notes, "payable to the bearer on demand." They were supplemented by bills of exchange instructing the goldsmith to transfer a part of the depositor's gold to the man who presented the signed note. This too seems to have happened first in China about the middle of the third century B.C.

So convenient were these slips of paper that they traveled around the world, changing hands at every market, while the gold they represented remained undisturbed in the strong boxes of the goldsmiths. In this way the goldsmiths built up large stocks of idle gold, a fact well known to both robbers and honest people in need of funds.

Partly to make their establishments less attractive to thieves and partly to increase their own wealth, the goldsmiths began to lend out at interest a part of the gold that had been left with them. In so doing they became the world's first bankers, the fathers of our modern system of credit finance.

The birth was not painless. All the world's philosophical and religious sages railed against the practice of usury. So did the merchants whose gold the goldsmiths risked.

Often they had reason. How much gold could safely be loaned, and for how long, was a matter of guesswork. Goldsmith bankers who had been too greedy for interest frequently found themselves unable to honor the slips of paper that were supposed to represent gold in their vaults.

As a result of such miscalculations laws were passed which made lending money for interest a crime, often punishable by death. Despite the laws, the new banks continued to do business. They met important needs. There was no place else that people could borrow money or place their wealth for safekeeping.

In major cities goldsmiths' rows grew into financial centers and remain so today. London's famous Lombard Street was once exclusively reserved for goldsmiths. Many of her first bankers, including Richard Martin, founder of the Bank of England, started their banking careers there as "goldsmiths who keep running cashes."

When laws forbidding goldsmiths to lend money failed to eliminate the practice, governments set limits on the amount of interest that could be charged and the percentage of gold on deposit that could be let out on loan. Occasionally governments themselves went into the business of banking or offered the use of treasury vaults to private citizens for the protection of their valuables.

Governments were even less experienced in banking than were the goldsmiths, and they were subject to the same errors in judgment and the same temptations. In 1640 King Charles I of England, finding himself financially embarrassed, seized the valuables that had been placed for safekeeping by private citizens in the Royal Mint on Tower Hill.

The king was finally persuaded to relinquish his booty but, wrote Pepys in his diary, "the thing will never be forgot." Like most other Englishmen after that, Pepys left his gold with a goldsmith.

He continued to deplore the "most horrid shame" of the usury of the goldsmiths even as he availed himself of their services. Despite their many vocal critics, the new banks were there to stay.

And the usury of the goldsmiths was regarded in a different light, even by Pepys, when he found his own gold earning interest. In a diary entry of March, 1666, he recorded that for £2000 in gold he had left with his goldsmith three months previously he had received £2035.

"It hath produced me this profit," he wrote happily, "and hath been a convenience to me as to care and security of my house and demandable at two days warning."

World Conqueror *a desperate search for gold in new lands*

THEY CALLED HIM MARCO MILLIONS and he was the biggest liar in all of Venice. Everybody listened to him, but nobody believed. Marco Millions talked about traveling thousands of miles to a land where there were millions of people and millions of ducats in gold and silver and precious gems.

It was true that Marco Millions had gold and silver and precious gems. They were nothing to what he had seen, the liar insisted. In the land of Cathay, to the east, where he had spent twenty years, such miserable specimens of wealth were worn by the animals. Marco Millions didn't even try to make his stories plausible.

Everybody in Europe in the thirteenth century knew that gold and silver and gems were much too precious and scarce to be wasted on animals. The people of Europe had been fighting over their limited supply of such wealth for more than five hundred years—city against city, nation against nation, ruler against pope.

Since the fall of the old Roman Empire, Europe's supply of gold had shrunk until it was practically nonexistent. The mines of Spain that had once enriched the Romans produced gold for the Moors. Elsewhere on the Continent the mines produced nothing at all. Not since the Romans had they been owned by people who could operate them.

Through the centuries the gold coins had deteriorated, each new issue containing less gold, until at last the mints turned out nothing but coins of silver and copper. Even this money was scarce, and many markets had reverted to trade by barter. In once-rich Sicily, Frederick II, having no gold at all, made money out of leather.

Gold, of course, was not the only thing Europe lacked in the time that has since been called the Dark Ages. The Mediterranean was an Arab lake on which European ships dared not sail, and all the riches of the eastern world were cut off from the isolated continent by the hostile Moslems who controlled the old trade routes.

The merchants of Venice and Genoa dreamed of finding new ways to the spices and other luxuries of the East, the sale of which had once enriched them. It was on such a quest that Marco Polo had seen the wealth that earned him his nickname, Marco Millions.

The boy had grown up in Venice in a family of traders. It was not an ideal calling in those lean years, and in 1270, when Marco was seventeen years old, he set out with his father and uncle in an attempt to reach India. After traveling for more than two years the men were captured by Mongols who treated them kindly and took them to the court of their king, Kublai Khan, to show him the curious men from the West.

Kublai Khan ruled in Peking. His people, led by Genghis Khan, had swept out of Mongolia to take China in 1214. They had been on the march ever since. By the time the Polos reached the Mongol capital the former nomads controlled northern India, the Middle East, and the lands that are now Siberia, Russia, Poland, and Hungary.

From all these conquered territories gold made its way to Peking to enrich the fabulous court of the Khan. Nor did much of it leave the city, for the Khan, accepting taxes and tribute only in gold, paid his own debts with "flying money." He made this money from the underbark of the mulberry tree, "with as much solemnity and authority as if it were pure gold," Marco Polo related.

The ceremony with which the paper money was issued was supposed to guarantee its acceptance. Actually the Khan's power did this—and the docility of the Chinese people. They had been accepting flying money from their rulers since the third century B.C. when the Emperor Shih Huang Ti killed an albino stag and had the white skin cut into foot-square pieces of leather cash.

So luxurious was the court of the Khan, and so well were the visitors treated, that the Polos stayed for twenty years. During much of this time they lived in Kublai Khan's golden palace. They sat on chairs like golden thrones, were served from golden vessels six feet across, and were protected by golden idols sixteen feet high. The gifts the Khan gave them included golden ornaments sparkling with precious gems and silk robes glittering with threads of gold.

Young Marco was a special favorite of the Khan's. He was allowed to see, and he later described, the wealth of the Khan's great empire and even the wealth the mighty ruler did not control. This lay tantalizingly close, on the island of Cipango, now Japan.

On this island, roofs gleamed with gold and glistening yellow spires pierced the sky. Every palace, temple, and public building was richly ornamented with the precious metal. Lords and ladies wore golden jewelry artistically fashioned by Cipango's expert goldsmiths. But little of the metal was minted as money or used in trade.

Commerce was considered undignified by Japanese gentlemen. Even the Samurai, hired to kill, prided themselves on never touching money and not being able to count. When the Japanese were forced to handle coins they did so indirectly, keeping the currency in a bag. The amount of gold the bag contained was inscribed on it. No one risked contamination by opening the bag and checking its contents. Year after year the bags passed from owner to owner, the seals unbroken.

Kublai Khan tried, without success, to capture Cipango. After Marco Polo described the wonders of the East, European traders tried, with indifferent success, to reach the fabled island, the gold of Cathay, and the riches of India. Those who followed the overland trail pioneered by the Polos insisted that the wealth in the East was only exceeded by the perils of the journey.

Cautiously, ships set out to look for a sea route to spices and gold. Both trade goods, such as spices, and the gold that would serve as a medium of exchange were needed if European trade was to be revived. Portuguese sailors sought a new route to the East by sailing south along the west coast of Africa, stopping to claim the land they touched for their monarch. They brought back so much gold from the Niger and Senegal rivers that the king of Portugal referred to himself proudly as "Lord of Guinea." Enviously, geographers of other nations marked Portugal's new possession on their maps as "the place where gold is collected."

In 1488, Bartolomeu Dias succeeded in rounding the southern tip of Africa. He called it the Cape of Storms. Portugal's King John II renamed it the Cape of Good Hope. That it proved to be. Over the new sea route the gold of southern and eastern Africa and the riches of India finally found their way to Lisbon.

It was to King John II that a penniless Genoese sailor named Cristóbal Colón, later to become famous as Christopher Columbus, first presented his plan for reaching rich Cathay in the east by sailing due west. It wasn't a dreamer's get-rich-quick scheme. The sailor was thirty-two years old in 1483 when he asked the Portuguese king to finance his voyage. He was an experienced seaman, navigator, and map maker. He had been studying, documenting, and charting the proposed trip for years.

With gold from Guinea, the Portuguese king could afford to outfit such an expedition and he did, though he turned down the man whose idea it was. The surreptitious attempt to cross the Atlantic was unsuccessful. When the sailors found that the ocean was larger than Columbus' charts indicated they mutinied and the captain turned back.

In the meantime Columbus had found no one to finance his scheme. Friends and relatives had spoken for him at almost every court in Europe. No monarch felt he could afford the venture.

Spain was poorer than any nation, but King Ferdinand and Queen Isabel were the only ones who seemed interested. So Columbus waited year after year for a decision. In the meantime the Spanish monarchs were concerned with driving the Moors from their country. When the Moors were defeated, the treasury was exhausted. There was simply no gold to send out ships to look for new ways to reach the spice islands of the East and the gold of Cathay.

Desperately and drastically Columbus pared his anticipated needs to a minimum. Queen Isabel's confessor, the friar Juan Pérez, and her treasurer, Santangel, both urged her to make every effort to place Columbus' expedition under the Spanish flag.

She donated her jewelry and household funds to the cause. Santangel set himself the task of finding the rest of the needed money. He also found the three merchant and mariner brothers Pinzón who equipped the little ships for a promised part of the profits, commanded two of them on the voyage, and rounded up the men for the crews.

Finding men was almost as difficult as finding money. Reasonable seamen preferred to ship to known ports. Even offering pardons to sailors convicted of crimes didn't bring a rush of volunteers. It took ingenious methods of persuasion to bring the roster of the crew to ninety. In their three little ships the men set sail in August, 1492.

Columbus commanded the largest and slowest of the vessels, the *Santa María,* which could carry a hundred ton and boasted a deck. The *Pinta* and the *Niña* were open boats just half her size, like little tubs in the ocean. Columbus pronounced them "very suitable." Among his official papers was a letter from King Ferdinand and Queen Isabel addressed to the Grand Khan, in Cathay. To reach Cathay's gold was his main objective, wrote his son Fernando, who accompanied him on later voyages.

As the Portuguese had found out nine years before, the ocean exceeded Columbus' calculations. Sailing on, day after day, week after week, with no sign of land, the men threatened mutiny. Their commodore would not turn back. But when at last he saw birds flying overhead he changed his course to the southwest hoping the birds would lead him to land.

They did. At dawn, October 12, 1492, the ships reached an island, one of the Bahamas. Columbus was sure he had accomplished his objective, according to Fernando. Consulting his maps, on which there was no place for the large continents of North and South America, he decided that the island he had found and those that lay near it were located off the eastern coast of India. He called them Las Indias, the Indies, and though the natives were naked and poor he was encouraged to see that they wore rings of gold in their

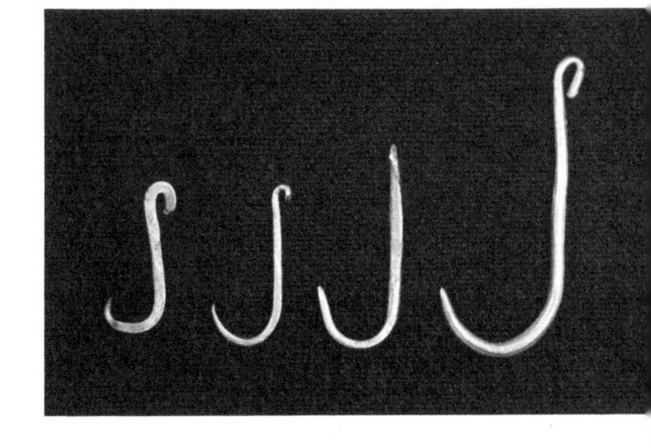

In the West Indies, Columbus found naked Indians wearing gold nose rings and fishing with gold hooks, shown here in actual sizes.

Museum of the American Indian, Heye Foundation

pierced noses. He took possession of the islands for his king and queen and hurried on to find Cipango.

The island he chose for Cipango, now Cuba, was a disappointment. No gold-roofed palaces or temples rose from its shores. There were only the same naked Indians he had found on the other islands, living in the same poor huts. But they too had gold. They brought it to him in the form of nuggets, fishhooks, ornaments and masks, happy to exchange their treasure for fishhooks of steel, glass beads, buttons, and bells.

Asking always for Cipango, Columbus followed native directions to Cibao, and wrecked the *Santa María* on the shores of Haiti, which he named Isla Española. He used the wreckage to build a fort.

Leaving a small settlement behind, he returned to Spain. He took with him the gold he had received from the natives and several Indian chiefs in full regalia. The effect was all that he had hoped. He announced that he had found a land of rich gold mines and great rivers filled with gold. Instantly he became a hero.

The grateful Spanish sovereigns granted him the titles Admiral and Viceroy, and gave him castles and a coat of arms. Rich men, poor men, sailors, farmers, priests, princes, and vagabonds begged to join him on his return trip. Setting out again in September, 1493, he had seventeen ships instead of three. His crew numbered fifteen hundred, and a hundred more managed the trip as stowaways. The admiral himself took thirty personal servants.

When the fleet reached Española the weary voyagers saw no rich mines or rivers flowing with gold. They disembarked to face hostile natives, the ruins of the Spanish fort and one lone survivor of the men Columbus had left behind. The newcomers, who had envisioned themselves picking up nuggets of gold in a land of plenty, scrounged for enough food to keep alive and built crude huts for shelter.

Their admiral searched for a gold mine. Finding none, he levied a poll tax of gold dust on the natives. When they couldn't pay the tax, he shipped five hundred of them back to Spain as slaves. With them went the colonists who were ill, injured, or disgruntled. Happily home again they spread the disillusioning word that there was no gold to be found in the Indies. There was only hardship and hunger.

When Columbus himself returned to Spain, in 1496, to get sup-

Antonio de Herrera, *Historia General de las Indias Ocidentales . . . ,*
The New York Public Library, Rare Book Division

Apparently Herrera, who was official Spanish chronicler for the New World, believed Columbus' glowing reports of a land heaped with gold. The truth is that when an eager fleet of seventeen ships made a second voyage to Española, they found little but hardship and hunger.

plies for his colony he announced that the island of Española was the long lost Ophir, from which much of King Solomon's wealth had come. But the Spanish sovereigns had lost faith in their admiral's tales of gold. They sent provisions back to their subjects and instructed Columbus to win souls for Christ among the distant heathen.

Winning souls was not as alluring as winning gold. Once again criminals had to be given pardons in order to make up a crew for the admiral's six ships. On this voyage the fleet reached the mainland of South America, touching Venezuela.

Although the Spanish conquerors levied a poll tax of gold dust on West Indian natives, the returns were small. To replace the Indians, who died in great numbers from hard work and bad treatment, the Spaniards imported African Negroes. In this grossly exaggerated drawing printed by the Flemish engraver De Bry, Negroes present gold dust to their masters. Others mine a hillside.

Theodoro de Bry, *Americae,* The New York Public Library, Rare Book Division

According to his son, Columbus thought he had come at last to the continent of Asia. On these shores he would find golden Cathay. His dreams renewed, he claimed the land for his country and continued on to Española with provisions.

On this unlucky island there was nothing but illness, both natives and colonists dying in alarming numbers. Instead of bringing the Indians civilization and Christianity, the Spaniards had brought measles and smallpox. In return they had received dysentery and syphilis in place of gold.

Tales of disease, dissension, and mismanagement reached the Spanish sovereigns from the colony. In the year 1500 Christopher Columbus, admiral of the ocean seas, was arrested and shipped back to Barcelona in chains.

They were removed when he reached Spain, and the charges against him dropped. But in the six years that were left to him of life he never forgot, wrote Fernando, and he kept the chains always near.

Once he had written: "Gold is most excellent. With gold the possessor of it does all that he desires in the world and arrives at sending souls to paradise."

He had spent a quarter of a century searching for that which was most excellent. He had found a new world that would make Spain rich and yield more gold than men had collected in all the thousands of years of history. But for himself there had been only hardship and suffering and, at the end, the humiliation of the chains.

AS GODS

SAILING SOUTH FROM CUBA IN 1517, Hernández de Córdoba was blown off course by a storm. When the winds abated, the sailors found themselves in strange waters with an unfamiliar shoreline before them. As they drifted nearer this land, of which there was no record on their maps or charts, they were surprised to see stone walls rising from the plain and, above them, the top tiers of great pyramids holding aloft elaborately carved temples. Not in all their voyages exploring the lands and waters to which Columbus had led them had they seen such evidence of civilization.

Landing near one of the cities, they were so impressed with its size and beauty that they thought they must have stumbled on fabulous India. They called the city Cairo. Advancing toward it, they were attacked by warriors armed with lances and bows and arrows. When the Spaniards fired their muskets, the warriors retreated, leaving the nearest temples deserted.

Córdoba and his men climbed the pyramid steps and entered the stone buildings. Without and within, the walls were carved with animal figures and row upon row of hieroglyphic inscriptions. But the thing that most impressed the Spaniards were the idols and images, for they were made of gold.

The men carried off what they could and set sail along the coast looking for another city to plunder. A warning had preceded them. This time the warriors who guarded the walls refused to flee before the muskets. They pushed the Spaniards back to the sea and their ships, killing and capturing many and wounding all. Córdoba died of his wounds, but not before he had taken his strange story and his golden trophies back to Cuba.

The land he had discovered was the peninsula of Yucatán. It lay less than two hundred miles from the western tip of the island of Cuba, yet it had eluded the Spaniards for a quarter of a century. The cities he admired and the gold he stole belonged to the nation of the Maya.

The Mayan calendar and the sequence of events in the rest of the world have not yet been satisfactorily correlated, but strong evidence supports the theory that the lost Mayan civilization was as old as the Egyptian. Some scholars say it was older.

The Mayans believed that they had come originally from the north. When their culture was at its peak they lived in Central America, in what is now Honduras and Guatemala. Like the Greeks in the Mediterranean world, the nation of the Maya absorbed the culture of their neighbors, preserved it, and spread it. The mark of the Maya was everywhere.

But by the time Córdoba found the Mayan cities of Yucatán, the jungles of Central America had already covered the deserted temples of their past. Why they kept building and moving on, no one knows for certain. The ruins show no evidence of an attack by enemies. It has been suggested that they were forced to move when their agricultural lands wore out.

Their society was sharply divided into two classes. There were the artisans and intellectuals, who were also holy men. And there were the farmers and laborers. The latter did not live in the beautiful stone cities built with their toil. They lived in primitive huts on the edges of the fields they tilled with forked sticks.

Though the metalworkers in the holy cities could make beautiful images of gold and silver, they had never made a metal digging tool for the farmers whose labor fed them. Though the priests were excellent astronomers and mathematicians, and had devised an ingenious and accurate round calendar, no one had ever invented a wheel or used an animal as a beast of burden.

While the farmers scratched at the earth with their inadequate sticks, the priests watched the stars, reckoned time, and erected stone monuments inscribed with hieroglyphs. They also wrote books, or codices, which were stored in an official library.

Each year the peasants were invited to bring their harvest and their sacrifices to the city. The sacrifices were live—captive warriors, beautiful maidens, and children.

On the appointed day, at dawn, the high priests, dressed in their elaborate robes and laden with jewelry, left the Temple of Kulkulcán, the Sacred Serpent, and led a procession to the Sacred Cenote, or Well of Sacrifice. At the edge of the well the human sacrifices were ceremoniously laden with golden ornaments before they were hurled into the murky waters.

Occasionally the heart was cut from the living sacrificial victim and the knife thrown into the well with the heart and the body. Images of gold and jade were sacrificed too, but unlike the humans they were killed, or broken, first.

In the latter part of the nineteenth century a young archaeologist named Edward Herbert Thompson devised a special dredge and learned deep-sea diving in order to explore the depths of the Sacred Cenote at Chichén Itzá, in Yucatán. Besides the skeletons he brought up from the slimy water, half of them children's, he retrieved vast quantities of gold in many forms—figurines, pendants, bells, axheads, and knife handles. After he had taken these from the country, the Mexican government sued him for half a million dollars, their estimate of the treasure he had removed from the Mayan city.

Chichén Itzá was already in ruins when the Spaniards discovered Yucatán, and its crumbling walls sheltered at least one army of conquistadores. The name of the city memorialized other invaders who had preceded the Spaniards by centuries. They were the Itzás, probably Toltecs, from the Valley of Mexico. Though they conquered the Mayas, the two cultures merged and dominated the surrounding territory.

According to one version of the story, the Itzás were led out of the Valley of Mexico by their great god, Quetzalcoatl, whom the Mayan made their own and called Kulkulcán. Under both names, the god was represented by a plumed serpent, but he was described as a tall, bearded white man. Powerful and wise, he had left his people long ago to sail away to the land of the rising sun, promising to return one day and put down their enemies.

The Aztecs were their enemies. They had conquered Quetzalcoatl's people and built their own capital in the Valley of Mexico about 1325. They knew about the god's promise and feared his return.

In an effort to prevent his wrath they adopted him and made him the greatest of their many gods. They built their highest temples to him and worshiped him with lavish offerings of gold and silver and human beings. These they exacted from subject tribes in a vast empire that embraced most of what is now the country of Mexico.

Their capital city was built on an island in the middle of a lake, where Mexico City stands today. Called Tenochtitlán, it was a beautiful place protected from attack by the water around it. These waterways were used as thoroughfares. Canoes filled with people and produce plied up and down them, and floating barges of flowers added color and fragrance. Causeways connected the city with mainland suburbs to the east and west.

On the island the Aztec king, Montezuma, lived and ruled. His palaces were filled with treasure. His tax collectors stuffed great warehouses with the produce they brought back from subject tribes.

When the tax collectors failed to bring back enough tribute, the warriors were sent out to capture young men and women as living sacrifices to the gods. The temples where these sacrifices were made

The Mayan people cleverly got rid of Cortez by saying that if he wanted gold he should go to the Aztecs, who were rich. In this Indian drawing from the Codex Florentino, *an Aztec goldsmith makes a turquoise-and-gold ornament. The* Codex *is a history of New Spain written in the sixteenth century by a Franciscan monk, Fr. Bernardino de Sahagún, who devoted his life to the welfare of the Indians. They contributed to his historical work by supplying facts and making drawings.*

Codex Florentino

Warned for some time by portents of doom, Montezuma was instantly alarmed when messengers brought reports of an invading army. To keep the foreigners away, he sent his sorcerers to offer bewitched food to Cortez and his staff. They refused it.

Codex Florentino

were raised on pyramids and dominated the city. From them came the smell of blood.

The many gods of the Aztecs demanded many sacrifices. In times of peril twenty thousand victims might be offered in simultaneous and continuous ceremonies that kept the steps of the pyramids flowing red for weeks.

In the spring of 1517 Montezuma's tax collectors brought alarming news from the east. Quetzalcoatl had returned from the land of the rising sun with many other superhumans. They had appeared in the sea on floating houses. They rode over the land on tame deer, and they killed many people with thunder and lightning.

In the temples the priests increased their sacrifices. The city echoed with the screams of the captives as the ceremonial knives cut their beating hearts from their breasts. To the living gods in the east Montezuma sent messengers with golden tribute.

The living gods in the east numbered five hundred. Their floating houses were eleven ships. Their tame deer were horses. Their thunder and lightning were their muskets and seven small cannon. Their leader had never heard of the god Quetzalcoatl, nor of the mighty Montezuma. His name was Hernando Cortez and he had sneaked away from Cuba to capture more of the gold that the dying Córdoba had seen on Yucatán.

Much to his surprise the Maya greeted him with gifts, carefully fumigating their visitors first. Among the offerings of gold, women, and slaves were two translators. One was a Spanish priest named Aguilar who had been shipwrecked seven years before and captured by cannibals who kept him in a cage while they fattened him. He had escaped to live with the Maya and he spoke their language.

The other was a beautiful girl named Marina. She had been sold to the Maya as a slave by her people, the Aztecs. She knew the Aztec language and the way to their island city. Later she was to bear Cortez a child and to prove her loyalty by saving his life.

If Cortez wanted gold he should follow Marina, the Maya people told him. The gold they had given him was all they had. They were poor, but the Aztecs were rich.

Cortez might not have believed them, nor have undertaken the long journey to the Valley of Mexico, but as he explored the coastline, looking for cities to loot and a suitable spot for his headquarters, Montezuma's messengers arrived. They brought mantles of iridescent feathers, bolts of cloth, many golden ornaments, and a golden disk, representing the sun, as large as a cart wheel. They presented their gifts in Montezuma's name and begged the great white god to stay in the east. They did not know how desperately the great white god wanted gold.

Having seen a sample of the treasure to be found inland, Cortez

Montezuma sent gifts of gold to Cortez, begging him to stay away. But the treasures only convinced Cortez that he should discover their source. In this drawing, he and his army ask the way to Tenochtitlán; behind them smoke rises from the volcano Popocatepetl.

Codex Florentino

determined to go after it. He established a headquarters at Vera Cruz and then, to increase his fighting strength and to make sure that none of his men could desert, he destroyed his ships and added the sailors to his troops. He left 150 men at Vera Cruz and marched inland with 15 horses, 400 marching soldiers, and 1000 Cempoalan Indians who wanted to fight their enemy, the Aztecs.

The Aztec capital was two hundred miles away, a three months' journey through rugged mountains and the territory of unfriendly tribes. Doggedly the Spaniards marched and fought their way toward Montezuma's stronghold. They were spurred on by the frequent messengers who arrived from the Aztec king bringing gifts of gold and begging the white gods to turn back.

After slaughtering three thousand in one village alone, making a sumptuous feast for the cannibal Cempoalans, the invaders met fewer and fewer enemies. Most villages greeted them with gifts and protestations of friendships, always carefully referring to them as gods. The Tlascalans joined them in their campaign against the Aztecs.

As they reached the causeway that led to the city of Tenochtitlán, Montezuma came in person to meet the strangers. He was carried on a golden litter and dressed in rich robes. Even the soles of his sandals were of gold. He welcomed the Spaniards as his guests and led them into the city where a palace had been prepared for them.

For a week they enjoyed the luxuries Montezuma provided—women and slaves, exotic food served from golden tableware, clean linen, and soft robes. Behind a concealed door in the palace, which had once been occupied by Montezuma's father, they found a room filled with treasure which they divided, setting aside a fifth for the king of Spain. Montezuma himself sent them rich gifts regularly.

They were magnificently treated, but they were also prisoners. The causeways that led from the city were fitted at intervals with drawbridges which could be quickly raised to cut off their escape. Nervously they listened to the shrieks of less fortunate prisoners who were being sacrificed to the gods. The smell of blood came from the temple towers.

Their situation was desperate and Cortez took a desperate chance to remedy it. He seized Montezuma in his palace, placed him in fetters and kept him prisoner in the palace of his father.

Charles V, king of Spain, now had a new subject, and a wealthy

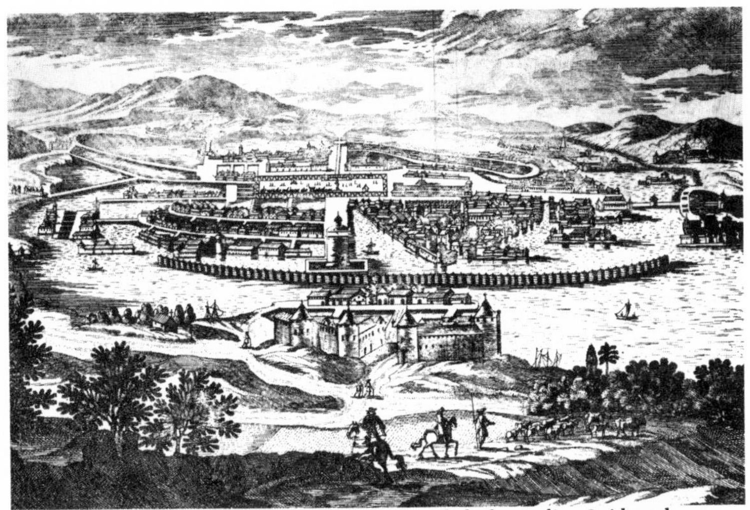

Antonio de Herrera, *Historia General de las Indias Ocidentales . . . ,*
The New York Public Library, Rare Book Division

Tenochtitlán, island capital of the Aztecs, is now Mexico City. Then, as now, it was beautiful. Except for three broad causeways connecting it with the mainland, there were no roads. Canoes filled with produce and barges filled with flowers plied along the city waterways.

one. Montezuma's tax collectors went out over the Aztec empire collecting gold for the king across the sea and the powerful white gods who controlled the city.

The treasure mounted so rapidly that the king's fifth was soon equal to a shipload. Cortez had it carried by a train of porters to Vera Cruz with instructions that a boat should be built to speed it on the way to the Spanish monarch.

Cortez's purpose in hurrying the gold overseas was to receive official recognition of his conquest and the king's permission to continue to govern the territory he had seized. He had left Cuba against the orders of the Spanish administrator there and he feared that once the news of Mexico's riches reached the island, rivals would appear to try to take from him all that he had won.

He was right in his fears. His hasty attempt to ship off the treasure alerted the Cubans to the fact that it was there. While they raised an army to conquer Cortez, the ship carrying gold to the king of Spain was captured by the French.

Charles V protested. Francis I refused to give up the stolen gold. Quite possibly some of it was used later by Cellini to create his famous salt cellar. The quarrel between the two monarchs grew into war.

In Mexico, too, trouble was brewing. The men from Cuba, one thousand strong, landed on the eastern coast. They were led by Pánfilo de Narváez who had what Cortez hadn't—the official authorization from Spain's representative in the Indies to take and hold the country in the name of the Spanish king.

Taking as many men as he dared from the Aztec capital, Cortez hurried over the mountains to meet the Spanish foe. He surprised Narváez in the middle of the night, wounded him in the eye, and took him prisoner.

The thousand men didn't really care who was their leader, as long as they received their share of the gold. They gladly swelled Cortez's forces and they brought with them another ally—smallpox. Within the next year the disease killed more natives than the Spanish could have slaughtered in a decade.

During Cortez's absence, the Aztecs in the city of Mexico had revolted. Returning to the city, Cortez found his troops besieged in their quarters. He managed to reach them and led the captured Montezuma onto the palace balcony to ask his people to stop their war on the white gods. Their answer was immediate and violent. Montezuma was killed in the Aztec attack.

The prince Cuitlahuac led the fight, which was fierce and ceaseless. No matter how many Indians the Spaniards killed, more came to take their place. The Spaniards themselves had no reinforcements. Steadily their number decreased and even those who survived were wounded.

Their only hope was escape. They built a movable bridge with which to span gaps in the causeway and divided the treasure, carrying in the midst of their ranks the fifth that had been set aside for the king. On the night of June 30, 1520, they dragged their movable bridge into place under the cover of darkness.

The men and the gold they carried proved too much for the bridge. It buckled under the load and could not be moved to span the next gap in the causeway. By this time the Aztecs were in full pursuit. Men who had weighted themselves with too much gold were captured. Others discarded treasure, packs, and muskets, and plunged into the lake to swim for safety through water filled with enemy canoes and the bodies of their comrades.

The rich leavings in treasure and the many live captives to be taken back to the temples diverted the pursuers. A few hundred Spaniards and twenty-three horses survived La Noche Triste and escaped to the mainland. Wounded and weary, without food, weapons or ammunition, they limped toward the friendly village of their Indian allies, the Tlascalan.

On the night of July 8, the Aztecs struck again. There were two hundred thousand of them, according to Cortez's report. Their leader was arrayed in golden armor and carried a battle flag of gold net. The Spaniards had neither weapons nor ammunition.

Their only choice was to die bravely, for death appeared certain. Cortez led the way, charging straight for the Aztec commander. One of his companions threw a lance, wounding the Indian prince. Cortez leaped from his horse, thrust his dagger through the general's heart and rode off again, waving the captured battle flag high.

The fall of their leader confused the enemy and heartened the Spaniard's Indian allies, the Tlascalan. They seized the arms of the Aztecs and used them to help the Spaniards win a miraculous victory.

Known as the battle of Otumba, it was, wrote the historian William H. Prescott, "one of the decisive battles of all history." It won Mexico for the Spanish. Bernal Díaz, one of the heroes, wrote simply, "What a hard thing it is to go and discover new lands."

Victorious, the Spaniards and their Indian allies went on to Tlaxcala to rest and recover from their wounds. The Spaniards were now reduced to the number Cortez had originally brought to Mexico. With these he had conquered Tenochtitlán once and he meant to do it again.

Because he was not officially recognized as Spain's representative, Cortez was careful to do everything properly. At each Indian village he read the required "requisition" which warned the heathen that unless they accepted Christian theology and the authority of the Church and the emperor, their lands would be taken and they would be enslaved.

Since the natives did not understand the requisition, their lands were inevitably taken and they were inevitably enslaved. To make their enslavement permanent and apparent, Cortez branded their faces. Reading, conquering, and branding, he moved across the country to the Valley of Mexico.

For the attack on the island city, the Spaniards constructed thirteen boats and dug a canal half a league long to float them to the lake. At the end of April, in 1521, the boats were launched, and the soldiers marched across the causeway. One division of infantry was captured immediately and for ten days their screams issued from the Aztec temples. Their comrades tried to drown them out with the noise of their ruthless, systematic destruction of Tenochtitlán.

It was, Cortez declared, "the most beautiful city in the world." Within three months not a fourth of it was standing. The streets

It is clear that the Spanish illustrator of Herrera's book had never seen the great temple of Tenochtitlán, which in reality had a double row of steps with two temples at the top. This drawing nevertheless gives us an idea of what many Aztec temples looked like.

Antonio de Herrera, *Historia General de las Indias Ocidentales . . .*, The New York Public Library, Rare Book Division

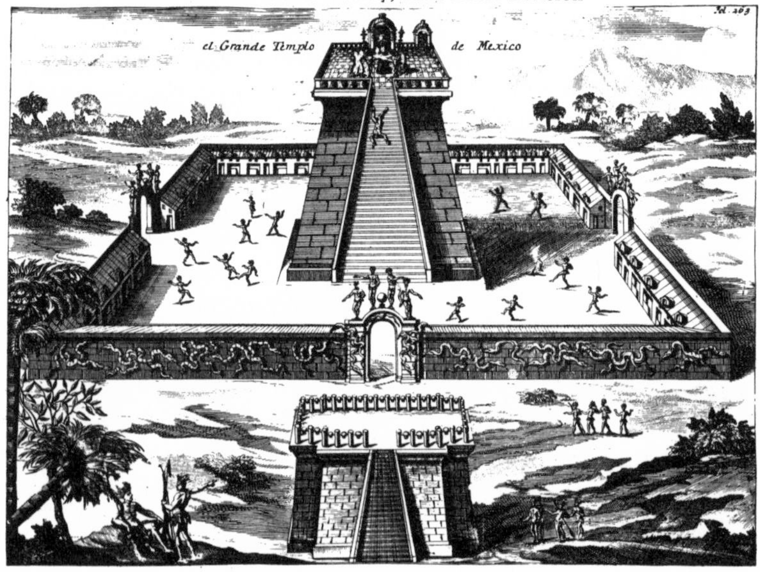

were filled with the bodies of the dead. Those that still lived were starving or dying of pestilence.

On the thirteenth of August, Guatemoc, the Aztec king, surrendered. Cortez ordered the city evacuated. For three days the refugees streamed over the causeways, "so thin and foul and yellow and stinking that it was a pity to see them," wrote Díaz.

Not the torturing of Guatemoc, later hanged, nor a thorough searching of the city revealed the treasure the Spaniards had lost in their retreat nor any other treasure. The men who had fought for gold received parcels of land and assignments of Indian vassals. For lack of anything else to leave his children, Bernal Díaz wrote a book about the conquest in which he had taken part.

Cortez achieved the appointment he coveted as Governor of New Spain, but his glory was brief. As it happened with most of the conquistadores, he fell into disfavor, and others reaped the harvest from the land he had won.

As for the Mayas of Yucatán who had craftily sent Cortez to the kingdom of the Aztecs, they gained for their people a twenty-year respite. Then, in 1541, they were captured by Montejo the Younger. The conquerors spent the next few years tearing down the Mayan temples, smashing the altars, and melting the golden artwork.

In 1549, a Franciscan monk named Diego de Landa found the great library of leather-bound parchment codices, pronounced them the work of the devil, and burned them all. Later he wrote a history of the Mayan nation, but it did not replace the volumes of history he had destroyed. Nor did it provide a key to the hieroglyphic language.

One of the few words scholars have been able to translate is the name of the city in which the library was stored. It was called Mani, which meant, "It is finished."

OF NEW LANDS

THE CONQUISTADORES were few in number and their enemies were numerous. The foe included cannibals, poisoned arrows, jungles, mountains, wild animals, disease, exposure, and, above all, hunger. "Often I have searched in various directions, desiring more to find a sack of corn than a bag of gold," Balboa wrote from Darien.

Yet he pursued the gold. It led him to the Pacific Ocean. It took Cortez from Mexico to California. It lured Hernando de Soto from Nicaragua to Peru to his death on the Mississippi River. It sent men scrambling over the length and breadth of South America.

It was a big continent and it held much gold, but there was always more just over the mountains or where the river began. Everybody heard about *el hombre dorado,* known since as El Dorado. Nobody ever saw him. He was a gilded man, a king, who ruled a kingdom so rich in gold that every morning he was painted with gum and sprayed from head to foot with gold dust. Each evening his golden attire was washed off in the waters of a lake.

El Dorado's habitat kept changing, as did the story. In some versions of the tale all the people in his kingdom dressed in nothing but gold dust, which enriched the waters of a lake each night. Sir Walter Raleigh placed the kingdom in Guiana but reserved the golden attire for special feast days. Then the natives covered their bodies with gum and blew gold powder at each other through hollow canes, "until they be al shining from the foote to the head." In this way they prepared themselves for a week of eating and drinking, for they were "marueylous great drunkards."

As El Dorado was sought to no avail, the goal became the lake in which the gilded one bathed. The lake was said to be as big as a sea. In the center of it there was an island of gold on which a city was built, named Manoa.

Manoa became a permanent fixture on maps. Schoolchildren in the United States through the first half of the nineteenth century were required to memorize its location—near the headwaters of the Orinoco River. The conquistadores could never find it and gave up the attempt. They searched instead for the Seven Cities of Cíbola which lay to the north and proved just as illusive.

In Darien, now Panama, El Dorado was not gilded and he had a name. He was a *cacique,* or chief, called Davaive. In his house were bags of gold so heavy that a man could scarcely lift one. A hundred workers melted gold constantly for his store of treasure.

Davaive got his gold from a tribe of cannibals who controlled the richest mines in the world, and the easiest to work. When it rained in the mountains, the water rushing down the hillsides laid bare the gold. It gleamed in the gullies like a crop of fallen oranges. All the miners had to do was pick the rich harvest.

In the dry season, the Indians exposed the gold by setting fire to the brush that covered the ground. They gave their riches to the *cacique* Davaive in return for boys and pigs, on which they dined, and for women to serve them.

Vasco Núñez de Balboa had been in Darien three years. He had heard much of Davaive but had never seen him. Still the stories made the amount of gold the Spaniard weighed and divided among his men seem small and insufficient.

As he was performing this chore one day in 1513, the son of an Indian chief struck the scales, scattering the gold. Pointing south, he announced that in that direction lay a sea and beyond it a kingdom of gold. If the Spaniards wanted gold they should go there.

Balboa started out. With a handful of men from Darien, including Francisco Pizarro, he reached the Pacific Ocean. From this new sea, it was reported, he pulled out quantities of gold and pearls in nets. Still he dreamed of the kingdom of gold to the south and made plans to go there. Before he could carry them out, he was beheaded by his father-in-law, a rival for power in Darien.

The kingdom of gold was real. A land rich beyond any the Spaniards had yet seen, the country known to the Indians as Biru had been attracting invaders for millennia.

Archaeologists have found evidence of primitive cultures in Peru dating back to the year 3000 B.C. The earliest examples of goldwork have been ascribed to the first millennium B.C., about the time King Solomon was gilding his temple.

Two thousand years after that two powerful nations began to march over the land. The Chimu took the coastal area, lacing it with roads which led from their placer workings to their capital city, Chanchan, near modern Trujillo. Here their goldsmiths fashioned gold in a variety of shapes—vessels, masks, helmets, shields, and large idols intricately formed by welding small bits of the metal together. Gold wire was welded to plain expanses of the metal to create decorative patterns, and the gold was chased and worked in repoussé. Often it was painted.

As the Chimu established themselves on the coast, a people called the Quechuas spread through the mountains of the interior. In a valley high in the Andes they built their holy city, Cuzco. They have been known in history by the name of their ruler and god, the divine son of the sun, the Inca.

It took the people of the mountains more than four hundred years to conquer the nation on the coast and unite Peru under the Inca. The Spaniards gave them less than a century to savor the accomplishment.

When the Spanish met the Incas it was as if the pages of history had been jumbled. Nothing illustrated more vividly man's never-changing desire for gold and the change in the uses to which he put it.

Both the Spaniards and the Incas had fought for gold and would fight each other for it. To the Spanish its value was economic. The golden art work of the Incas could be melted into bullion and used to buy all the good things of life. To the Incas, gold was holy, the actual sweat of the sun. The bullion that came from their mines could be fashioned into shapes that were pleasing to the sun and would bring his blessings on his child, the Inca, and on all his people.

For modern men, living in a society which has long regarded gold as wealth, the Spanish reasons for seeking gold are more easily grasped. The Sumerians and Babylonians, raising their ziggurats to the sun, and the Egyptians, burying their divine pharaohs with the divine metal, would more quickly have appreciated the motives of the Incas. The historian, looking backward through the ages, sees that wherever men discovered gold, in places widely separated in space and time, they learned to value it for its mystic qualities and sought it for religious purposes long before they used it in trade.

To the Spanish, gold was money. The Incas had no money. Theirs was a barter economy. Gold, reserved for religious purposes, rarely appeared in the market as a commodity. The metal belonged to the Sapa Inca, son of the sun and shepherd of the sun. He was both ruler and god.

Gold was captured and mined to serve him. It made beautiful the sacred city of Cuzco. Gold straws mingled with the straws that thatched the roofs of the city, reflecting the brilliance of the sun and bringing his blessing to every building reserved for his descendants, the wives and relatives of the Sapa Inca. They numbered thousands.

Thick gold plate was also fastened to the walls of the buildings, and formed their cornices, so that the first Spaniards who saw the city described it as ablaze with gold. Then they ripped the sheets of metal from the temples and palaces.

Cuzco's most ancient and beautiful shrine was the Curi-cancha, the Golden Enclosure, built around the Field of the Sun. Here the chief priests presided over one of the strangest, richest gardens in the world. In it every gift of the sun was represented in a golden likeness. A fountain encased in gold stood in the center of the enclosure spreading jets of golden water upward toward a round metallic sun. From ground of gold, molded to represent the turned earth, flowers blossomed and crops of maize grew, their golden ears encased in furled silver sheaths. Twenty full-sized llamas, with their young, nibbled blades of grass. They were tended by remarkably sculptured shepherds equipped with slings and crooks. All were made of gold. The statues of humans and animals were so perfectly cast that, according to one of the Spanish soldiers who inventoried the booty as it went into the melting pot, "they looked as if they were alive."

In the palace where the Sapa Inca lived—and in every place he might stay as he visited his vast empire—the interior walls were sheathed with gold, beautifully engraved with sacred figures. The Inca sat on a golden stool, in place of a throne, and was served by his "chosen women" from golden tableware.

Although his queen was his sister, as in the case of the Egyptian pharaohs, he might have as many as seven hundred lesser wives and concubines selected from among the most beautiful and talented women in the kingdom and trained in the arts of spinning, weaving, and serving. These women made his tunics from the finest vicuña

Golden ear spools were a mark of nobility in Peru. The Inca men pierced and stretched their ear lobes until they were able to insert spools as large as eggs. For this practice the Spaniards called them "Big Ears."

Photograph by Charles Uht, The Museum of Primitive Art

wool. The garments were elaborately decorated with mosaics of jungle-bird feathers and tiny particles of gold.

Tunics for special occasions were often woven entirely of gold. Others were hung with tiny gold bells and bangles in intricate patterns. Months of labor went into each article of clothing worn by the Inca. Because he was a god, the apparel was worn only once. Nothing the Inca touched could be touched by anyone else.

When the Inca traveled he was carried in his royal palanquin which was plated with gold and set with precious stones. One of the treasures of Peru not immediately melted down by the Spaniards was the Inca Atahualpa's palanquin, which Francisco Pizarro kept for himself.

The Inca and all male members of his family had their ear lobes pierced and stretched until spools of gold as large as an egg could be inserted. Golden ear spools were a mark of nobility which lesser men copied in silver and copper. The Spaniards called the people "Big Ears."

When the Inca died, his concubines and royal servants were strangled to accompany him on his journey to the sun. His body was mummified and placed in his palace, which then became a shrine. Along with the mummy the shrine contained a life-sized golden statue of the deceased, which continued to sit on the golden stool and was served as if it were alive.

Before his death the old Inca was expected to choose a successor from among his sons and pass on to him the gold-headed mace which was the symbol of office and the fringe of red wool which was the crown. The red wool fringe had tassels lined with gold lamé and trimmed with golden spangles which hung down before the Inca's eyes.

Once he received the fringe of wool, the son became the ruler of all the land that lay under the sun. A new palace was built for him in Cuzco. From it he ruled an empire that stretched from Argentina to Colombia, contained ten million people of five hundred different tribes, and covered some 350,000 square miles. All points of the empire were linked to Cuzco by highways along which couriers were stationed to run important messages back and forth.

Among the more important roads in this elaborate highway system were the gold roads, built through passes twenty-three thousand feet high to the mining region around Lake Titicaca. The gold roads were sacred, as were the mountains which held the gold. Digging the metal was consecrated duty and the miners prayed as they worked. Still, the people of the communal villages, who paid their taxes in labor, did not like to be assigned to the gold mines. So, as it had in many other civilizations, mining became a form of punishment.

Though criminals worked the mines, they were not mistreated. Mining was done in the cold elevations of the mountains only during the warmest months of the year. Wives accompanied their husbands and helped the farmers cultivate the crops on the terraced hillsides from which the miners were fed.

Such care contrasted sharply with the negligence of the Spaniards. Eyewitnesses reported that it was impossible to walk about their mines without stepping on the bones and bodies of those who had died or been killed at their labors. The swarms of birds who scavenged about the workings cut out the light of the sun.

Besides their hard rock mines, the Incas built stone riffles to catch the gold in the mountain streams. The metal from both sources was melted into bullion over fires built on mountaintops so that they could be fanned to greater temperatures by the trade winds.

The Incas had no written language. Records were made by knotting strings of different lengths and colors. These were the quipu, interpreted by official rememberers trained to the task. As the gold flowed over the gold roads to Cuzco, the string records went along to be checked against the amount of gold delivered to the city.

Although the Spaniards destroyed the quipu library, official rememberers recalled that gold traveled into Cuzco at the rate of seven million ounces a year, an amount that would be worth $145,000,000 at the official price of $35 an ounce today.

In Cuzco, in 1527, the Sapa Inca, Huayna Capac, lay dying. Couriers, running along the highways from the coast, relayed the message that white men had landed at the coastal city of Tumbes. It wasn't a very important message. The strangers numbered fifteen.

The fifteen men were the remains of several armies from Darien who had been trying for three years to reach Peru. All the attempts had been commanded by two determined men. One of them, Francisco Pizarro, had been with Balboa when he discovered the

Pacific Ocean while trying to get to the rich country of the south. Pizarro inherited the dream.

In 1527 he was past fifty years old but still strong and durable as tough leather. The illegitimate son of a peasant, he had been a swineherd in Spain and had shipped to the Indies with Columbus after losing some of the pigs placed in his charge. He could neither read nor write.

Also illiterate, past fifty, and of peasant parentage was his partner, Diego de Almagro. Almagro had set sail for the new world after stabbing a man in the old. He was small and wiry, unbelievably homely, and had, in the course of his adventures, lost an eye.

In Tumbes, the fifteen Dariens were treated well and given gifts of gold, cloth, and llamas. They were impressed by the wealth of the city, and sailing slowly along the coast of Peru they saw evidence of more wealth. Since there were so few of them they dared not try to grab what they saw. They sailed back to the isthmus.

In Darien there was gold close at hand, beside which the gold brought back by the travelers was not impressive. Their glowing descriptions of the wonders they had seen were discounted. Too many men had suffered too much on previous attempts to reach the land to the south. They were unwilling to try again.

So Pizarro took his Peruvian trophies to Spain. He arrived at exactly the right time. Cortez was there, fresh from his conquest of Mexico, and everybody was quite willing to believe that the mountains of the new world were made of nothing but gold and silver.

In Spain, Pizarro found money and volunteers, including his own four brothers. He also managed an appointment for himself as Governor of Peru for life. To his partner, Almagro, he took back the official title of Governor of Tumbes, the coastal city at which the fifteen Dariens had first landed.

The difference in their official ranks caused the first of many quarrels between the two friends. Still, preparations proceeded for the expedition. Toward the end of 1530, Pizarro and his brothers sailed for the kingdom of gold with 180 men and 28 horses. Almagro was to follow later with more men and provisions.

The Peruvians were embroiled in a civil war. The Sapa Inca, Huayna Capac, had died without naming his successor. For three years his sons, Huáscar and Atahualpa, had been fighting for the right to rule. The conflict had weakened the nation and continued to occupy its divided forces as the conquistadores established themselves on the coast.

The inhabitants of the first town they approached fled before they arrived, leaving behind their gold and silver and precious gems. The Spaniards loaded the treasure on a ship and sent it back to Panama to encourage others to join them.

News of the boatload of booty from the south spread quickly through Central America. By the time Pizarro and his men had captured Tumbes they were joined by volunteers from Nicaragua, commanded by Hernando de Soto. With these reinforcements Pizarro felt strong enough to march into the interior without waiting for Almagro to join him.

Leaving detachments at strategic places along the coast he started inland, traveling over Inca roads. He was accompanied by 62 horsemen and 106 infantrymen. His weapons consisted of twenty crossbows, three muskets, and a few small cannon which shot stone balls.

It was almost two years since the Spaniards had landed on the coast of Peru. The civil war was over and Atahualpa, the victor and now Sapa Inca, was resting and taking the hot sulphur baths at the health resort of Cajamarca. When he had purified himself by bathing and fasting he would make his triumphal entrance into Cuzco.

The new ruler was not at all dismayed to hear that a little band of strange white men was traveling toward him along his highway. Camped around Cajamarca were his own troops, numbering thirty thousand. The white men could be walking into such strength for only one reason—to throw themselves on his mercy. Magnanimously he sent messengers with gifts to greet the strangers.

After a forty-five day march, Pizarro and his command reached Cajamarca on November 15, 1532. They found large empty buildings available to them in the town. They sent friendly greetings to the Inca inviting him to break his fast with his white brothers the next day. He accepted the invitation.

He arrived at the camp of the Spaniards in a palanquin which his hosts later described as "a castle of gold." He was accompanied by five thousand warriors, but since he had been invited to visit his white brothers as a friend his attendants were unarmed. So, in the

Antonio de Herrera, *Historia General de las Indias Ocidentales . . . ,* The New York Public Library, Rare Book Division

When the Inca ruler Atahualpa was captured, he promised Pizarro a roomful of gold for his freedom. Pizarro gave his word, and the gold was brought from temples all over Peru. Atahualpa was then strangled.

words of Hernando Pizarro, "they were defeated without danger to any Christian."

At a given signal the Spaniards leaped from their hiding places and attacked their guests. At least two thousand defenseless Indians were killed, according to Hernando Pizarro. De Soto reckoned the number higher. Francisco Pizarro was wounded by his own men. The Inca Atahualpa was taken prisoner.

The next morning the Spaniards looted the native camp, which contained the Inca's golden vessels and ornaments. Watching the eagerness with which his captors collected the treasure, Atahualpa knew why they were there.

Lifting his arm above his head he offered to fill the room with gold to the height his fingers reached if the Spaniards would set him free. His jailers accepted his proposal. They drew a line around the walls to mark the height Atahualpa had indicated. The line was over seven feet from the floor. The room was twenty-two feet long and seventeen feet wide.

Over the Inca highways runners were sent to all the villages to order the gold brought from the sun temples and the palaces in which the Inca stayed when he traveled. Over the same highways the gold was rushed to rescue Atahualpa. Day after day it came, loaded in *cargas,* which were slings fastened to long poles the ends of which were balanced on the shoulders of four porters.

The gold arrived in many different shapes from many parts of the kingdom. Massive pieces of gold plate from the walls of the sun temples weighed fifty to seventy-five pounds apiece. There were golden statues, goblets, ewers, salvers, vases, plates, and platters. All were dumped on the floor, and daily the pile grew higher, but not fast enough to suit the Spaniards.

Three of the conquerors were sent to Cuzco to hasten the collection. They tore seven hundred sheets of gold from the walls of the sun temple and robbed the Field of the Sun of much of its artwork.

Other adventurers went to other major cities of the realm, but the priests knew that enough gold was on its way to Cajamarca to ransom the Inca. They hid the temple treasures. The Spaniards went away empty-handed.

Within three months the collection of gold filled the room to the line on its walls, but the Spaniards weren't satisfied. They realized that they had underestimated the amount of gold the Inca controlled. Peru was filled with precious metals, and they had settled for a roomful.

Moreover, Almagro had arrived with reinforcements, which meant more men wanting to share the gold. It also meant more strength with which to capture more gold. They would take all the gold in the country—the sun temples, the palaces, and the mines. This could be accomplished with greater ease, some argued, if the warriors of the nation had no leader. Some disagreed, but their voices weren't heard. Having paid his ransom in gold, Atahualpa was strangled.

Goldsmiths were brought to Cajamarca. For a month they worked melting down the art they had created into bars of bullion that could be divided among the conquerors. A few exceptional pieces were saved and some of these were sent to Spain to please the king. He never saw them. They were minted into coins at the port of Seville.

The official yield was 1,326,539 *pesos de oro,* a weight of gold not to be confused with the modern peso. The value of the gold at today's set price would be almost twenty million dollars.

Every cavalryman received ninety pounds of gold as his share. In Spain this amount would have kept him comfortably for the rest of his life. In Peru, gold was so much more plentiful than the necessities of life and war that in most instances the ninety pounds were soon gone.

Almagro gave a pound of gold for a domesticated cat. The price of a horse, if one could be bought, was never less than twenty-six pounds of gold. Lacking iron, horses were shod with silver shoes and gold was made into stirrups.

In the bloody war between Pizarro and Almagro which climaxed the conquest of Peru and cost both men their lives, Almagro's soldiers were forced to turn their gold and silver booty into swords and pikes with which to fight. Next to silver, gold was the cheapest thing in Peru, yet the men from Spain continued to fight and die for gold.

In Cajamarca the Spaniards divided Atahualpa's treasure and set out for Cuzco. Their burdens were carried by Indian porters whom they controlled throughout the conquest in a cruel but effective manner. A continuous chain passed through rings fastened around the necks of the carriers. None could escape and whenever one faltered or fell he could be removed from the line with a single swipe of a sword which severed his head from his neck ring and his body.

The conquerors reached Cuzco exactly a year after they had marched into Cajamarca. They housed themselves in the palaces and shrines, ripping the gold plate from the walls and destroying the mummies of the Incas as they stripped them of their ornaments.

The beautiful disc of the sun from the Golden Enclosure was, for a brief day, the property of a soldier named Leguizana. He lost it that night in a gambling game. A companion, rushing from house to house, claimed to have gathered two hundred pounds of gold in the form of water pots alone.

The city's inhabitants were tortured, burned, and mutilated to force them to reveal where treasure was hidden. When a young priest objected to the cruelty, reminding Pizarro that these souls might be won for Christ, the conqueror cried: "I have not come for that. I have come to take from them their gold."

IN NEW WAYS

THE FLOOR OF THE OCEAN between Cuba and the tip of Florida is littered with the broken hulls of Spanish sailing vessels and the gold they carried. Twenty ships were sunk there in a hurricane in 1502. All were loaded with gold for Spain and one carried a nugget that weighed thirty-six pounds. A part of Montezuma's treasure lies beneath these waters, valued at thirty million dollars and now completely grown over with coral.

For those who wish to try deep-sea prospecting, the United States Treasury Department maintains a list, called the Treasure Trove, of the ships that are known to lie in the territorial waters. A permit to conduct salvage operations is necessary, and the government claims a percentage of anything recovered.

The trip between the Spanish Indies and Spain was not an easy one in the years of the conquest. Many a gold-laden clipper was lost to the stormy Atlantic. As many more fell prey to pirates. Some of these ocean robbers were official naval officers of Spain's rivals in Europe.

One of the most famous was England's Sir Francis Drake who intercepted Spanish treasure ships to provide Queen Elizabeth with gold for coinage. In 1577 this experienced pirate set out on a trip around the world in his ship, the *Golden Hind.* On his way he looted Spanish vessels and Spanish ports in Central and South America. By the time he reached the coast of California, claiming it for England, he was carrying between twenty and thirty tons of gold.

There, just north of San Francisco, he waited for favorable winds to help him complete his journey. His sailors whiled away the days picking up "a resonable quantitie of gold and silver" almost three centuries before gold was "discovered" at Sutter's mill.

Pirates such as Drake, and the treachery of the ocean, forced Spain to take elaborate precautions with the ships bearing gold from the Spanish Indies. The treasure was collected at specified departure ports from which it was sent out in well-armed convoys, sometimes numbering more than one hundred vessels. Routes across the ocean changed frequently to keep the pirates guessing. It was reported that King Charles cried with joy when the great armadas sailed safely into Seville.

Despite the dangers of the trip, they arrived regularly. In the decade of the 1550's, 100,000 pounds of gold, which would today have a value of $56 million, reached Spain without mishap. All in all, for more than a century after 1503, Spain received from her new world possessions 6000 to 7000 pounds of gold a year, plus large amounts of silver and precious gems.

This steady stream of wealth upset the established order of things in Europe. The nation that had been the poor step-sister of the Continent was suddenly the rich and powerful queen. Her armies marched and conquered. Wars financed with gold from the Americas, and bribes paid with gold from the same source, brought King Charles the coveted crown of the Holy Roman Empire. It brought the rest of Europe's monarchs nothing but hard times.

For wherever it traveled, and it traveled everywhere, this gold had a tendency to enrich the poor at the expense of the mighty. As Spain outbid all rivals for ships and supplies for her new colonies, prices rose, merchants and manufacturers prospered, and kings and nobles found themselves suddenly impoverished. Their lands were worn out, and the peasants that had once tilled them were off to other climes or to work for wages in Europe's busy ports and factories.

In the case of ruling monarchs their plight was not irremediable. They had the power to force the merchants to share the wealth, one way or another. So their pirate ships, exploring expeditions, armies, and navies continued to go around the world to search and fight for gold. The landed gentry had to confine their search to their own back yards where they revived the ancient custom of looting the buried graves and cities of past civilizations.

The practice proved so profitable in Italy that it continued for two hundred years. Roman graves and cities were ransacked for anything of value and were often destroyed in the process. The sites of Pompeii and Herculaneum, Roman cities buried beneath lava and lapilli when Vesuvius erupted in A.D. 79, became particularly popular with diggers.

When Vesuvius exploded, the people had sought to save their gold as well as themselves. They had gathered it together in sacks, sheets and skirts before they fled to the city gates or took refuge in their basements.

This proved a great convenience to the gold diggers who came sixteen hundred years later. Almost any skeleton uncovered was worth a lifetime's savings in gold. The stakes were high, and excavation was carried on as secretively as possible. A building was dug up, the treasure removed, and the pit filled and camouflaged.

When the archaeologist J. J. Winckelmann arrived on the scene, early in the eighteenth century, half the twenty-two laborers digging up the ruins of Pompeii were criminals. The landowners could hire them for the job at a pittance since they pocketed much of the treasure they found. Nobody was very glad to see the archaeologist. Time and again they drove him off until he convinced the gentry who were overseeing the work and reaping the profits that he was interested in science, not gold. Then they allowed him to view the wealth they unearthed.

It was a decision they surely regretted later, for Winckelmann's writings put an end to haphazard prospecting for gold in Pompeii and in many other places of historic significance. The man who was thus responsible for protecting the buried remains of past civilizations from treasure hunters was himself murdered in a hotel in Trieste in 1768 for the antique gold coins he carried in his pockets.

All through history, men had searched for gold in the cities and graves of their ancestors. It was the only place ordinary men knew to look for the precious metal. The ways of locating veins of gold in the ground, of mining and milling the ore and refining the final product were closely guarded secrets passed on from father to son and carefully guarded from outsiders. Thousands of slaves and criminals were employed in digging and washing gold, but the knowledge that made all this labor productive was possessed by the select minority who directed the work.

The knowledge was often lost, along with the men to whom it belonged, when mining areas were conquered by people who did not understand that there was more to getting gold than just digging. This happened in Europe when the Roman Empire fell. The result was a drought of gold that lasted until the discovery of the West Indies. Europe's mines were not exhausted. They were simply mismanaged by their new owners.

Hungary's auriferous mountains invited a long succession of invaders, many of whom knew not the first thing about working the mines they had fought so hard to capture. Sigismund, who ruled the country at the beginning of the fifteenth century, has been much criticized because he did nothing to stop the torrent of blood and water that poured for days from one of his richest gold mines in the hills above his summer home. To get to and from his castle, his carriage had to splash through the rank river.

The ruler may have been indifferent to the fate of the miners whose blood had been added to the raging stream when a rush of underground water caved inadequate supports, but he was surely not indifferent to the loss of the mine itself. Had he known what to do to save it, he undoubtedly would have acted. But then, had anybody known anything about saving mines the tragedy would have been less gruesome.

A century later a man named Dr. Georg Bauer decided it was time that everybody knew how to save a mine—and how to find one and dig and treat the ore. With the help of the printing press, he made available to the public for the first time in the history of civilization a complete, detailed, and meticulously illustrated textbook on mining and metallurgy.

The book was *De Re Metallica*, and it was written under the name Georg Bauer chose for himself, Georgius Agricola. He wrote it in Latin, the universal language, that it might be read and understood by everyone. It was not his only literary contribution in the scientific field, but it was the one most needed.

Educated as a physician, Agricola joined a gold rush to Bohemia as soon as he had received his degree in medicine. There he practiced as a physician in the mining camp of Joachimsthal and took the opportunity to learn all he could about mining and metallurgy from observation and personal contact with the miners.

He mined too, trying out old ideas and new in the mine he called

"God's Gift" in gratitude for the riches it had bestowed. This preparation for his book was important. In a secretive, noncompetitive craft, as much misinformation as information had been passed along through the centuries, and new ideas had been more often mistrusted than used.

Agricola disposed of much of the misinformation, if not all. He argued against the divining rod for locating gold and described

Georgius Agricola's sixteenth-century book De Re Metallica *was the first work on mining based on research rather than imagination. It had world-wide influence for many centuries. In it Agricola tried to dispel the popular belief that a divining rod would lead to the places where gold veins lay hidden in the earth. This drawing shows that the man who uses a divining rod is likely to find nothing more than a tree stump, while the one who looks for natural signs and digs trenches will strike gold.*

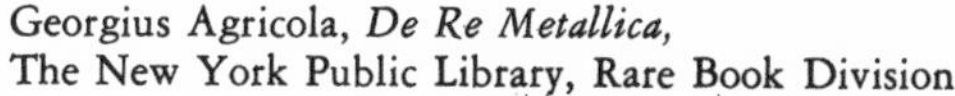
Georgius Agricola, *De Re Metallica,*
The New York Public Library, Rare Book Division

the natural indications of auriferous veins "which can be seen without the help of twigs." He also tried to dispel the prevalent fear of underground demons, though he did not deny their existence.

Most of them were less than two feet tall, he explained, and more mischievious than dangerous. Unless ridiculed, they would do nothing more harmful than throw pebbles at the miners and might be "put to flight by prayer and fasting."

Believing that "a miner must have the greatest skill in his work," Agricola instructed his readers in every mining procedure and in those aspects of philosophy, medicine, astronomy, mathematics, architecture, and law that applied to the industry. His English translators, former President Herbert Hoover and his wife, Lou Henry Hoover, credit him with the first scientific explanation of the part erosion plays in mountain sculpture, and the gathering of gold, and with the first discussion of the importance of circulating underground solutions in the deposition of metalliferous ores. Scores of new mining methods and processes received detailed descriptions in his manual.

Wrote the Hoovers, who mined for gold themselves in America and the Orient: "There is no measure by which we may gauge the value of such a work to the men who followed in this profession during centuries, nor the benefits enjoyed by humanity through them."

Agricola himself held in great respect the miners for whom he wrote. "Nay, not even the common worker in the mines is vile and abject," he insisted. "For, trained to vigilance and work by night and day, he has great powers of endurance and easily sustains the fatigues and duties of a soldier . . . . Therefore, experts in military affairs prefer the miner."

De Re Metallica was printed by the publishing house of Basel in 1556, one year after the author's death. Nothing as comprehensive on the subject was to appear for centuries. The manual was immediately translated into three additional languages and went into ten printings.

Though the English translation of the work did not appear until 1912, the information it contained was used wherever men searched for gold. Most of the prospectors and miners who followed Agricola's directions, and even quoted him, would not have known his name. Few of them could read.

Georgius Agricola, *De Re Metallica,*
The New York Public Library, Rare Book Division

Ancient methods of washing sand from gold are still used today. Several are shown here. Water and gold-bearing sand are poured into the head of the sluice and stirred; grooves (B, C) or pockets (D) catch heavy gold as the sand is washed away into a bucket. Canvas (A) or animal skins (G) stretched over the sluices and swept with a wooden rake (H) or broom (F) catch small grains of gold. A sluice made of rough planks (E) catches gold grains in its splintery surface.

Georgius Agricola, *De Re Metallica,*
The New York Public Library, Rare Book Division

Draining water from underground mines has always been a problem. Here Agricola demonstrates one method of hoisting it out. A stream (B) is diverted into a wooden reservoir (A) with two gates that are opened and closed by levers (C, D). When one gate is opened, a trough underneath (E or F) pours water from the reservoir into a row of pockets (G or H) in the wheel. This turns the wheel, which hauls up a bucket of water (M). Then the man controlling the levers closes the gate and stops the wheel. When the bucket has been emptied, he opens the other gate so that the other set of pockets will be filled with water and will turn the wheel in the opposite direction to haul up another bucket.

His textbook quickly became part of the mining tradition, passed on from old timer to neophyte as the secrets of the trade had once been relayed from father to son. But now there was a difference. The knowledge belonged to the world.

And it was used by the world, not only in mining but in many other endeavors. The shops of craftsmen became factories by borrowing the techniques of mass production, the twenty-four hour day, and the division of labor that had been used in mines since the

Fires built to crack the rock in underground mines took oxygen from the air and filled it with deadly fumes. These ventilating machines, used in Agricola's time, diverted fresh air into the mines.

Georgius Agricola, *De Re Metallica,*
The New York Public Library, Rare Book Division

time of the Egyptians. Machines that developed in the mines were copied topside to speed the production and distribution of the world's goods. From the mine came the steam engine, the railway and subway, the elevator and escalator, artificial light and artificial air.

The search for gold that found the Americas spurred this mechanization. Almost at once industry and commerce needed more gold to finance growth and expansion.

To meet the demand, Europe's miners, with their picks and the knowledge Agricola had given them, crossed the ocean to find gold in New England, Virginia, the Carolinas, and Georgia. Finally, almost three hundred years after Agricola's death, they used his methods to dig the treasure that was hidden in the mountains of California.

For Everyman *prospectors strike it rich*

FORTY-NINER

JOHN A. SUTTER HAD A PROBLEM. The fact that he shared it with the United States government did not make it less annoying. People insisted on discovering gold on his property. They did it in 1843 and again in 1844. Then in 1848, James W. Marshall, who was supposed to be building a mill, repeated the performance. As he had before, Sutter swore all hands to secrecy. He hadn't a clear title to his land.

The United States government was in an even more embarrassing position. Gold kept popping up all along the western seaboard. The land belonged to Mexico. Acquiring it would take time and probably a war. Until the land was transferred nobody wanted a gold rush, but several times it appeared that there might be one anyway.

The Indians kept bringing gold dust in willow baskets to the California padres. These good men, more interested in winning souls than gold, discouraged the practice. They taught that the little yellow *chispas* were "bad medicine."

Not everyone was as cooperative. In 1816 a book on mineralogy, published in Great Britain, discussed at length the gold to be found in the California mountains. Ten years later the fur trapper Jedediah Smith panned a pouch of gold flakes in the Sierra Nevadas.

In the meantime every ship that stopped at a California port took gold dust back to the East Coast, a fact that Richard Henry Dana made public in 1840 when he published his *Two Years*

Before the Mast. Two years after that, a caballero named Francisco López was searching for stray horses in the Santa Feliciana canyon, forty miles northwest of the little pueblo of Los Angeles. He stopped to rest and to pick some wild onions. Their roots were spangled with gold.

By this time a gold rush was inevitable and so was war. The discovery that set off the rush didn't wait for the end of the military conflict. The peace treaty of Guadalupe Hidalgo, by which Mexico transferred California to the United States, was signed on February 2, 1848. James Marshall made his historic discovery of gold at Sutter's mill on January 24.

Like the war, the mill was not finished. Sutter asked his employees to keep the news quiet, finish their work, and confine their search for gold to their leisure hours. When the mill was built, he promised, he would give each man a grubstake. At the same time he sent a trusted friend to Monterrey to check on the title of his land.

The friend was more interested in gold than titles. Like the other men at Sutter's place, he knew the gold was there but he didn't know how to get it. In Monterrey he found an old placer miner from Georgia who could build and use a rocker. He took him back to Sutter's ranch.

As fast as Sutter's employees learned to make and rock a cradle, as it was often called, they stopped work and devoted all their time to placer mining. With a cradle a man could gather fifty dollars a day in gold, a good deal more than he could earn in wages.

Even employees who stayed on the job could not resist advertising their new wealth. One of Sutter's teamsters, stopping at a way station for a drink of whisky, paid his tab with gold dust. The news was out and Sutter was ruined.

There weren't more than fourteen thousand people in California at the time. Most of them hurried to Sutter's ranch, at Coloma, to search for gold. The place was swarming with men, but Sutter could hire none of them to finish his mill or harvest his crops. Instead they dug up his ground, camped in his buildings, used his horses for transportation, and butchered his cattle for food.

In Monterrey and Yerba Buena, now San Francisco, buildings were left unfinished as carpenters took off for Coloma. Stores closed, lacking both clerks and customers. Ships lay in dock unable to sail or load or unload cargo. All hands had gone to the gold field.

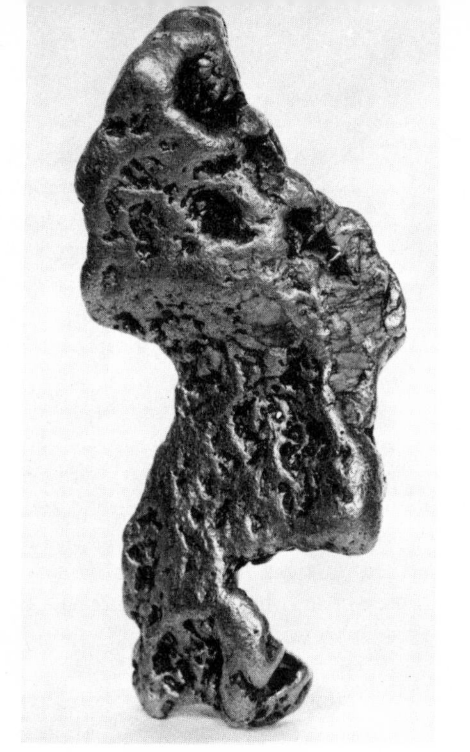

This gold nugget, weighing eighty-two ounces, was found near Greenville, California.

Smithsonian Institution

Oregon heard about the strike when a boatload of excited Hawaiians landed at Salem. Half the male population of that territory followed the islanders south. More prospectors arrived from Mexico, South America, and Australia.

By the end of the year an official messenger bearing an oyster can filled with gold nuggets reached Washington D.C. President Polk relayed the news to Congress on December 5. Said he calmly, "It was known that mines of precious metals existed in California at the time of its acquisition. Recent discoveries render it probable that these mines are more extensive and valuable than was anticipated." By this time California had produced ten million dollars worth of gold, and the rush was not yet started.

Announcements less reserved than the President's stirred up excitement on the East Coast. Newspapers printed letters from California which stated: "These are the richest placer mines in the world!" and "Many instances are known of persons having obtained from $800 to $1000 in a day."

To laborers in the East, making a dollar a day, such figures were irresistible. More than forty thousand hopefuls began preparations for the overland trip. Publishers wrote and printed guidebooks by the thousands. Harness and wagon makers from Philadelphia to St. Louis, the jumping-off place, worked day and night to meet the sudden demand. With luck, starting early in the spring from the Missouri frontier, a wagon train could reach the promised land before the winter blizzards.

The eager ones started before the spring thaws. By the time summer came, the trail across the western plains was deeply rutted by wagon wheels and marked with broken vehicles, discarded equipment, and the rough wooden crosses that denoted graves.

News of the trail was scratched on rocks, burned on planks, and tacked to trees. It gave the names, fortunes, and misfortunes of those ahead, plus advice and encouragement or discouragement for those who followed.

Thirty-five thousand California gold seekers chose the sea route. On a good ship, with favorable weather, the trip around Cape Horn took five months. Not all the ships pressed into service to accommodate the Argonauts could have been described as sea worthy. Many were rescued from the graveyard and kept afloat by nothing more substantial than their owners' fervent prayers for profits.

The California-bound passengers were satisfied if the craft managed to get them to the Isthmus of Panama. They crossed the isthmus by foot and in canoes. Those who didn't succumb to malaria waited on the Pacific side to be picked up by ships sailing to San Francisco. The wait was often long and the prices charged for the voyage north were exorbitant. One impatient party put out to sea in canoes but quickly paddled back to await sturdier means of transportation.

When the S.S. *California* steamed through the Golden Gate to a booming salute of guns from the Pacific Naval Squadron on February 28, 1849, the gold rush was officially under way. It was the largest the world had ever seen. It produced a bigger yield of gold in less time than any rush before or since. And it was a unique experiment in private enterprise and democracy.

For the first time in man's relationship with gold, the metal belonged exclusively to the man who picked it up, and he could do with it as he wished. No god demanded a tithe. No king expected a fifth. No landowner kept a percentage.

There weren't even any laws to prescribe who could dig for gold, or where, or in what manner. The laws of Mexico no longer pertained. The United States had no legislation to cover the situation. The military officers in charge of the newly acquired land had no orders. California had no government.

It was every man for himself, and there were one hundred thousand of them before the year was out. They came from every part of the globe, spoke a dozen different languages, and represented every walk of life. Enough of them were escaping the grasp of the law that it was considered a breach of etiquette to ask anybody for a last name.

Few of them knew anything about finding or mining gold. They learned the hard way, by buying the worn-out placer claims of those who had been first on the scene. When these yielded nothing but gravel, they followed the experienced miners to new locations, took up claims near theirs and learned from observation.

In this way they spread themselves through the Sierra Nevadas along what the Mexican miners called the Veta Madre, or the Mother Lode. On the edges of cliffs, in gullies and inaccessible canyons, they staked their claims and built their tent-and-shack communities. Some of these sprang up one week and were ghost towns the next, as news of a richer strike lured away the fortune hunters.

Nothing could be kept secret along the Mother Lode. It was said that a story told in Mariposa, at the southern end of the gold territory, would be repeated in Downieville, two hundred miles to the north, within two hours. The human grapevine took the place of telephone, telegraph, and newspaper.

Over it sped the report of the nugget found near Carson Hill. It weighed 195 pounds and was valued at $74,000. North of Carson Hill, at Angel's Camp, a prospector named Raspberry, who had found no gold, went out to hunt for meat. He had trouble with his gun, struck it against a rock, which broke away revealing signs of gold. By himself he dug $7000 worth of ore in three days, opening the mine that eventually made him a millionaire.

In Grass Valley, George Knight found a fortune by stubbing his toe on a piece of gold-bearing quartz that proved to be an outcrop of a rich underground vein. At another mining camp the prospectors stopped work to bury one of their number. As they bowed their heads while the volunteer preacher prayed, they saw the sheen of gold in the open grave. The service stopped abruptly, the coffin was removed and the mourners staked claims and began digging.

These were the stories that passed from camp to camp along the Mother Lode, and they were true. Many lucky prospectors made fortunes in the California rush, and the big discoveries were often the result of lucky accidents. Other men found rich claims that brought them from fifty to five hundred dollars a day. When the claims petered out, their owners retired to live comfortably on the proceeds. A larger number of fortune hunters found no fortunes and were lucky to make expenses.

The end product of a day's work was, on the average, an ounce of gold. Depending on its purity, this could be sold at an assay office for from twelve to sixteen dollars. Traded for supplies at a nearby mining camp, where everything but gold was scarce and dear, the metal was worth about half its cash value. With his ounce of gold, the miner might be able to buy half a dozen eggs, if eggs were available. They sold for a dollar or more apiece.

Most prospectors ate flapjacks, made of sourdough, without eggs. Flour cost fifty dollars a barrel. When they could afford it, the forty-niners added salt pork to the menu, at two hundred dollars a barrel. Tenderfeet at new sites used their frying pans for cooking and for panning gold. When supplies caught up with them they might invest in a prospector's pan.

This was a circular sheet-iron or tin-plate dish with sloping sides, three or four inches deep and a foot across. In it the prospector swirled sand and water, letting the water carry the light sand over the lip of the pan while the heavy material settled to the bottom where he could examine it for "color."

Color meant gold, which was often as fine as the sand itself. In this form, washed free of extraneous matter and dried, it was referred to as "gold dust," carried in a pocket pouch, and used for money. A pinch of dust was worth about a dollar. Since the seller did the pinching, clerks and bartenders with large thumbs were in demand. Their pinch was bigger.

Even in a rich stream, it took a lot of swirling to produce a decent

John Sherer, *Adventures of a Gold-Digger*

Prospectors tested sand for gold by swirling it with water and dexterously tilting the pan to let the water carry off the sand and leave the gold. This method didn't produce much gold except in the Klondike, where a pan of earth sometimes yielded fifteen ounces.

When panning showed that the earth was rich enough to mine, the prospector made a box with a sloping floor and mounted it on rockers. He then poured in sand and water while gently rocking the box—or cradle. The cleats on its floor caught the gold grains as the water carried the sand out of the cradle's lower end.

Harper's New Monthly Magazine

An improvement on the cradle was the long tom. The box was lengthened so that the gold grains would have time to settle before the water washed the sand away.

Harper's New Monthly Magazine

day's wage with a pan. Once he found color, the prospector built himself a cradle. The cradle resembled one in which infants were put to bed except that its construction was cruder. It was a wooden box about three feet long, mounted on rockers. Cleats, or riffles, were nailed across the bottom to trap the gold. If the gold was very fine, pieces of the miner's rough wool blanket might be added to help snare it.

The miner poured sand and water in at one end of the cradle, which was inclined. Rocking the contraption back and forth, he helped gravity separate the heavy gold from the sand and dirt. The gold settled behind the riffles. The water carried everything else out the open, lower end of the cradle. It was an inspiring sight, said one contemporary observer, to watch all those bearded, burly men gently rocking their cradles like so many mothers putting babies to sleep.

The cradles proved less efficient than picturesque. Gold spilled out along with the waste matter. To give the grains of metal more time to sift to the bottom of the box, the cradle was elongated to eight or ten feet. If a steady stream of water was available to be run through it, the rockers were eliminated.

This gold sluice was called a long tom. In time the long toms were arranged in series and the prospector needed partners or hired hands to help him run the operation. The flow of water through the sluice boxes had to be regulated. Auriferous dirt had to be shoveled in at the upper end of the series of boxes. Along the way, workers lifted out large stones that interfered with the downward movement of the water and sand. They stirred the mixture with pitchforks. It was the hardest kind of work, no less strenuous than digging ditches.

That, too, often had to be done to get water to gold-bearing ground. Some of the ditches were many miles long. One group of prospectors investigating a stop in the flow of water found their ditch had been dammed by a fall of rock much richer in gold than the gravel they were working. More often the miners found that their water had been diverted to a ditch dug by others. Sometimes the gold-bearing dirt had to be dug and hauled by the ton to a stream of water.

At best the life of a forty-niner was a hard one. His days were spent in taxing physical labor. His shelter, made of brush or canvas, scarcely protected him from the elements. His diet was monotonous and inadequate. He suffered from scurvy, dysentery, typhoid, and a vague but disabling ailment known as ague.

He sought relief from all these discomforts when he went to town on Sunday. He was as often relieved of any gold he had gathered. Merchants, saloonkeepers, prostitutes, and gamblers lay in wait for him. If he had gold dust in his pouch he spent it freely, but sometimes what he craved most was food.

A hungry miner who had struck it rich originated California's most famous dish when he went into a restaurant in the mining camp of Hangtown and ordered the three most expensive things in the house. The proprietor scrambled together eggs, oysters, and bacon for the customer's breakfast. This unlikely combination is still a favorite morning repast in the Mother Lode country.

Sunday was the busy day in mining camps. Rich or broke, the prospectors flocked to town. Those without gold dust to spend offered merchants a percentage of any gold they might find in the future for a grubstake. Storekeepers who accepted the proposition gave the miner food and supplies and wished him luck. His prosperity would also be theirs. Most merchants had a grubstake interest in many claims.

Generally the agreements were oral and disputes often arose. In fact, disputes were the order of the day in the California goldfields. They frequently involved thousands, sometimes millions, of dollars and there were no courts in which they could be settled.

Anarchy might have reigned under these conditions. According to the mining engineer and gold-rush historian, T. A. Rickard, what developed instead was "the nearest approach to a democracy, that the world had ever seen." Wrote another gold-rush chronicler, Bayard Taylor, "The capacity of the people for self government was never so triumphantly illustrated."

It was an informal kind of government. Few of the rules and regulations were written and they were not the same in Mariposa as they were in Downieville. As a strike was made, and prospectors gathered in number, they met together and agreed on laws for the new district, the boundaries of which varied with its fortunes. These laws regulated the size and number of claims each man could locate, the way they should be marked and protected from trespassers, the actions that were to be considered crimes and their punishment.

L. Simonin, *L'Or et l'argent*

Powerful jets of water, aimed at California hillsides, broke down thick gravel banks and washed the gold-bearing earth through a line of sluices. This method of mining, called hydraulicking, was also used by the Romans, who channeled rivers to fall from great heights and wash down the earth.

Town meetings were held on Sunday, when most of the prospectors were in camp. The majority ruled and the decision was final. Since there were no jails, crimes were punished immediately. Theft was the most heinous offense. A man accused of stealing tools or provisions from another's claim could be tried, convicted, and hanged within an hour.

If the crime was a lesser one, the culprit might be banished from the district. Sometimes he was branded, that his criminal record should be known to those he met later.

It was a harsh sort of justice, but it created law and order in an environment that might have taxed the ingenuity of experts. Life and property were protected. Arguments were mediated. Laws were established and enforced.

The laws that pertained to mining and mineral rights form the basis of the rules that govern the mining industry throughout the United States today. Their principles and many of their provisions were incorporated into the national code when the government drew up mining regulations in 1865.

The California forty-niners confined their mining to techniques which had originated in antiquity and had been given to the public by Agricola hundreds of years before. They even rediscovered the long-forgotten Roman method of breaking up ore with pressurized water. They called it hydraulicking.

For this method of getting gold, water was piped under pressure to the auriferous ground and powerful jets of it were aimed at the gold-bearing hills. The force of the water washed away mountains. Where hydraulicking was used, nothing remains to this day but barren, tumbled rocks. Soil, forests, farms, and towns were destroyed before laws were passed prohibiting hydraulic mining.

In the ten years after the discovery at Sutter's Mill, California produced $555 million in gold. This was $135 million more than Spain had collected in the hundred years that followed the discovery of the Americas.

Remembering the way in which Spain's gold had upset the old order in Europe, many economists predicted that dire economic consequences would follow the sudden flood of wealth from California. W. Stanley Jevons argued that the government might as well inflate its own currency. Others asked Congress to halt the mining of gold in the West.

The financial experts were not in agreement, however. Some blamed the increase in gold stocks for the depression that became a panic in 1857. Equally qualified observers insisted that the economic slump would have been much worse without the western gold country which gave work to the unemployed, provided new markets for industry's products, and primed the pump of the economy with a greater flow of money.

There could be no difference of opinion on the economic effect of the California strike on the two men who were responsible for it. John Sutter lost his property, had a ring made from the gold that was responsible for the loss, and lived out his life on a small pension granted him by the State of California. A statue of James Marshall was erected on the discovery site, and while he fought for a pension to keep himself from starving he summed up his version of the gold rush he had precipitated: "Yankeedom $600,000,000; myself individually $000,000,000."

TENDERFOOT

THOUSANDS OF FORTY-NINERS, nearing the end of a long overland journey to California, stopped at the edge of Carson Creek, near Gold Hill, in what is now Nevada, to rest and water their stock. They were in sight of the towering, snowcapped Sierra Nevadas, on the western slopes of which they hoped to find gold. The end of the trail was but a hundred miles away.

The travelers stayed no longer than they had to in this place called Washoe. It was sorry-looking country. The creek was scarcely more than a trickle. The land was dry and grew nothing but sagebrush and scrubby cattle. The ranchers round about were poor, and spent odd moments scratching for gold in Gold Hill's tortured gullies. The forty-niners hurried on toward the majestic mountains in the West.

Ten years later many of them hurried back, deserting the Mother Lode country of California to claim a piece of the Comstock lode in the Washoe goldfield of Nevada. For all its ugly exterior, Gold Hill of the Washoe was exactly what its name said it was, and the sagebrush in its gullies and on the surrounding undulations was rooted in treasure.

This underground storehouse of gold and silver, later called the Comstock lode, was discovered in the spring of 1859 by two Irishmen, neither of them named Comstock. Like most of the prospectors digging desultorily at Gold Hill before the rich strike, McLaughlin and O'Riley were poor and faring badly, making less than a dollar and a half a day. Near their digging, ground squirrels were digging too, mounding up a strange black dirt of a kind the men had not seen before.

They ran a sample of it through their rockers and were surprised at the amount of gold it yielded—and slightly suspicious as well. The gold was a peculiar color. It was extremely pale. They feared it might not be gold at all but some worthless, bogus metal instead.

It was, in fact, a gold-and-silver alloy exactly like the pale gold that Croesus had taken from the River Pactolus. The ancient Mediterranean world had called it electrum. The black dirt proved to be the outcrop of a rich gold-and-silver-bearing ore which became famous in America as the Comstock lode.

The product did not test as high as brighter gold and the men from Gold Hill received less per ounce for it. But where they had once worked a week to get an ounce of gold now they extracted it from the black earth by the pound. On some days they made a thousand dollars a day. At other times they ran into a clinging, blue-black dirt that yielded no gold at all and clogged the riffles in their rockers. They called it "that blasted blue stuff" and threw it aside.

Despite the annoying blue stuff, McLaughlin and O'Riley were doing well enough to attract the attention of a neighbor, Old Pancake Comstock, who claimed they were working on his land and threatened to cut off their supply of water. He managed to bully his way into the mine the Irishmen called the Ophir and has been known ever since as the discoverer of the Comstock lode.

The mysterious Ophir of the Bible made King Hiram and King Solomon rich. By revealing the treasure of the Washoe country, the Ophir of Nevada created dozens of bonanza kings and broke as many again. It was the first mine on the Comstock.

The news of the newly discovered wealth of Nevada reached the outside world when an experienced mining man from California visited the Washoe and suspected that "the blasted blue stuff" which would not give gold was rich in silver. He took some of it back to California where an assayer confirmed his suspicions. Both men struck out at once for the new gold and silver field.

Not far behind them was George Hearst who contracted to buy an interest in the Ophir, then hurried back across the Sierra Nevadas to raise the cash for his investment. He sold his California mine and borrowed a thousand dollars from a hotel owner to finance his new undertaking.

The gamble paid off in gold, silver, and experience. Though the Comstock became famous as a silver strike, the ore yielded forty-three percent gold, which, at its higher and steadier price, produced the larger profits over the twenty-year period of the Comstock boom.

The Comstock lode brought many new features to the mining industry in western America. Deep mines were necessary to get to the Comstock ore, and men who had served their apprenticeship in the California placer country found themselves faced with the problems of ground support and ventilation.

Both problems had been met and solved satisfactorily in deep mines throughout history. Agricola had described the way in which ore was removed from stopes, or rooms, and pillars of rock left standing as supports.

This tried and tested procedure didn't work in Comstock mines. The ore body was soft. The pillars collapsed, and several serious cave-ins taught the operators that they would have to find a new way to support the ground.

In the Ophir, Hearst and his engineers developed the square-set method of timbering. As rock was removed from a stope, the walls and roof of the room were braced with heavy timbers placed upright and horizontally and fastened securely at the corners to make a wooden cage. As the working was extended, so were the square sets, which multiplied outward and upward like stacked boxes. The miners used the timbered roof of one square set as the floor on which they stood to break out the rock above. This method of mining shored up many an underground working on the Comstock. Hearst used it later to open the famous Homestake gold mine in South Dakota.

Heat, too, threatened to keep miners out of the Comstock workings. Temperatures increased three degrees with every hundred feet the mine deepened. At three thousand feet beneath the surface the muckers could work for only fifteen minutes at a time and ran the danger of being scalded by underground water that steamed around them at 170 degrees Fahrenheit. Double crews of workers spelled each other, and large quantities of ice water were provided

To keep the Comstock mines from caving in, engineers built square-set wooden supports. This practice, called timber-stope mining, is used today. In the modern photograph shown here, wedges hold the timbers tight against the roof of the mine. Beneath the workers, ore has been removed and the space is being filled with waste rock. To mine the ore above them the men will use the timber roof for a floor and put up another roof.

Homestake Mining Company

for drinking and dousing while the operators experimented with air shafts, blowers, and a tunnel meant to ventilate all the mines.

In many ways the Comstock was a harbinger of things to come. Hallidie's flat hoisting cable made deeper shafts possible. Improved explosives and drills speeded the extraction of the ore. The deep mines, needing large amounts of capital for their development, were bought and sold by stock-market speculators in San Francisco, who made millions or went broke without ever having seen the mines.

There was no room on the Comstock for the little operator with his cradle or sluice boxes. He found himself working underground for wages, and in an unsuccessful attempt to keep his rate of pay at four dollars a shift he formed the Miners' Protective Association which later became the Miners' Union, affiliated with the once-strong Western Federation of Miners, no longer in existence.

The Comstock lode produced $300 million in the twenty years from 1860 to 1880. It also produced literature, in the writings of Dan De Quille, editor of Virginia City's *Territorial Enterprise,* and Mark Twain, his chief reporter. In the pages of the *Enterprise,* and in Twain's *Roughing It,* the Washoe boom days remain for all to experience.

In the sagebrush country of Nevada they were over by 1880. The mines closed, the bonanza kings went back to San Francisco to build their mansions, and only a few destitute miners, too poor to move on, were left in the deserted streets of Virginia City and Gold Hill.

In the meantime, in the Rockies, another landmark had been heralded as a mountain of gold. It was Pike's Peak. As far as William Green Russell was concerned the "Pike's Peak or Bust" gold rush of 1859 was a mistake. He should have known. He was the one who found the gold that caused it.

A miner from Georgia, he had been caught by snows in the Rockies on his way to California in 1849. With six companions he built two log cabins at the junction of Cherry Creek and the South Platte River. There the men spent the winter—the first residents of Denver, Colorado. They prospected the sands of Cherry Creek and found good color, but not enough to keep them in the vicinity. They went on to California.

Nine years later, in the summer of 1858, they returned to the cabins in Colorado. The next spring, after prospecting all winter, William Green Russell took his gold dust to St. Louis to trade it for supplies. There wasn't much of it, less than a thousand dollars worth.

To the merchants in St. Louis and the other towns of the Missouri frontier it looked like millions in potential trade. Remembering the profits of the rush to California in 1849, they advertised Russell's few ounces of gold as if it were a wagonload.

"Gold! Just a few days away! Running in rivers from the slopes of Pike's Peak!" So went the ballyhoo. Special agents were hired to spread the good word. "Guides" to the Pike's Peak goldfields were printed speedily and in vast quantities.

Alarmed at the sensation his little poke of gold dust had caused, Russell raised his voice in protest, pointing out among other things that Cherry Creek and Pike's Peak were separated by many mountainous miles. Few people listened. Those who did were sure that Russell only wanted to discourage competition and keep the Pike's Peak gold for himself.

The propaganda had an immediate effect. The "jumping-off places" along the Missouri frontier swelled with Argonauts, as green as they were eager. They bought provisions faster than the merchants could stock them.

Steamboats plying up the Missouri River were filled to capacity. A stagecoach service was set up between Fort Leavenworth, Kansas, and the new mining camp of Denver. With characteristic optimism the month's trip was advertised as taking only a week. Everything was underestimated except the amount of gold waiting on the slopes of Pike's Peak.

The atmosphere in the frontier towns was much like that surrounding preparations for a Fourth of July picnic. Some impatient and penurious gold seekers set out for Colorado armed with nothing but hand carts or knapsacks slung over their shoulders. After all, the guidebooks said it wasn't far.

It was, in fact, a six-hundred-mile obstacle race, even with the best of covered wagons and the sturdiest of draft animals. In the spring, the Kansas and Colorado plains were swept by snow and rain and fierce, biting winds. Wagons bogged down in mud or were carried away by flooded rivers. There was no forage for the animals and no wood for fires.

John Sherer, *Adventures of a Gold-Digger*

This digger has given up. Frontier-town merchants lured gold seekers West with advertisements of wealth to be mined at Pike's Peak. When the eager hordes arrived in their wagons, they found no gold at all.

Later in the summer, the rivers dried up and so did the vegetation. There was no shade and no water. Fires swept over the prairies in great hissing sheets, devouring the dry grass and anything else in the way.

The gold hunters with their guidebooks left the Missouri frontier gaily advertising their mistaken destination on handcarts and wagon canvas: "Pike's Peak or Bust!" By the time they reached Denver, or its sister city, Auraria, they were thoroughly disillusioned. There was nothing in either of these primitive and crowded camps to cheer them up.

Housing was limited to tents or hastily built log cabins with mud roofs and floors to match. There was no glass for windows and not enough food for all the newcomers. Men dreamed of steaks and lived on gritty bread.

Worst of all there was no gold. Before summer had warmed the mountains, the early arrivals were trekking back East again. Now their carts and wagons bore the unhappy sign: "Busted!"

Some of them, hoping to avoid the hardships they had endured on the way West, built boats and rafts and tried to sail home down the South Platte River. Brand-new Denver, suffering from a surplus of people and a lack of everything else, responded eagerly to this chance of establishing herself as a port. A boat-building yard accommodated the emigrants, but the Platte proved unnavigable. The boats and rafts were wrecked, and the survivors scrambled out of the muddy river, defeated again.

The stampede for home was almost as large as the stampede for gold had been. For a while the enraged voices of the men who had been there drowned out the sweet talk of the gold-rush promoters. Nobody knew what to believe.

While the debate thundered in the East, a prospector named John H. Gregory walked into Denver with gold—lots of it. The whole town followed him back to his claim. It wasn't far; just thirty miles—straight up.

Since it wasn't possible to go straight up, the gold seekers wound around mountain ledges, leaped crevices, forded rushing streams and took chances that frightened even the stoic mules. With luck, the thirty-mile trip took only three or four days. And at the end of it there was gold.

When news of the Gregory Gulch strike reached the East it

only added to the confusion. Was it real or just another pipe dream? Determined to find out, three conscientious newspaper editors hurried to the diggings. They were A. D. Richardson, of the *Boston Journal;* Henry Villard, of the *Cincinnati Commercial Enquirer;* and Horace Greeley, of the *New York Tribune.*

"The solitude in these mountains was sylvan and perfect until a few weeks ago," Greeley wrote back to his newspaper. "All is now being rapidly changed, and not entirely for the better."

The newspaper editors found four thousand men at the diggings, and a dozen women, half of these the Indian common-law wives of the miners. Men often kept squaws at the gold camps, leaving them behind with the mules when they returned to civilization.

Nowhere in Gregory Gulch was there a chair or a table, Greeley reported. The miners cooked and ate in the open air. The aristocrats slept in tents. The rest of the populace used shelters made of pine boughs.

The prospectors called the ore they mined "blossom rock." It was the crumbly quartz outcrop of an underground vein of gold, but it was so weathered that it was easily crushed and sluiced and it was exceedingly rich. No man digging in the area made less than a hundred dollars a day.

This was gold enough to satisfy anybody, but the Colorado miners had developed an inferiority complex. Their publicity had been bad. If it continued that way, civilization might never bring its charms to their mountains. They wanted to impress the eastern editors, so they fired a shotgun loaded with gold into the trench from which Mr. Greeley had been invited to take a sample of ore.

This method of "salting" a claim was not uncommon. Miners more experienced than Horace Greeley would have scraped away the surface of the rock before testing it for gold. For such wary customers, a claim could be salted by placing gold dust in a charge of dynamite. The explosion forced the gold into the rock so that the salting could not be detected.

Some miners did their salting while the dirt was in the pan. Gold mixed into ashes from a cigar or pipe, a squirt of gold-laden tobacco, or a fingertip with gold dust concealed beneath the nail were easily introduced into a pan of dirt and water. They left enough gold to give promising color to the most ordinary garden soil.

Had Horace Greeley written back to his newspaper that the gold he panned in Gregory Gulch was introduced to the rock by means of a shotgun, Colorado's reputation for dishonesty would have been permanently established. Fortunately for posterity, and the region's future prosperity, the editor never found out that the color in his pan had been enriched for his benefit.

He wrote about the gold he had washed from the blossom rock in his pan and the gold he had watched others take from their sluice boxes. He also reported the difficulties he had encountered getting to Gregory Gulch, the primitive living conditions, and his firm conviction that "next to outright and indisputable gambling, the hardest way to obtain gold is to mine for it." He did not advise his readers to go West. He advised them to stay put. They went West.

For a while they poured into Gregory Gulch at the rate of five hundred a day. Before the summer was out there were more than ten thousand men crowded into an area less than four miles square. They hardly left each other room to swing a pick, but they kept digging.

They followed the rich blossom rock farther and farther into the mountain. They set up a mill, called the woodpecker, to crush the ore. Gold mining in Gregory Gulch took on all the aspects of a permanent industry. And then, suddenly, the blossom rock turned rebellious. It refused to yield its gold.

Gold, which rarely combines chemically with other elements, does mix with them in alloys. Gold is usually found in nature as an alloy, its atoms intermingled with those of other metals, as clay and lime are mixed in a mortar. Unlike gold, nonauriferous metals do form chemical unions, and when gold is alloyed with these metals it may be locked in the resulting chemical combination.

This had happened in the blossom rock. The iron alloyed with the gold and abundant in the ore body was chemically combined with sulphur as an iron pyrite. Other metals too appeared as sulphides.

Where the ore was exposed, nature had released the gold through oxidation. Deep in the earth, and unoxidized, the sulphides imprisoned the metal and the miners could not find a way to free it. The woodpecker ground finer and finer, but still only a tenth of the gold was retrieved.

Mercury was ordinarily used to help gravity in rockers and sluice boxes gather gold and separate it from impurities. The quicksilver was placed in the bottom of the box between the cleats or riffles, and as the heavy gold sank beneath the dirt or sand, it mixed with the liquid mercury to form an alloy called amalgam.

The amalgam was squeezed through leather, to remove excess quicksilver, and then heated. The mercury vaporized, taking impurities with it, and the gold was left. With "sulphurets," as the miners called the refractory ore they had run into in Gregory Gulch, the mercury treatment was useless. The sulphides prevented the gold and mercury from mixing.

The gold miners cursed the sulphurets and left them. They fanned out through the Rockies finding color in almost every

Although the Pike's Peak gold rush had turned out to be a mirage, the Rockies were rich in both gold and silver. Camps that had grown up around gold mines remained to extract silver. The miners in this camp

stream. The metallurgists and capitalists were interested in the gold left behind. There was lots of it; it was rich; and if a way could be found to treat it, there were profits to be made.

They shipped the stubborn sulphurets to experts in Great Britain and Europe. They set up a milling and smelting center in Blackhawk and brought the experts to the mountains to help work out a milling and smelting process that would efficiently and economically divest the unoxidized ore of its gold.

Strangely enough, though gold is chemically sluggish, rarely combining with other elements, modern metallurgy has forced the metal to make such chemical unions to extract it from its ores. In this way the problem of the sulphurets was solved. The ore was

at Quartz Hill set themselves up in houses instead of the usual tents. Some later camps added luxuries such as running water, electric lights, and trolley cars.

Frank Fossett, *Colorado: Its Gold and Silver Mines*

roasted over low heat to oxidize it and drive off the sulphur. The resulting mass was permeated with chlorine gas.

Chlorine gas is bubbled through molten gold-silver alloys in refineries to remove silver as a silver chloride. In this brief exposure it does not affect the gold. But the men working with the sulphurets found that if the contact of gold and chlorine was sustained for several hours the gold would form a terchloride which was soluble in water. The gold could thus be removed from the roasted ore in solution. Since its chemical union with the chlorine was unstable, it was easily precipitated.

In developing this process the metallurgists not only found a way to extract gold from rebellious ores but learned much about extracting and saving the other metals found with gold. This knowledge enabled Colorado to successfully treat refractory silver ores in the silver boom that followed the gold rush. By the time the sulphurets were conquered, Colorado was ready for a long and profitable career mining and milling the rich assortment of metals which are still coming out of her mountains.

Actually the region had two gold rushes, with a silver boom in between. Leadville, for instance, began life as a gold camp and produced eight million dollars worth of placer gold before it became famous for creating millionaire Silver Kings. When the price of silver tumbled in the 1890's, the Silver Kings tumbled too.

The game was played rather like musical chairs. In the 1870's silver made Horace Tabor a millionaire. Before he ran off to Washington with a chorus girl named Baby Doe, he built Leadville an opera house. At that time Leadville Johnny Brown was so poor he couldn't buy a ticket to a performance.

With the silver slump, Tabor's fortune vanished. He got a job at three dollars a day hauling trash from the back door of the Tabor Opera House. At the same time Leadville Johnny found gold in an old silver mine, made several million, and decided he didn't want a ticket to a Tabor Opera House performance after all. He married his favorite waitress, Molly Tobin, and bought two tickets to New York.

After a long and happy career as one of the wealthier and more eccentric members of New York society, Molly Brown became a real-life heroine in the *Titanic* disaster. Fifty years later she was still dazzling New York as she lived again in *The Unsinkable Molly Brown,* the Broadway hit musical based on her life.

Almost thirty years after the "Pike's Peak or Bust" pioneers had trudged back from Colorado "Busted," gold was discovered at Cripple Creek, on the south slope of the Peak. It was one of Colorado's biggest strikes and did more than anything else to pull the mining region out of the silver slump.

W. S. Stratton, a carpenter from Colorado Springs, was the man who discovered the riches of the area in 1892. Stratton had been searching for gold in his spare time for twenty years. Like many another prospector, he had often seen, but never tested, a worthless rock, called sylvanite, which was so abundant that it was used for building purposes.

After twenty years experience, Stratton's eye grew trained enough to see what others couldn't. He tested the gold and found that it was a telluride of gold and silver. He traced it to its source in the mouth of an old volcano, staked out his claim, and mined it until the turn of the century. Then, wishing to retire and enjoy his profits, he sold the mine for ten million dollars.

The mining camps that grew in the Pike's Peak region had little in common with earlier camps, like the one in Gregory Gulch. Almost from the beginning they had running water, electric lights, and trolley cars.

Among the muckers in the mines was Jack Dempsey, who started his boxing career by fighting another underground shoveler who aspired to be a boxer. Dempsey won the match, fought in the mining camp of Victor, forcing his opponent to look for another field in which to excel. The defeated fighter was Bernard Baruch.

In neighboring Cripple Creek, for a time, the groceries were delivered by Groucho Marx. The residents were less impressed with the delivery boy than with the fruits and vegetables, brought in fresh by rail from eastern farms. Such luxuries had been unknown in earlier mining camps.

In the years between the first Colorado strike, in 1859, and the last, in 1891, gold had been discovered all over western America, from Arizona and New Mexico, in the south, to Idaho and Montana in the north. In every place but Utah, where the Mormons preceded them, the prospectors leaped ahead of the frontier, often into all but inaccessible mountain areas where transportation was a major problem.

A combination of steamboats and mule trains first brought these isolated mining communities the necessities of life. Provisions were carried by steamer as far as possible and then loaded on pack mules. From St. Louis, steamers traveled up the Missouri to Montana. From San Francisco, they steamed up the Sacramento, San Joaquin, and lower Feather rivers, and up and down the coast.

From Portland, ships sailed up the Columbia and Snake rivers, deep into the Northwest, taking supplies to mining camps along the way. Miners in the arid Southwest were serviced by ships which navigated the Colorado River from the Gulf of California to ports now covered by Lake Mead, in Nevada.

Not until roads were built were the pack mules that trudged between inland steamer ports and mining camps replaced by ox-drawn wagons and stagecoaches. The first roads were privately owned toll roads, little gold mines in themselves. They in turn were replaced by railroads.

When the gold diggers started their rush for the Black Hills, in 1876, those who could afford it traveled as far west as Sydney, Nebraska, by train. They were still some three hundred miles from their destination, but they had accomplished the greater part of their journey with an ease no previous gold seekers had known. It was a rude shock to get off the train to face not only the discomforts of stage or wagon travel but Indian trouble as well.

In the beginning the Indians had tolerated the gold seekers as they tolerated missionaries and mountain men. The West was big and there was room for all. But they soon saw that towns grew where the white men found gold, farms and ranches spread around the towns, roads and railroad tracks invaded the plains, the wild game disappeared, and the land was swallowed up.

The tribes of the West stopped fighting each other and joined against the intruders. They forced the gold seekers to travel in groups and keep armed guards posted around camps and diggings. As the miners streamed into the Black Hills, sacred home of the thunder god of the Sioux, the Indians massacred Custer and his regiment. The brief victory came too late.

For a quarter of a century prospectors looking for gold had been blazing trails across the West, preparing the way for those who were to follow. Perhaps, more than the gold they found, that was their contribution to civilization. In recognition of this service, the railroad track that first linked the East Coast with the West was joined, in 1869, at Promontory Point, Utah, with a golden spike.

SOURDOUGH

IN THE WILDERNESS of British Columbia an Indian knelt to drink from Thompson River. He saw something glittering in the water and scooped out a bright yellow nugget of gold. Indians had been doing this for centuries as they fished and trapped along the Thompson and Fraser rivers. This particular nugget was important because it started a gold rush.

In the 1850's the whole world was infected with a disease called gold fever. It was particularly virulent in the western half of North America. Many of the thousands of young men who went to California in 1849 gathered little gold but much experience. In fact, prospecting was the only thing they knew. It was their profession and their way of life.

Known as sourdoughs, in honor of the sourdough flapjacks they consumed, they followed the scent of gold in all directions. In 1858, because of a nugget found in the Thompson River, thirty thousand of them headed north.

In hollowed-out logs and homemade rafts they paddled up the Thompson and Fraser rivers. The treacherous waters wrecked their flimsy craft. The Indians attacked them. The Hudson's Bay Company resented them. And at the mouth of the Fraser, the British government greeted them with a gun boat and a proclamation.

The proclamation stated that all gold in its natural place of deposit belonged to the Crown and was not to be dug without authorization from the colonial government. Authorization was granted upon payment of a monthly fee of ten shillings. Royal Engineers followed the prospectors to their diggings to collect the fees and supervise the mining. Gold diggers who disturbed the peace, polluted the streams unduly, or recklessly destroyed trees and vegetation forfeited the right to mine in British territory.

It was a new experience to sourdoughs from the States, used to making their own rules and regulations, keeping all the gold they dug, and destroying whatever they dang well pleased. At first the Royal Engineers were resented, but when they saved the claims and the scalps of the miners from the Indians, their presence was tolerated if not welcomed.

Year by year the prospectors kept pushing north. By 1880 they were washing gold from rich placer deposits in Gold Creek, near Juneau, Alaska. Among the late-comers to this bonanza country was Pierre Erussard, generally known as French Pete. He was also known as a squaw man because he had an Indian wife and lived with the natives.

By the time French Pete got his relatives to Gold Creek, the best claims were taken. So Pete and his in-laws tried their luck on Douglas Island, west of Juneau. They found gold in the sand of Paris Creek and an outcrop of gold-bearing quartz on the hillside above.

French Pete located two claims, one called Bear's Nest and the other called Paris. For a year the family worked the claims, but the yields were disappointing. They decided to move on. Stopping in Juneau for provisions, French Pete sold the Paris claim for five dollars to John Treadwell. Then he went off to seek his fortune.

In the next thirty-five years the Treadwell mines, located on and around the Paris claim, yielded $67,355,050 in gold. More than $25,000,000 of it was profit. The mine on French Pete's original claim followed the outcrop of ore the squaw man had discovered to a depth of 2,300 feet beneath the sea, using the stope and pillar method of mining.

The pillars were not strong enough to hold up the sea, pounding above the hanging wall. About 1912 the pillars began to collapse, shaking the ground around and tumbling solid rock in the mine. Four years later salt water seeped into the stopes. In 1917 the thin hanging wall that separated the ocean floor from the underground caverns gave way. The ocean rushed in with a roar and the unmined gold of the Treadwell and two neighboring mines was added to the bounty at the bottom of the sea.

Another squaw man was responsible for the discovery of gold on the Klondike in 1896. He was an American, George Washington Carmack. With other sourdoughs he had been prospecting for some years along the Yukon River where several small mining camps had grown. The one called Circle was in Alaska. Forty Mile was over the border in Canada.

All the old-timers at Circle and Forty Mile knew that the streams flowing into the Yukon from the north held no gold. This knowledge was so common that nobody ever questioned it. Carmack and two of his wife's brothers were heading for one of these northern streams, the Thron Diuck, an Indian name meaning "plenty of fish." They were going fishing.

On their way they met some Indian friends returning from the Thron Diuck. These fishermen told them that the stream with plenty of fish also had plenty of gold. They really didn't credit this information because everybody knew that gold in the Thron Diuck was impossible no matter what men said who had been there. But Carmack was willing to pass the word along to Bob Henderson, a Canadian prospector they met later. He was even ready to invite Henderson to accompany them to the river to try his luck, which had been so bad that even a few fish would be a marked improvement. But at that moment Henderson insulted Carmack's Indian companions so they went on without him.

On the Thron Diuck, the men used the frying pan in which they had expected to fry fish to test for color in the river. The color was so rich that they forgot about fishing. They staked out claims, panned more gold, and took the evidence of their strike back to Forty Mile. When the sourdoughs there saw the gold, the rush was on. The Thron Diuck, once noted for its fish, became the Klondike, famous for its gold.

Years later, Carmack, a millionaire, wrote a book about his experiences in the north and his discovery of the Klondike gold. In it he pointed out, with not a little satisfaction, that Henderson's prejudice against Indians had cost him his big chance to make a fortune.

Henderson, in the meantime, was convincing the Canadian government that he had panned gold on the Klondike long before

Carmack got there. As the discoverer, who had received no other reward, he felt he was entitled to a pension. He got it: $200 a month!

Within a week after Carmack showed up with his Klondike gold the mining camp of Forty Mile was empty. A new camp, Dawson, sprouted where the Klondike joined the Yukon. It grew daily despite its isolated location and the difficulties of reaching it. It was a mean voyage from Forty Mile to Dawson. The trip from Circle was even harder and longer.

In the vast, sparsely settled north country news traveled slowly. Word of the Klondike gold didn't reach Circle until Christmas, six months after the strike. It was then mid-winter and fifty degrees below zero. Nevertheless the sourdoughs at Circle began bargaining for dog teams to pull them over the frozen river to Dawson. Many a good Yukon claim was exchanged for a team of Huskies, priced at $250 per dog.

By the time the miners from Circle reached the Klondike, the claims around and below the discovery site had been taken. It was a long way up the river to unclaimed ground and they had already traveled three hundred miles. The lazy ones staked ground lying closer, on the rivulets running into the main stream. These creeks were known as "pups" and scorned by the old hands.

But nobody could lose that first year on the Klondike. The "pups" panned out as well as the Klondike itself. The gold was good quality and brought $16.20 an ounce. The average take was $866 a day.

By spring, diligent miners had collected enough gold to keep them comfortably for the rest of their lives. Some of them decided to enjoy their profits and booked passage on the steamers *Excelsior* and *Portland,* bound for California.

The *Excelsior* reached San Francisco first, on July 14, 1897, carrying forty miners and a half million dollars in gold dust. The men came down the gangplank minus toes and fingers, ears and noses, mutilated by the bitter cold of the north land. But they carried gold. It was the first news the outside world had received of the fabulous riches to be found in the Klondike.

When the second ship, the *Portland,* arrived at Seattle three days later, the world was waiting. A tugboat carrying newspaper reporters crossed Puget Sound and lay off Cape Flattery for two days, awaiting the treasure ship.

"The *Portland* has brought a ton of gold," was the news they flashed to the mainland. The dock at Seattle was crowded with the curious who watched the sixty-eight bearded, weather-beaten sourdoughs come ashore, each carrying his hard-won Klondike gold, all guarded by rows of armed Wells Fargo officers.

After that there weren't enough steamers heading north to carry the hopeful. Ships built for twenty-five passengers took aboard a hundred more. Many of those destined to sleep on the floor paid a premium for the privilege.

Those who had the fare could book passage to St. Michael and then up the Yukon River, all the way to the goldfield. It was expensive, but it was supposed to be the easiest way to reach the new El Dorado. The ships that set sail too late also provided the slowest

A team of strong dogs was a good guarantee of making it safely to the Klondike with supplies. Thousands of dogs were shipped north to join in the gold rush, but most of them were not fit for the work or the weather. Huskies, shown in this 1898 photograph, sold for $250 per dog.

Alaska State Historical Library and Museum, Juneau

way to the Klondike. Many cheechakos, or greenhorns, who had expected to spend the winter digging gold, spent it instead on an icebound vessel in the Bering Sea or the Yukon River.

Poor men bought passage to Juneau or Skagway and then packed six hundred miles over Chilkoot or White Pass. Men were the only pack animals who could make it over the passes. Dogs were not to be had at any price, and horses perished in such numbers that their rotting carcasses in the spring and summer obliterated all other odors for miles around.

At any time of year the passes were perilous, yet some thirty-three thousand gold hunters made their way over them in the dead of winter in 1897. Many more tried and failed.

Since there was absolutely nothing in the country to which they were going, the men had to carry everything they would need on their backs: stoves, sleighs, tents, mining equipment, fuel, food, clothing, rifles, and ammunition. Some made several trips back and forth over the mountains to bring across their belongings.

It was a strenuous climb just to get to the foot of Chilkoot Pass. No wood was available on the steep approach or on the pass itself. Those caught in severe winter storms found themeslves burning the very possessions they had struggled so hard to bring up the grade.

Glaciers overhung the pass, and the trail was narrow and treacherous. Horses, sinking into the snow and trying to fight their way out, fell from the trail to be dashed to death on the jagged rocks a thousand feet below. Over the worst part of the trail, men crawled on hands and knees to better distribute their weight on the shifting snow.

A wind blew constantly from the overhanging glaciers, filling the air with sharp ice pellets that obscured vision and lacerated exposed skin. Men crawling over the pass were hung with icicles like Christmas trees. The breath from their noses and mouths and the perspiration from the exertion of their climb froze quickly in temperatures that hovered around forty degrees below zero.

When the wind on the pass turned into a blizzard, the men wriggled forward slowly on their bellies. The wind whipped up the snow beneath them into such dense clouds that they couldn't see or breathe. A blizzard also blew down great masses of glacier ice. They could hear the roar as the ice fell. If they were lucky, they weren't under it.

Not all of them were lucky. Their chances of perishing beneath a descending chunk of glacier increased as the weather warmed and the ice melted. The worst such disaster occurred on White Pass, in April, 1898, when sixty-three men were killed in a glacier slide. Only seven bodies were ever recovered.

Once over the pass, the long journey to Dawson was just begun. In the spring, mosquitoes contributed to the torture of the rest of the journey. The men who fought them insisted that they were as thick as thunder clouds, as big as buzzards, and could bite through anything but the heaviest buckskin.

They battled the insects as they built the rafts and boats that would carry them through lake after boulder-strewn lake. If they survived these hazards, they arrived at the Whitehorse rapids where all but the most expert sailors were apt to see the possessions they had brought so many miles dashed to pieces between rock and water. Crosses on the river bank below the rapids testified to the number of men who had been lost along with their belongings.

To add to the hazards of the trip were sudden and violent wind storms which blew away tents. And there were hungry wolves and bears, and the lynx, who had a habit of dropping out of trees on any human morsel he fancied.

The object was to reach Dawson before the freeze congealed the waterways in September. Dawson! Men dreamed of it, fought toward it, and finally reached it—a scrawny array of rough timber shacks and tents stretching along the river banks.

Dawson could easily accommodate a population of four hundred. By the spring of 1898 it held thirty thousand, with more arriving every day. There weren't enough beds, or enough houses and tents, or fuel, or whisky, or food.

Many of the spring arrivals, who had fought their way over one of the mountain passes in the bitter cold of winter, reached Dawson with frozen limbs already turning gangrenous, or with the brown circlets of scurvy crawling up their legs. There were no doctors, no hospitals, not even a decent place to die.

Those who had lost their outfits on the long, hard journey found that they couldn't replace them. Everything was scarce in Dawson, especially the basic necessities of life.

Even rich men, coming in from their claims with pokes bulging with gold dust, slept in the streets for lack of other accommodations.

They might not be able to buy food or clothing, but they could always buy women and liquor, of a sort.

The whisky was red-eye—a home-distilled, watered-down, poisonous liquid, richly colored with tobacco juice. The women were red-eyed too, a remarkably ugly lot, according to contemporary accounts. They lived in the center of town, in what was known as Hell's Half Acre, and not a few of them made fortunes.

For lack of anything else to do with their gold, the men gambled it away through the long summer nights. Any entertainment was automatically a sell-out, even if it consisted of nothing more exciting that the reading of a newspaper several months old.

One enterprising Dawson gentleman bought a newspaper a cheechako had brought with him from the States. He paid one hundred and fifty dollars for it in gold. To hear him read it aloud, Dawson residents paid a pinch of gold dust (about a dollar). The man shouted himself hoarse through one Sunday afternoon reading every morsel of news, including the want ads, but he cleared over a thousand dollars.

As Dawson grew, the stores and restaurants sold out everything they had to sell and closed their doors. Frantically the miners sent calls for food and supplies to the outside world, but the outside world was a long way away. The men didn't know if their appeals for help had reached anyone. They only knew that they faced starvation. Young men in the prime of life were so weak from hunger they fainted in the streets. A week before Christmas, in 1897, the last business house shut down.

The miners called a town meeting, or "roll up," to decide what should be done. The poet Joaquin Miller hobbled out to the gathering on frozen feet, his long white hair straggling over his shoulders, his back bent with hardship, age, and worry. Hardly a man who raised his hand in a vote could count five whole fingers on it. The Klondike had demanded a price for its gold.

The men agreed unanimously that they should share and ration food. There was a difference of opinion as to what else they should do to better conditions. Joaquin Miller felt that they should wait in Dawson, conserving food and strength, until supplies reached them. Others wanted to send the strongest men, with a part of the precious food, over the pass to Juneau to bring back provisions. This opinion carried the day.

The army of men, two hundred strong, set out just after Christmas on a dangerous, mid-winter trip in weather that was 65 degrees below zero. Some of them had made the journey in the opposite direction just a few months before.

Now they found the going even harder. The ice on the river was ten feet thick. It was impossible to chop through to water. They quenched their thirst with snow, which covered everything, also several feet thick. To wade through it required a prodigious amount of effort. Their exertions caused them to perspire beneath their fur overcoats. The perspiration froze, sealing clothes to skin, and the next movement tore away the frozen flesh.

They had few tents. Most of them slept in hollows in the snow. All of them were desperately hungry. Their share of Dawson's limited food supply was not enough to keep up strength on such an arduous journey.

One evening a man was caught stealing an extra handful of precious flour. No one would waste scarce ammunition on the thief but an angry group strung up a rope and tried to hang him. His rescuers were forced to strike out ahead of the larger party. It was the first of many quarrels that finally broke Dawson's rescue team into a dozen different groups. Fortunately for those waiting in the mining camp, supplies reached them in answer to appeals they had sent out earlier. They survived, but not without a struggle.

A fire destroyed the town the next winter, but by that time a saw mill was turning out lumber and steamers rushed supplies up the Yukon all summer. Within two years there was a railroad and a telegraph.

In return for these benefits, Dawson gave the rest of the world Jack London's stories, Robert Service's poems, and Joaquin Miller's vivid accounts of life in the frozen North. It also produced $32 million dollars worth of gold in two years. And then, as most mining camps do, it died.

The miner who had brought his gold to Dawson moved on to other, richer benches in Alaska and northern Canada. At the turn of the century he was finding gold around Nome.

He had, for the most part, given up panning gold from running streams. The richest placer gold was found in benches, or shelves, above the streams. There, gold had been left behind when rivers changed or narrowed their channels. Rich deposits were also found

Bureau of Mines, U.S. Department of the Interior

This sourdough, with pan and cradle, is posing for his picture in the Klondike about 1900. Prospectors who moved on to Nome didn't pan gold in streams. Where rivers had changed course, they dug in the abandoned banks and under dry riverbeds.

deep beneath soil and tundra on the bedrock of waterways that had long since disappeared.

The only way the miner could reach this gold was by digging. He dug in the winter when the ground was frozen, using the miner's ancient friend—fire.

With fire he thawed the frozen ground so that his shovel could remove a layer of dirt. In this way, lighting fires at night and digging by day, he could burrow as deep as necessary without worrying about ground supports or flooding. The earth was frozen solid and so was the water in it.

He spent the winter digging, piling the auriferous ore on the surface. When the spring thaws came, flooding the land, he used the water to wash the gold from the dirt.

His enemy was the cold. To protect his face from frostbite he mixed ashes from his fire with bacon grease and spread the black goop lavishly. Even so, the freezing temperature might give him a permanent shave and remove the skin along with the beard.

His thermometer couldn't tell him how cold it was. At 42 degrees below zero the mercury froze. After that he measured the drop in temperature by the other things that froze. When his kerosene refused to pour, it was 55 degrees below zero. His pain killer turned solid at 72 degrees below. If the Hudson's Bay rum froze, it was 80 degrees below and he didn't venture outside.

Even inside, at that temperature, his beard froze tight to the covers. If he tried to chop wood for his fire, his ax splintered. Then he burned rockers, sluice boxes, sleighs, extra clothing—anything to keep warm. Or he might develop a common form of madness known as cabin fever, set fire to his hut, and wander off to freeze to death in the snow.

Despite the cold, the search for gold continued. In 1899, the beach on either side of Nome was covered for seventy miles with pans, rockers, and ingenious contraptions invented for the purpose of washing gold from the rich dark blue sands at the edge of the sea.

There is still gold in Alaska where the mining of many metals has been a major industry, second only to fishing. But things have changed. Gold is increasingly a by-product of base metal mines. Machines do the digging. And when the miners want to know how cold it is, they pick up their telephones and dial the numbers that will give them the time and the temperature.

FOSSICKER

GOLD FEVER IS CONTAGIOUS. In the latter half of the nineteenth century it swept around the world. California forty-niners joined the gold-seeking fossickers of Australia. Across Bering Strait, rumors of gold in Siberia reached the Alaska sourdoughs.

The gold rush in Siberia differed from the one in Alaska even though Siberian streams and mountains were as generous as the Klondike country and created as many millionaires. These millionaires were not free to return to their homes with the riches they had collected. They were convicts who had been sentenced to the vast Siberian wasteland for crimes or unpopular political activities. Each exile carried a police certificate stating his offense and his sentence.

Nor were they allowed to keep the gold they collected. They turned it over to the government, which paid them for it in paper money of fluctuating value.

Even so, they grew rich. They ordered necessities and luxuries sent to them by steamer along the Irtysh and Ob water systems, or hauled in on a sledge, known as a tarantass, when the ground was covered with snow. Though there was only one man for every five square miles of country, they began to gather in towns near their gold mines.

Their homes were log cabins, but those of the millionaires were large and ornately furnished. They hired less lucky criminals to work for them as servants and miners. They entertained one another at dinners and all-night gambling parties. Even in the middle of the day, when venturing out, they wore formal evening clothes.

When the news spread that there was gold in Siberia, men began to go there voluntarily and the government started building the trans-Siberian railroad to take supplies to the miners and bring back the gold they collected. Before the turn of the century, mining camps had become cities, boasting every convenience. The millionaires at Tomsk had built a university.

Much of the mining in Siberia was done by the tribute system. A mine owner farmed out portions of his claim to teams of miners, paying them for the gold they got out. The tribute workers stripped the land of the gold that was easy to get, letting the fine grains run through their long toms with the waste.

They did not develop a mine; they ravished it. When the yield went down, they moved on to another contract, often leaving rich ground so burdened with tailings, collapsed shafts, discarded equipment, burned-over forests and rotting timber that any future development was economically impossible.

Siberia is a large land, rich in mineral resources. Despite early mismanagement of many of the gold properties, gold is still mined there, raising Russian gold output to second place, just under South Africa, in present world-production estimates.

Russia was not the only country that, quite unintentionally, sent her criminals to a land rich in gold. Great Britain did the same thing when she established a penal colony in Australia. There, early in the nineteenth century, convict laborers employed on road-building gangs began picking up gold nuggets, an offense that was quickly and severely punished.

The last thing anybody wished to find, at that moment in Australia's history, was gold. The continent was large—as big as the United States in area. The white population numbered less than fifty thousand and three quarters of them were convicts. Nobody wanted the convicts breaking loose and running over the land searching for gold.

Though it was difficult to do, with gold lying around in chunks as big as boulders, everyone was careful not to see any. Occasionally a newcomer claimed to have discovered some, but he was quickly convinced of his error. In the interests of public safety, the existence of gold in Australia was denied so often by so many respected officials that its absence became an established fact.

As often as people have been fooled by fool's gold—iron or

Convicts in Australia greatly outnumbered the law-abiding, and so murders and robberies were frequent, as this old drawing suggests. In the vast solitude of the country, prospectors found it safer to travel in groups.

John Sherer, *Adventures of a Gold-Digger*

copper pyrite or yellow mica—they have been fooled by the real thing, passing it by because they were not trained to recognize it or because they had been trained to discount what they saw. Civilized men trust the opinion of experts and authorities even when these opinions contradict the evidence before their eyes.

So in 1849 Australians who wanted to search for gold joined the rush to California. Among them was Edward Hammond Hargraves. He had shipped off once before, when he was seventeen, leaving England for Australia to seek his fortune. At forty, he was still seeking.

In California he found no gold, but he did learn what gold country looked like. It looked like home. California gold came from geological formations much like those he had left behind in the land Down Under.

"I have been in a gold region in New South Wales, within three hundred miles of Sydney," he wrote to a friend. "Unless you know how to find gold, you might live for a century in the region and know nothing of its existence."

In California, Hargraves taught himself to recognize gold-bearing ground, prospect for color, and estimate yield. Then he sailed for home again, not at all disappointed to be leaving the States as poor as he had arrived. He expected to find plenty of gold in Australia where nobody else was looking for it.

In actually preparing himself for his task, and setting out deliberately to open a new goldfield, Hargraves did something unique. Most gold rushes have resulted from accidental discoveries without benefit of preliminary testing of the yield or the extent of the auriferous deposits.

Hargraves set about the business of finding gold scientifically and systematically. In February, 1851, he began to prospect on the Macquarie River and its tributaries, mapping, sampling, and testing. When he had proof that there was at least seventy miles of auriferous land along the Macquarie, he took the news to Sydney.

The government officials greeted the good tidings with mixed emotions. They still feared the effect of a gold strike on their forty-five thousand convicts. On the other hand, without gold, they kept losing large numbers of citizens to California. After some hesitation, it was decided that the gold in Australia should receive official recognition. The governor announced Hargraves' discovery and appointed him Commissioner of Crown Lands.

The citizens were so used to reminding each other that there was no gold in the country that at first they refused to believe the news. The word spread that Hargraves had really found his gold in California, and it was to California that the young men kept flocking.

But then a few daring gold seekers went out to test the Macquarie River for themselves. Just as Hargraves had said, there was gold. Instead of sailing for the States, the young men began a rush to New South Wales.

As the government had feared, there was trouble. Not with the convicts but with the prospectors, who suddenly poured into the territory from everywhere, even from California. In Australia, these gold seekers were known as fossickers, a word which meant, originally, to dig a ditch.

The trouble developed over the monthly fee the British charged for authorization to dig gold that belonged to the Crown. Unlike the sourdoughs in Canada, the Australian fossickers resented the fee and refused to pay it.

They called the officers sent to collect the stipend "digger hunters." Whole camps went into hiding when the digger hunters appeared. When the miners couldn't hide, they fought. In one pitched battle between the diggers and the hunters, two officers and thirty prospectors lost their lives.

The warlike aspect of the Australian rush did not discourage participants. Hopeful fossickers kept pouring into Sydney on their way to the goldfields. Melbourne, to the south, became a ghost town.

The citizens that were left in this capital of the territory of Victoria met together to discuss the town's predicament. It was unanimously decided that what Melbourne needed was a gold rush of her own. A reward of £200 was offered to anyone who discovered gold within two hundred miles of the city.

Within the year the reward was claimed and the rich Ballarat goldfield, just east of Melbourne, began to lure fossickers from New South Wales. With the discovery of the Bendigo mines, north of Ballarat, the population of the province of Victoria increased fourfold.

This was nugget country. Prospectors used to measuring gold by the grain, the pennyweight, and the ounce were amazed to stumble over chunks of gold weighing anywhere from ninety to two hundred pounds. The nuggets, worth thousands of dollars apiece, were even more valuable because of their oddity. They were named, and gained fame all over the world. Finders who were farseeing enough to preserve them in one piece earned money displaying the golden rocks before they sold them for the value of the gold they contained.

The first of the big nuggets was found on the farm of Dr. J. W. Kerr by an aborigine who had been hired to build a sheep run. Trying to hack out a boulder of quartz from the ground with his tomahawk, he broke away the rock and found it had been sheltering a great chunk of glittering gold. Just how big it was, no one knows.

Dr. Kerr, deciding it was too large to move in one piece, broke it to bits, some of which vanished before the total could be weighed.

Another of the big nuggets was unearthed when a discouraged prospector, who had found no gold to present to his fiancée, decided to pick her a bouquet of wild flowers instead. Clumsily he pulled some of them up by the roots, surprised to find the tendrils bright with golden bangles. He began to dig and struck a nugget that weighed ninety-three pounds.

Accounts of the discovery of the famous Welcome Stranger nugget differ, but all agree that it was found near Ballarat, in 1869, by John Deason and Richard Oates. It weighed two hundred pounds.

According to the most popular version of the events, the partners were trying to move their cart of provisions when it bogged down in a mud hole. Digging it out, they struck a rock. Even in the mud, they could see it was gold.

Since the country was full of prospectors, they feared they might be forced to share the wealth if they exposed their find in daylight. They waited until dark when they dug up the boulder of gold and loaded it into the cart, not without some difficulty. It was extremely heavy and of beautiful color, so they felt sure they would be rich if they could just get it safely to Melbourne.

They didn't quite get it home before the cart broke beneath the load. They dragged it to their cabin and decided that, in case strangers happened by, they had better hide it. But where do you hide a two-hundred-pound nugget in a one-room cabin?

Having just dug it up, they began to dig again, and buried the nugget in the fireplace. When they built a fire over it they were ready to welcome strangers. They welcomed several before the cart was repaired and ready to carry its golden burden to Melbourne.

The Welcome Stranger was the largest nugget ever found. Had it merely been worth its weight in gold its value at today's price for bullion would have been slightly over one hundred thousand dollars. As an oddity and showpiece it was worth many times that.

Nuggets still turn up in the Victoria gold country. In the 1950's, a citizen of Wedderburn, near Bendigo, spotted gold in a crack in the pavement of High Street. He dug up a nugget that brought him two thousand dollars. Immediately people started staking claims and digging up pavements all over town. As in most gold rushes, the majority found nothing, but one man picked up ten thousand dollars worth of gold in his own back yard.

When gold was discovered in California, the world's total stock of the metal was estimated at $1,500,000,000. In the next ten years, the output from the new mines in the United States, Canada, and Australia almost doubled the amount of gold in the world. The production for the decade was $1,200,000,000.

Wherever gold was found, people and prosperity followed, at least for a short time. During the gold-rush days, Western Australia looked enviously across the continent at Victoria, New South Wales, and Queensland with their busy ports, growing populations, and new mining camps. Western Australia was blessed with little but desert, but if the area contained gold it might attract settlers despite its drawbacks.

The government called in E. H. Hargraves who had discovered gold in New South Wales. Mr. Hargraves examined the desert country and gave his opinion. There was no gold.

Even experts can be wrong. Western Australia became, and remains, one of the most productive gold-mining regions in the world, but the gold in the desert eluded the man first sent to find it.

Discouraged by Hargraves' report, but not willing to give up hope completely, the government, in 1869, offered a reward of £5000 for the discovery of gold within three hundred miles of any port in Western Australia. This sent large numbers of hopeful prospectors into the desert. They found the gold Hargraves had failed to find, but no water.

At Coolgardie, John Ford and Arthur Bayley found the rare combination of gold and water. The rush Western Australia had hoped for became a reality—twenty-three years after the government had offered its reward.

Even Coolgardie afforded only enough water to sustain life—not enough to wash gold. The miners of Western Australia developed their own method of separating gold from desert sand. They used two pans—the fossickers called them dishes—and the wind that blew constantly over the dry, arid land.

The miner lifted a dish of auriferous sand above his head and poured it slowly into a dish on the ground. The wind blowing through it scattered the light dust and the heavy gold fell into the waiting receptacle. This was called dry blowing.

Bureau of Mines, U.S. Department of the Interior

In the waterless desert of Western Australia, prospectors developed their own method of panning, which they called dry blowing. Filling a dish with gold-rich sand, they poured its contents slowly into another dish on the ground. The constantly blowing wind carried away the light sand, leaving the gold to fall into the waiting dish. This picture also shows a shaker, the Western Australian version of a cradle.

Not long after the Coolgardie strike, outfitters began selling a contraption called a shaker. Built like a wheelbarrow, it was a two-man dry blower. One miner shoveled sand into the hopper on wheels. The oher shook it and forced gusts of wind through the dirt by operating a bellows attachment. The bellows forced the light sand out the open end of the box while the shaking helped sift the gold to the bottom.

On the Western Australia desert *el hombre dorado,* for whom the Spaniards had searched so diligently in South America, appeared everywhere. The desert sand was as yellow as the gold it harbored. Without water for bathing, the dry blowers, wandering from place to place with their dishes and their shakers, were thickly gilded with layers of golden dust.

Many of them were almost as rich as El Dorado was reputed to be. The gold rush that was twenty-three years late produced, in the twenty-three years after 1892, more than fourteen million ounces of gold with a value at today's prices of over five hundred million dollars.

One of the last of the Oceania goldfields to be opened was on the island of New Guinea. The island had received its name from Portuguese navigators who found gold there in such quantities that they were reminded of the riches of Guinea, on the western coast of Africa. Malaria, impenetrable jungles, and the fierce New Guinea headhunters kept them from harvesting New Guinea's wealth. It was still untapped at the beginning of the twentieth century.

Prospectors who ventured into the island jungles often failed to return. Finally, after World War I, two fossickers known as Shark Eye Park and Money Bill packed into the New Guinea wilds and settled down for a while with a friendly tribe of natives who were not headhunters.

These aborigines led their new friends to Edie Creek, sixty-five hundred feet high and seventy miles through thick jungle from the coast. Here the tribesmen demonstrated their own method of getting gold. The newcomers called it "specking."

Lying flat on the sand, the sharp-eyed men spotted the bits of gold and flicked them up with the tips of their tongues. In this way they collected gold faster than the prospectors could winnow it in their dishes.

Returning to Australia with their gold, Shark Eye and Money Bill, who had been given up for lost, demonstrated that it was possible to come back from New Guinea alive and enriched. Even so, it was not until 1926 that an expedition of gold diggers was organized to go to Edie Creek.

It was an opportunity that many a man who valued his head turned down. On the other hand, one woman, Doris Booth, went along with her husband. Later she wrote of the experiences of the group in the New Guinea jungle.

On Edie Creek they found much gold, but they were always hungry, Mrs. Booth reported. They hired the natives who had befriended the first prospectors to pack provisions in over the jungle trail to the coast.

For every miner on the creek, a porter was needed on the trail. The round trip to the port town of Salamaua took sixteen days, and not more than fifty pounds could be packed over the rugged trail by one carrier.

The flow of provisions to the mining camp was often halted by the headhunting tribes through whose territory the supply trail passed. The headhunters swooped down on the caravan and carried off the porters. The native carriers who survived refused to make any more trips. To avoid starvation, the miners themselves set out for the coast and very often failed to return.

Obviously, if gold was to be mined from the rich New Guinea deposits, a more dependable method of getting supplies to the miners would have to be found. A road to Edie Creek was mechanically and economically impossible. But in 1927 there were airplanes in the sky. The natives, regarding them with wonder, called them big pigeons.

The big pigeons solved New Guinea's transport problems. In and out of the gold district they flew, making two trips a day, carrying six hundred pounds of cargo at a time. They brought food, clothing, medicines, household supplies, stamp mills, amalgamators, diamond drills, explosives, and miners. In the twentieth century, in New Guinea, the search for gold took to the air.

CAPITALIST

IN EVERY NEW GOLDFIELD, in 1868, there was a mine called Ophir, proving that prospectors read their Bibles and dreamed of matching King Solomon's wealth. The location of the original Ophir from which King Solomon's ships returned, laden with gold, had been a matter of speculation for thousands of years.

Columbus thought he had discovered it in the Caribbean. Ben Jonson decided the king's gold had come from Peru. In the sixteenth century, Sir John Frobisher found Ophir west of Greenland, on Baffin Island. He loaded a ship with the gleaming ore and took it back to England. It proved to be muscovite, a type of mica.

Some said Ophir had been in Arabia, others in India. Milton wrote that King Solomon's gold had come from the East African port of Sofala, just south of the modern port of Beira, in Mozambique.

Sofala had been an important export point for gold in the Middle Ages. Much of the gold that enriched the Baghdad court of the famous *Arabian Nights'* caliph, Harun al-Rashid, in the eighth century, came from Sofala. And even before that, perhaps even before the days of Solomon, ships from Egypt, Persia, India, and China sailed into the natural harbor, now filled with silt, to exchange trade goods for gold.

The silent-barter method of trade had not changed when the Portuguese took over the port in the sixteenth century. The visitors did not see the mines from which the gold came nor the men with whom they did business. They were given no chance to bargain. They laid out their wares on the ground and retired. When the visitors were out of sight, the natives appeared, picked up the merchandise and left gold in its place. In medieval times the gold was usually in the form of beads. The pile of beads was larger for offerings of iron and salt.

Throughout all the centuries that men had traded for gold in East Africa, the jungle interior remained a mysterious wilderness. The Portuguese, claiming the country in the sixteenth century, confined their activities to the coast and the Zambezi River. Their missionaries, venturing farther, brought back reports of a city built of such massive stones it could not be the work of men but must have been constructed by the devil himself. They had seen Zimbabwe.

Three centuries later, in 1868, other adventurers cutting their way through the forests of Southern Rhodesia came across fortresses built of thick stone, each protecting an ancient mine long since abandoned to the jungle. There were hundreds of them. And in their midst, rising from two hills, the towering granite walls that the Portuguese had attributed to the devil, the walls of Zimbabwe.

The walls were twelve feet thick and in some places rose thirty feet high. Equally massive was the palace, on one hill, and the elliptical temple on the other. In the valley between were the remains of a village of thatched huts and abandoned gold mines. The ruins of both the palace and the temple yielded an abundance

This Greek coin shows the elliptical temple at Zimbabwe, site of the abandoned gold mines in the jungle of Southern Rhodesia. Inside the wall stands a great stone tower, thought to symbolize the majesty of the king. Its base is about fifty-six feet in circumference.

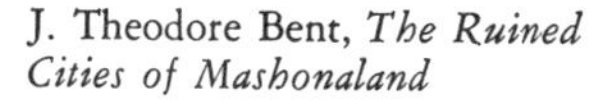
J. Theodore Bent, *The Ruined Cities of Mashonaland*

of gold. Even in the thatched huts gold wire had been used to bind together broken pottery pitchers.

So unusual was Zimbabwe, and so impressive, that it became at once the long-sought source of King Solomon's wealth. Ophir had been found again.

Before the year was out, Sir Henry Rider Haggard had written a novel set in Zimbabwe and called *King Solomon's Mines.* It took the treasure hunters a little longer to strip the Zimbabwe ruins of their gold. Had the walls not been twelve feet thick, the frantic digging that undermined them in many places might also have toppled them.

How much gold was removed from Zimbabwe, and where it got to, no one knows. Much of it was melted into bullion for easier transport through the jungle. By the time the archaeologists arrived everything but glass beads and potsherds had been removed.

The archaeologists put a prosaic end to the romantic notion that Zimbabwe was the long-lost Ophir. The majestic fortress had been built more than fifteen hundred years too late to be the source of King Solomon's wealth, they said. The oldest of the ruins dated no farther back than the ninth century of our era, though some of the mines showed signs of having been worked in prehistoric times.

These ancient diggings, filled with trees of great size and age, dotted the wilderness around Zimbabwe for four hundred miles in every direction. Mining engineers have estimated that from ancient through medieval times they enriched the world with $300 million worth of gold.

As archaeologists and historians worked together to solve the mystery of Zimbabwe they unraveled at least a part of the story of an empire built on gold. Unknown to the rest of the world except through its silent, unseen traders, the mighty kingdom flourished in Africa from the ninth century into the sixteenth. What brought it to an end no one knows.

Zimbabwe was the capital of this Bantu nation. The kingdom itself, and its king, were known as Manamatapa, which meant "Master of the Gold Mines." From his palace on one hill the king could look across at the temple on the other and down at the mines in the valley between.

As far as he could see in any direction there were fortresses protecting other gold mines. And there were more mines, far in the distance, that he couldn't see, though his very life depended on keeping the gold flowing from them to Zimbabwe.

Indeed, everything in Manamatapa depended on gold. Gold was all that the nation produced. Yet the people did not apply to their mines the engineering skill which had built the fortress of Zimbabwe. The underground passages of the mines were so narrow that when they were discovered it was assumed that the mining had been done by Pygmies. But the skeletons of both men and women removed from the workings were of normal-sized Bantu. Today their descendants dig the gold of the deep Rand mines.

The Bantu miners slithered through the adits like serpents, hacking out the rich ore. No nonauriferous rock was removed to give them room to work. And no pillars of gold-bearing rock were left to support the ground above. When a mine collapsed, it was abandoned, along with the miners it buried, and a new cut was started into the gold deposit.

The king ruled as long as his management of the mining properties satisfied the several thousand women in the palace harem, who kept him surrounded by a bodyguard of cannibals. When the women grew dissatisfied with his administration they elected a new ruler and ordered the cannibals to eat the old one. Between these feasts on royal flesh, the cannibals made do with ordinary citizens, arbitrarily selected by the king from any who chanced to be around when the cannibals were hungry.

The king's obligations did not end when the women of the harem gave his guards permission to devour him. His lower jaw, saved from the feast, and his umbilical cord, saved from the time of his royal birth, were preserved in the temple tower. This guaranteed that forever after his ghost would hover over the site, protecting the gold mines of the Manamatapa.

Even today the Bantu natives of the area avoid the Zimbabwe temple, believing it haunted by the ghosts of the dead kings. This may be the reason so much treasure was left in the ruins to be looted by nineteenth-century gold seekers.

There was gold in the mines too, its location thoughtfully marked by the excavations of prehistoric and medieval miners. In 1889, Cecil John Rhodes led two hundred prospectors and three hundred mounted police into Rhodesia, claiming the land for Great Britain. The prospectors opened new mines where their predecessors had dug and started a gold-mining industry that still yields twenty million dollars of gold a year, easily double the value of gold King Solomon received from Ophir.

To Rhodes, the riches of the country to which he gave his name were a disappointment. To the south he had seen, and invested in, a goldfield that promised more. He returned to the Witwatersrand.

The Witwatersrand, or white waters ridge, did not look like gold country. It was a treeless, windswept grassland inhabited by Dutchmen, the Boers, and their grazing cattle and sheep. Here and there the monotony of the landscape was broken by a weathered brown blob of conglomerate rock. The Boers thought the pebbles fused in the rock looked like almonds and called the outcrop *banket,* which was the name they gave to their almond cake.

In 1886 two prospectors, George Harrison and George Walker, found themselves stranded in this pastoral land. Both had been builders before they started to search for gold and they returned to their trade on the Rand in order to finance their way to a more likely spot to look for gold.

They found employment building a new house for the widow, Anna Oosthuizen, who lived on Langlaagte farm. The widow wanted her house made of stone. The banket that dotted her farm was too crumbly on the surface to cut into building blocks, but beneath the ground it was a slate-gray color and very firm.

The men began to quarry the banket, surprised to see that the rock shimmered with tiny particles which might be gold. They took some of it back to the bunkhouse, crushed and panned it, and learned that in this unlikely grazing country they had found a gold mine.

Within a few weeks men were staking mining claims on outcrops all along the Witwatersrand, a name they shortened, in their haste, to Rand. Near Langlaagte farm a tent city named Johannesburg sprang up where no one had expected anything but a new crop of spring lambs.

With picks and shovels the miners followed the banket into the ground. They were digging up a placer deposit that had developed along an ocean shore before there was any life on earth at all.

At that time, when the world was young, the ocean covered the land to the ridge of the white waters. Rushing rivers, long since gone, tumbled gold-bearing rock from ancient mountains to the

South African Tourist Corporation

The deep gold mines of South Africa require expensive hoisting equipment and special ventilation. Temperatures underground may reach 135°F.

edge of the sea. There the waves rolled and battered the broken rock to pebbles and sand, milling the gold.

Disturbances beneath the earth rearranged the surface. What had been the seashore heaved upward, pushing the ocean back. Pressure and heat fused sand and pebbles into new rock.

It is possible that during these turbulent periods the molten conglomerate was enriched with gold-bearing solutions from below.

It was also tilted like a barn roof, with a sharp dip toward the south. Except for a few high knobs, it was buried beneath new geological formations.

The first prospectors, following the gold-bearing reefs into the ground, dug up as much trouble as gold. Rich shoots of ore had a habit of wandering away under another's surface claim. The steep incline of the slanting shelves of gold-bearing rock demanded deep mines, expensive hoisting equipment, and ground-support timbers which had to be imported to the treeless veld.

At one hundred and fifty feet beneath the surface, the ore turned refractory. No matter how finely it was ground not more than sixty percent of its gold could be extracted by amalgamation. The other forty percent was sold with the tailings to the Johannesburg masons, making that growing city the only one in the world that could boast that the bricks of its buildings were cemented together with gold.

As the mines sank deeper, the costs rose higher and the gold yield shrank. Today it takes an investment of 50 to 100 million dollars to dig the first ounce of gold from a Rand mine. Earlier, mines could be developed for eight million dollars, but this was hardly the kind of cash a prospector carried around in his poke. The gold of the Rand belonged not to a poor man with a pick but to the investor with capital.

South Africa had such men. For fifteen years the diamond pits at Kimberley had been creating millionaires. Among them was Cecil Rhodes. As the sickly and penniless son of an English clergyman, Rhodes had gone to Kimberley in 1871 when he was eighteen years old. There he found health and wealth and began to dream of an empire.

The gold mines of the Rand attracted the wealth that had accumulated in Kimberley. Within a year of the original discovery on Langlaagte farm, Rhodes and his partner, C. D. Rudd, had bought up mining properties valued at $100,000 and had formed the Gold Fields Company for the purpose of acquiring more gold mines in the area. Stock in the company was offered to the public on the London market, and soon British capital and Britishers were pouring into South Africa. The problem of financing the development of the Rand mines was solved.

The problem of saving the forty percent of the gold that was being used to plaster Johannesburg's buildings remained. Extraction difficulties were not uniquely the Rand's. They had developed in every new goldfield.

Metallurgy had failed to keep up with the increased production of gold brought about through the discovery of new deposits all over the globe, the development of steam hoists and locomotives, the improvement in drills, blasting powders, underground ventilation and supports. The ancient method of smelting and the newer method of roasting and chlorination were expensive. Amalgamation was not always effective.

In 1887, in a laboratory in Scotland, J. S. MacArthur, R. W. Forrest, and W. Forrest tried treating auriferous ores with potassium and sodium cyanide solutions and announced that they had found in cyanidation a cheap, efficient method of extracting gold. Metallurgists scoffed at the idea, but practical mining men were ready to try anything. They tried the cyanide process in western America and Australia. It worked.

In 1890 a cyanide treatment plant was set up on the Rand. With

To separate gold from ore, modern mining companies grind the gold, air it, and immerse it in huge tanks containing potassium cyanide and lime. In a series of chemical reactions, the gold combines with the cyanide and is later released by the addition of zinc. These tanks were photographed near Johannesburg, South Africa.

South African Tourist Corporation

it, more than ninety-five percent of the gold content of the refractory Rand ores was recovered. A revolution had occurred in the metallurgy of gold.

Like chlorination, the cyanide process forced gold into a chemical union in order to extract it from its ores. In cyanidation, the ore is ground to a sand or slime, aerated, and wet thoroughly with a weak solution of sodium or potassium cyanide. In a slow and complicated series of chemical reactions, the gold in the ore combines with the cyanide and, as cyanide of gold, dissolves in the solution. It is released by zinc, which precipitates the precious metal as a black slime.

Without this efficient and inexpensive method of extraction the Rand gold mines would have died aborning. Not only were their deep ores refractory, they were also low grade. Even with ninety-five percent recovery, seventy tons of ore must be mined, milled, and leached to get a pound of gold.

As new mines opened and new cyanide plants were erected, the Johannesburg builders couldn't keep up with the tailings. To use them they would have had to build an Empire State Building a day. So the piles of refuse rose in great man-made mountains of sand that dwarfed the tallest buildings in Johannesburg and dominated the landscape for miles.

Unhappily the Boers watched these sandhills multiply on the ridge of the white waters. The *uitlanders*—outsiders—with their mines, had completely changed the peaceful countryside. Their cities sprawled where once there had been pasture. The roaring of their stamp mills drowned out the bleating of the lambs. The once-clean wind carried the dust from their pyramids of tailings until it covered even the green grass.

The *uitlanders* were mostly British. By 1899, they outnumbered the Boers four to one on the Rand and have outnumbered them there ever since. By that year the conflict between the farmers and the miners had become a war between the British and the Boers. By 1902, the British had won the war and the gold-rich reefs of the Rand. In 1910 the ruling British formed the Union of South Africa, bringing predominantly agricultural Boer provinces firmly under control of the British Crown and equalizing the British-Boer population in the newly formed country. African natives still form two thirds of the population in what is now known as the Republic of South Africa.

Today the mines of the Rand punctuate the high arc ridge of the veld for more than a hundred miles, and bring ore up from depths of ten thousand feet. Geophysical tests and diamond drills have traced the reefs of gold for three hundred miles. They extend into the earth deeper than men have learned to open it.

The gold mines of the Rand employ 500,000 persons, nine tenths of them African natives. The natives perform the hard physical labor of mining, most of it underground. In the Republic of South Africa this labor supply is plentiful and cheap. The policy of apartheid restricts the kind of work the Negro can do and keeps his wages at a subsistence level.

From the time the mines first opened, native miners have been brought to the workings by labor recruiters. Separated from their families, they are housed in compounds under constant surveillance. Most of the compounds are clean, and the food is nourishing. Any of them might be mistaken for a progressive penal institution.

Labor unions in South Africa exclude native workers, but strikes initiated by the all-white organizations of skilled and semiskilled Europeans produce the relaxation of supervision over native workers' compounds that allows the Negroes freedom to escape surveillance and express in violence their dissatisfaction with the restrictions under which they are forced to live and work.

In 1913 a dispute between a Rand mine manager and a miner brought on a bloody racial war which left Johannesburg at the mercy of the rioters until British troops arrived. The next year the trouble started in the coal mines and spread quickly to the gold mines and the city of Johannesburg. Troops of sixty thousand finally restored order and established martial law in the Rand's largest city.

In 1922, wage negotiations between Rand mines and the all-white labor union turned into a racial war, still called the reign of terror in Johannesburg. Both Europeans and natives were killed. Mines, buildings, and railroads were dynamited by the rioters. After more than a week of revolution, order was finally restored. Ten thousand agitators were arrested, their leaders were executed, and the natives were herded back to their barracks.

With the cheap labor corralled in the compounds, the mines of the Rand have doubled their production in the past quarter of a century. Today they produce close to a billion dollars worth of gold a year, more than seventy percent of the output of the non-Communist world.

TECHNICIAN

WHEN GENERAL GEORGE A. CUSTER set out to discover gold, he did it up right. He took along his famous Seventh Cavalry and a brass band mounted on white horses. There was also a small army of prospectors, geologists, mineralogists, newspaper reporters, and photographers.

At the head of this impressive parade the golden-haired young army officer advanced into the Black Hills of South Dakota. It was Indian territory, guaranteed to the tribes of the Dakota nation in perpetuity. This misplaced chunk of the Rocky Mountains, about one hundred miles square, was the home of the Dakota thunder god.

It was also rumored to be the place the Indians got gold, and in 1874 the prospect of more gold excited everyone. But prospecting in the area was a violation of the treaty with the Indian owners. To get around the conditions imposed by the treaty, Custer's entrance into the wooded hills was designated a topographical survey.

The prospectors found gold in paying quantities in the first cascading creek they reached. The geologists and mineralogists corroborated this evidence that there was gold in the hills. The general made a statement to the effect that the land was obviously too valuable to be left to the Indians. The band played. The news was flashed from coast to coast via telegraph. The rush began.

Under Crazy Horse and Sitting Bull, the Indians prepared to fight. General Sheridan, in charge of the western army, warned that trespassers in Indian territory would be removed by force. Some of them were. But by the spring of 1876, the trespassers outnumbered the western troops and outmatched them in determination. The army concentrated on eliminating the Indians.

Among the thousands who swarmed through the narrow wooded canyons of the new gold country in 1876 were the Manuel brothers, Moses and Fred, who had been searching for gold in the West for ten years. In a gulch in the northern hills they struck pay dirt.

Through the cold winter they worked the rich placer deposit. In the spring they traced it to its source, or lead (pronounced *leed*). The lead was a rich quartz outcrop which quickly brought them five thousand dollars and as quickly attracted the attention of the scouts sent out by the San Francisco mining syndicates.

In 1878, the Manuel brothers sold their claims for seventy thousand dollars to the Homestake Mining Company which had been incorporated the year before in California by George Hearst, John Haggin and Lloyd Tevis. In the 1960's the Homestake gold mine at Lead, South Dakota, was the largest in the western hemisphere. Excluding those operations where gold is a by-product in the extraction of other metals, Homestake was the only major producer operating in the fifty states. In 1963 the mine produced $20,278,195 in gold.

The Homestake mine began as an open cut which turned a mountain into a gaping canyon as miners followed the rich quartz lead deeper into the ground. The vein proved to be part of a mile-wide belt consisting of a dozen gold-enriched bands, fifty feet to several hundred feet wide and separated by barren slate. The veins ran vertically into the earth, decreasing in gold content as they descended but containing rich stringers of ore.

Following the gold beneath the surface, the Homestake gave up open-pit mining in favor of an underground operation. In those first years the ore averaged a thousand dollars of gold per ton, and the stringers often brought as much as ten thousand dollars from the same amount of rock. As the shafts sank deeper, the gold content of the ore changed radically.

The gold that is mined today appears in specks so small they can be seen only under a microscope. The ore is so hard it can't be broken with a pick. It is mined more than a mile under the ground.

One ton of ore has to be blasted, lifted, crushed, milled, amalgamated, and treated with cyanide, precipitated and refined, to get three tenths of an ounce of gold. That amount of the metal is no larger than the tip of your little finger.

The combined efforts of several cities above the ground and one large city below are required to transfer the gold in the rock to bars in the refinery. The city underground sinks ever deeper. All the gold in the first fifth of a mile below the surface has been mined. That city is deserted.

The city of Lead, which was once built on top of it, has moved higher up the mountain gulch as the old site shifts and settles into the hollowed ground. The move had already started when residents of the town's main street opened their doors one morning to find themselves peering into the five-hundred-foot level of the mine.

Advances in ground support and mining techniques have been made since these first levels were mined with the old square-set timber method George Hearst brought with him from his Ophir mine on the Comstock. In those days a mined-out section, or stope, was called a bull pen, which, laced with timbers, it much resembled.

Mice entered before men and if they lived the air was considered

Today it takes a ton of ore to yield three tenths of an ounce of gold—the amount in this little button in the man's hand. To find gold, the Homestake Mining Company must sink shafts at least a mile underground.

Homestake Mining Company

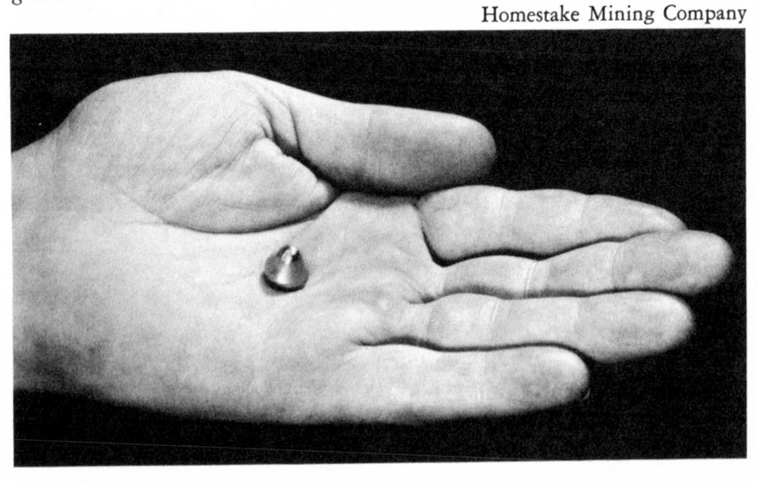

Homestake Mining Company

At the bottom of a timber stope, ore is dumped from a chute into a car, which will be hauled to the shaft.

capable of sustaining life even if it dimmed the candles. Hand-operated jackhammers drilled holes for the dynamite and sometimes broke the arms of miners learning to control them. The air was filled with dust from the drills. Blasts added more dust and sometimes ignited timbers as well.

The ore was shoveled into cars by muckers expected to handle sixteen tons of rock a shift. Trains of ore cars were pulled to the shaft by horses who never saw the light of day.

Now, ventilating systems keep the air fresh, and electricity

Homestake Mining Company

Where horses once pulled trains of ore to the shafts, compressed-air locomotives now do the work. Where suffocation once threatened, a ventilating system now brings fresh air to the mine.

spreads light. The miner's pneumatic drill spits out a sludge instead of dust, costs as much as a compact car, and is as easy to operate. Automatic mucking machines have replaced human muscles. Compressed air and battery-powered locomotives have sent the horses back to their pastures.

Instead of timbers, sand supports the ground above the mined-out stopes, which serve as tailings dumps for the cyanide plant. The sand is piped into the hollow rooms with water and packs them solidly as the water is released.

Today the upper sections, or levels, of the mine have been shored up to allow the removal of ore beneath them. This day-and-night operation takes place on thirty levels, each one hundred and fifty feet above the other. The lowest level is sixty-two hundred feet below the ground and about a mile square. As the ore is removed here it is also taken from other levels upward for a mile.

Underneath this mining operation, development work goes on as the next ore body is prepared for excavation. This preparatory work can take months and sometimes years.

The outlines of the gold-bearing veins are plotted through diamond-drill testing of the rock. Drifts and crosscuts, the streets of a mine, are blasted out to give access to the ore on each level. Underground water is ditched to sumps. Pumps are set up to lift it from the working area. Ventilation and elevator shafts are extended. Tracks, electric wires, and compressed air pipes are spread from shafts through drifts and crosscuts.

The deeper the mine goes, the more extensive and expensive development becomes. Underground man and ore lifts extend the mile-deep hoist operated from the surface. Cooling equipment must

These miners are using air-operated drills. Water lubricates the cutting bits and lessens dust in the stope.

Homestake Mining Company

overcome the sweltering temperatures, 113 degrees Fahrenheit at the 6200-foot level.

Rock below this depth is under tremendous pressure. Shafts and drifts must be supported with rock bolts and ever-heavier timbers to prevent cave-ins. Despite all precautions, the pressure may cause the rock to explode as the ground is opened.

Close to a thousand men descend into the mine every twenty-four hours, whisked down on double-deck cages which resemble express elevators in skycrapers. For safety's sake they wear goggles, hard hats, hard-toed rubber boots, and safety lamps with batteries clipped to their belts.

Safety is the watchword with both the men and the company that hires them. Still, four out of every thousand miners in the country will be killed each year and more than one hundred and fifty will be injured. Mining is not unlike trench warfare, which borrowed from the mines its poison gases and the gas masks that protect against them.

Chain-link fencing is bolted to the sides of this shaft to hold loose rock in place. At the bottom, an air-operated mucking machine digs up earth.

Homestake Mining Company

It takes brains just to stay alive in a mine. It takes both brains and training to become a miner, the man who does the drilling. In the words of a master miner, the late Jet Calhoon, "It ain't drilling the holes that's hard. It's knowing where to drill them."

A miner learns where and how to drill the holes for the dynamite by serving an apprenticeship under another miner. Holes are drilled ten feet deep into hard rock. In the wrong place, at the wrong angle, or allowed to fitcher to one side, they may cause the dynamite to misfire or to crack rock that can't be dislodged.

A misfire leaves a dangerous load of explosive to be dealt with before work can proceed. Cracked rock may be jarred loose while men are in the stope. Dangling rock prolongs the manual labor of barring down the roof and walls of the working at the beginning of each shift.

Ore is mined from a lower level upward to the one above so that gravity can be used to chute the heavy rock from the stope into the ore cars that tram it to the shaft. The ore is drilled, blasted, and scraped or slushed from the working in ten-foot slices.

As the slices of rock are removed they are replaced with the wet sand fill which makes a floor for the miners to use while breaking the next slice of ore. The stopes extend from the drift on one side of the ore ledge to the drift on the other, a distance that varies from 50 to 250 feet. They are 45 feet wide and are mined out to an arched crown just beneath the next level. The crowns are supported on either side by 30-foot-wide pillars of undisturbed ground. These are mined last, using timbers to give added support.

Locomotives pull trains of ore cars to the shaft where the rock is dumped, nine tons at a time, into skips that are hoisted straight up, a mile in two and a half minutes. Near the top of the hoist headframe, 150 feet above the surface, the chunks of rock, some of them two and a half feet square, are ground in gyratory and cone crushers to half inch chunks. Gravity carries these morsels downhill through the rest of the milling process.

Once the Homestake mill was a thundering operation that deafened employees and reverberated through the mountains as batteries of heavy, steel-booted stamps pounded the rock to sand. Now the stamps have been replaced by closed cylinders which grind the ore by revolving it with steel rods and balls until seventy percent of it is finer than flour.

Hard-rock mining is exactly that, and the rock wears out everything from the drill bits used underground to the specially tempered steel balls in their cylinders. Every year more than 2,500,000 pounds of these metal baseballs are ground to extinction by the rock they crush.

Water is fed to the rod-and-ball mills with the ore, which emerges as a flowing pulp. This passes through amalgamators where mercury catches the free gold, seventy percent of the precious metal content of the ore.

Before 1900 and the development of the cyanide process, this was the only gold retrieved. Now the pulp leaves the amalgamators to flow through classifiers which separate the sands from the slimes. The sands are run into huge vats where they are aerated and leached with a cyanide solution, a process that takes a week. The slimes, finer than sands, are packed into presses, each thin mud pie subjected to a bombardment of cyanide solution under pressure to ensure the contact of the solution with each microscopic bit of gold.

In the refinery, the gold precipitate from the cyanide solution and the gold retrieved from the amalgam through distillation are heated to drive off impurities and cast into bars weighing thirty-five pounds apiece.

Warm, the bars have a green cast. Cool, they are a soft, glowing yellow. Piled together, they tend to look orange. Each one of them was once the gold content of three million pounds of ore.

In the refinery, minute particles of gold are everywhere and everything is refined, from the dust on the floor to the dust in the chimney. The wash water in which the employees wash their hands and in which their clothes are laundered is treated to remove the gold. When the inexpensive overalls wear out they are burned and each pair yields more gold than it would take to buy three suits from the best haberdasher.

The refinery is also the stronghold in which gold bars are kept while they await twice a week delivery to the mint, via armored car and guarded train. Each shipment includes a dozen bars of gold, worth more than $235,000 dollars altogether, and a few bars of the silver which has been removed as one of the impurities in the gold.

To keep the treasure safe, every sound made in the refinery is amplified and every movement recorded. Two guards keep a twenty-four hour watch and a loaded gun is ready for use at every window. At night a powerful searchlight sweeps the surrounding area, discouraging romance as well as theft.

The company's surface operation includes logging camps and crews scattered through the mountains felling trees that become mine timbers and building lumber at the Homestake saw mill. Pattern makers design machines and machine parts which are cast in the foundry. Other shops service trucks and locomotives, repair mine cars, and sharpen drill bits.

The most impressive surface operations are the hoists, the headframes of which rise on mountains above the city like mechanical men of Oz. The hoists lift ore from the mine and raise and lower men and materials through vertical shafts that extend a mile into the ground. Deeper levels are serviced by underground hoists.

The three hoists now in use at the Homestake are electrically driven, replacing steam hoists that were once powered by wood-fired boilers. Coal is mined and water flumed from the mountains to generate electricity for present power needs.

In the eighty-six years of its existence the Homestake has mined almost a billion dollars worth of gold. Few mines in the history of the world have produced gold so continuously under one management for such a long period. The operation has been interrupted only four times. Twice the stoppage was the result of serious underground fires. In 1909 a strike caused the machinery to grind to a halt.

The strikers were members of the Western Federation of Miners, which was organized in Lead the same year the Homestake began to operate the mine. They were striking for a closed shop.

The strike lasted one long, cold winter, during which the pounding mill was silent, no blasts shook the earth, no whistles called the men to work. Though there was no bloodshed, it was a bitter strike which divided families and turned the town into an armed camp, Pinkertons on one side, angry miners on the other.

In the midst of the conflict the Miners' Union hall began to sag dangerously as the ground beneath it shifted and settled into the mine-hollowed earth. A truce was called while the company opened blacksmith and carpenter shops, lending tools and materials to brace the union hall.

Management won the showdown with labor in 1909 and today

Homestake workers are not represented by a union. Since World War II the National Labor Relations Board has repeatedly supervised elections called by the United Mine Workers and other unions seeking the right to organize Homestake employees. The employees have as often voted against them.

Despite their failure to gain a foothold, the unions have not been without influence. Knowing that dissatisfied workers could vote for a union in the future as they have voted against it in the past, the Homestake has kept a step ahead by offering top wages, frequent bonuses, free medical service, a pension plan, and extensive recreation facilities.

This paternalism was evident even in the days of the ill-fated Miners' Union when Phoebe Hearst, wife of George and mother of William Randolph, spread culture and educational opportunities through the gold-mining towns which grew around her husband's mines. Mining camps still built of canvas and logs found themselves blessed with a free public library, which usually included an adult-education program for those who couldn't read. Miners' children in Lead and other gold-rush towns were attending free Phoebe Hearst kindergartens when the idea was still so new the East was just learning the word.

In Lead many of the children attending the Phoebe Hearst kindergarten today represent the third and fourth generations that have started their educations in the same building and hillside play area. As in many another isolated mining town, the population does not drift away. Sons join their fathers in the mine or go off to college and return to become part of the large force of trained engineers, geologists, metallurgists, and other specialists on which a modern mine depends.

Before World War II, the Homestake had a hundred mining neighbors in the Black Hills of South Dakota. Throughout the West, wherever the nineteenth-century gold rush had discovered the precious metal, mines were digging gold at the rate of $210 million annually.

In October, 1942, the War Production Board declared gold a nonessential metal and ordered all gold mines shut down for the duration. The order, number L-208, was calculated to transfer several thousand miners to the shorthanded base metal mines.

"Gold mines cannot be turned off and on like water faucets," warned L. L. Huelsdonk of the California Ruby mine. It was a prophecy as well as a protest. Of the two thousand mines turned off in 1942 only one major producer is operating today.

To carry out the L-208 order, the United States employment service set up offices in each town affected, arranged for the transfer of the miners and their families and paid for the moving. As the mines closed and the population dwindled, the stores closed too. Buses took the place of schools and the towns died.

As it turned out, the War Production Board order left in its wake more ghost towns than the diggers of the gold rushes had deserted in half a century of scurrying from one rich strike to another. It was aided by the inflation that followed the war.

When the ban against gold mining was lifted in 1946, some of the mines were already past saving. Shafts were caved and underground workings collapsed, or flooded, or both. Without materials, skeleton maintenance crews had difficulty managing routine upkeep. Neglect had taken its toll.

To the expenses of three unproductive years, mines reopening had to add the cost of a major overhaul before they could bring gold from the ground. And the price of everything but gold had skyrocketed.

Squeezed between rising costs and a price for gold that had not changed since 1934, straight gold mines found that they could not operate in the black. By the hundreds they closed—in the United States, including Alaska, in Canada and Australia. Today the United States is producing about fifty million dollars worth of gold annually, one third the amount it mined in prewar years. Most of this production, which continues to decline each year, is a by-product of base metal mines, paid for by the profits from copper, zinc, or nickel. Even the Homestake has added uranium mines to its operation and now depends on these new enterprises for the larger part of its revenue.

"There is more gold left in California than ever was taken out," says Jack Sheedy, owner of the Telegraph mine in Downieville. But today, with a thousand other California gold mines, the Telegraph stands idle.

At the very time that technology has made it possible to mine gold that was inaccessible half a century ago, inflation has rendered gold mining economically unfeasible. The dollar that is legally worth one thirty-fifth of an ounce of gold cannot pay for the labor and materials to dig that amount of the metal from the earth.

Coined and Condemned *gold in the modern economy*

MONETARY MEASURE

"YOU SHALL NOT CRUCIFY MANKIND upon a cross of gold!" thundered William Jennings Bryan in 1896 as the United States debated the pros and cons of adopting the gold standard. There were many who joined his protest, not all of them with a political or financial interest in "the silver dollar of our daddies."

But the gold standard was not to be shouted down or wished away. Even as Mr. Bryan spoke, gold measured America's greenbacks and silver dollars and influenced their purchasing power. It would continue to do so regardless of decisions made by the government.

For the gold standard was not invented by nations and defies their attempts to control it. It developed when the value men placed on gold for religious reasons became a dominant factor in ancient barter markets.

No other commodity was so constantly and universally desired. This made it an ideal medium of exchange. The demand for it increased as merchants began to use it for money.

Gold was too scarce to fulfill satisfactorily this new economic obligation. Men who wanted gold often had to accept substitutes. They measured the worth of these offerings, using gold as the standard of value.

The most popular substitutes became tokens or little slips of paper, worthless in themselves but considered "as good as gold" because they represented gold in the safekeeping of a goldsmith or banker. Professional traders preferred this token money to the metal itself. It was more convenient to carry, less attractive to thieves, and acceptable everywhere.

As the new paper money began to circulate on its own, without returning to claim the gold to which it was entitled, the new bankers discovered they could issue paper promises that exceeded in value the gold in their vaults. Up to a point this added the virtue of abundance to the other advantages of the folding currency. Trade flourished as the medium of exchange increased to meet its needs.

When paper money exceeded the goods available in the markets, its abundance was a handicap. Then it was able to claim fewer commodities than the gold it represented, so it was withdrawn from circulation and exchanged for gold.

The process reversed itself when the resulting shortage of currency hampered the movement of trade goods. Gold was returned to the banks and mints as the demand for its paper representatives made them once again "as good as gold."

For centuries this alternating appearance and disappearance of gold was the only stabilizing factor in chaotic markets. Paper notes were issued indiscriminately by goldsmiths, money changers, merchants, banks, rulers. Trade extended beyond the reach of any government. Gold was the only authority the market would obey. Against it men measured the value of trade goods and currencies and kept all in a roughly balanced relationship through their demands on gold.

In the latter half of the nineteenth century more and more governments, led by England, made use of this traditional method of balancing and stabilizing an international trade conducted with many different domestic currencies. The United States, adopting the gold standard in 1900, was one of the last countries in the Atlantic trade community to do so.

Accepting the gold standard meant that a nation had to allow its currency to be evaluated in terms of gold and freely exchanged and converted into gold and the monetary units of other countries. In economic terminology this is known as convertibility.

If the established par value of the currency was realistic, and if the circulation of money was allowed to contract and expand according to the flow of gold in and out of the nation's monetary gold reserve, then the fluctuation of a currency's value was limited.

Many people objected to this tyranny of gold and foreign exchanges over the domestic economy, which was forced to expand and contract with the currency. But in the first years of the twentieth century, the gold standard accomplished what was expected of it. It provided an economic method by which the wealth produced by the world's new technology could be distributed among its nations. It was assisted by peace, world-wide productivity, and an increasing supply of gold.

Far from diminishing after the gold rushes of the nineteenth century, the world's annual output of gold continued to grow. In 1900 it reached $300 million. By 1910 it had jumped to $455 million, one fourth of which came from the United States. This meant adequate reserves of gold to back the increasing amount of currency necessary to finance expanding trade.

It wasn't the gold standard that broke down in 1914, but the world. War replaced trade, and winning the war became more urgent than maintaining balanced currencies. Governments allowed money to depreciate as gold flowed out of their reserves to buy, in America, the materials for the conflict.

When the hostilities were over, all currencies were inflated, and some were worthless. Again, nations looked to the gold standard to bring economic order out of chaos.

Among the obstacles they faced in accomplishing this objective was a severe shortage of gold. The rising production in the first years of the century had been seriously disrupted by the war. A shortage of men and materials had cut world output by twenty-five percent. Gold from the United States was down fifty percent.

Nor did production increase when the fighting ceased. Everywhere, inflation had driven up the costs of mining until they approached, and sometimes exceeded, the official price of gold. In the United States this price was $20.67 an ounce and had been since 1834.

To add to the scarcity, most of the world's stock of gold had gone into hiding. Half of it was in the United States' reserve. The rest was in private hoards and would not emerge until its hoarders had something "as good as gold" for which they could exchange it.

In an attempt to provide good-as-gold currencies, the nations of the Atlantic trading community agreed to return to the gold standard in 1925. With so little gold, this required radical changes in the system. The gold standard became the gold exchange standard, which padded out lean gold reserves with key currencies. To further conserve the metal, Britain gave up gold coinage. The pound note was convertible to gold only in quantities large enough to command bars of bullion.

The role of gold was changed. Instead of serving as a standard against which money was measured, it was expected permanently to prop up ailing currencies and render inflation as invisible as the emperor's new clothes. With more faith than wisdom, nations retained the prewar parities of their monetary units and bravely pronounced them "as good as gold."

More realistically, the public recognized that they were not as good as gold. The pound sterling, for instance, would buy only half as much as would the gold it represented. So the pound was exchanged for gold in amounts large enough to command bullion. In a vain attempt to defend the over-valued pound, Britain used up her gold reserve.

At that point, in 1931, England went off the gold standard. Nations can leave the gold standard, but in a very real sense money never does. On the free exchange the pound was measured against gold and at half its former valuation was once more accepted in place of gold.

For nations who had used the inflated pound note in their gold reserves, the sudden devaluation was disastrous. For everyone it was frightening. All currencies became suspect, and governments, banks, and individuals started converting money to gold on the London bullion market.

As a result, the price of gold rose. At the same time the worldwide depression had reduced the costs of mining. In the midst of hard times a boom developed in the gold-mining industry, and new gold rushes discovered more of the metal all over the world.

In many western states, and in gold-mining countries, prospecting was encouraged as a method of reducing unemployment. Canada offered courses in geology and mineralogy and grubstaked the newly educated gold seekers. In New Zealand, two government-subsidized prospectors, W. M. Kilgour and Percy Bell, discovered the Lucky mine which soon became one of the island's largest producers.

Even without such aids, many unemployed set forth with pan

and pick as their grandfathers had done before them. Some searched for gold in streams and mountain gullies. Others moved to ghost towns where they occupied deserted houses and tore up the bars, counters, and floors of saloons and stores, gathering the gold dust that had been spilled there in more prosperous times. Old tailings dumps were reprocessed, and discarded sluice boxes and mills dismantled to catch any gold that had been left behind.

Mines that had shut down during and after the war reopened. Small two- and three-man operations became profitable. Larger mines could afford to dig and crush lower-grade ore.

Gold-mining towns became islands of prosperity in a world that had all but forgotten the meaning of the word. The mines worked at full capacity. Stocks soared and paid handsome dividends. Regular pay checks lured former ranchers, farmers, businessmen, college graduates, and their professors undergound. On Main Steet business was brisk. The only signs of the depression that gripped the rest of the globe were the tent cities that grew around each mine as men waited for jobs and prospected for gold.

Faster than miners took gold out of the ground, a panicky public removed gold from United States banks. The war years had filled United States vaults with over $11 billion in gold. By 1933 the reserve had been reduced to a total of $3.5 million. Even America didn't have enough gold to prop up an inflated dollar in an emergency.

With the bank holiday, in March, 1933, the government gave up the struggle. After the banks reopened, President Franklin D. Roosevelt announced: "We are moving to a managed currency."

The dollar was no longer convertible to gold, and gold could not be exported from the country. All privately held gold and gold certificates were called in.

This latter requirement merely speeded a process that had been going on throughout the depression. It was almost possible to chart the relapses suffered by a sick economy as gold moved in and out of the possession of private citizens. When people were merely frightened, they traded their dollars for gold. When they were hungry and hopeless, they sold their hoards.

Trading in gold became a sizable business. Bullion brokers sent gold buyers from door to door to purchase jewelry, keepsakes, and heirlooms. Until the export of gold was forbidden, most of these articles were melted, cast into bars, and sold on the London market.

By the end of 1932, gold was pouring into the Philadelphia mint at the rate of $1.5 million worth a month. It arrived in every conceivable form. There were wedding rings, eyeglass frames, ornaments of every kind, medals, cups, tea sets, and elaborate dinner services worth hundreds of thousands of dollars. There were also numerous articles which had been bought and treasured as gold which contained little or none of the precious metal.

People who could afford to keep their gold looked for ways to evade the government's denial of the privilege. Nuggets in their natural form, coins in numismatic collections, jewelry, and artwork were allowed to remain in private possession.

In the spring of 1933 hundreds of people developed a sudden interest in collecting nuggets and coins. Women who had restricted their jewelry to gems set in newer, lighter metals became attracted to gold ornaments, the heavier the better. Gold subject to forfeit was melted down and fashioned into wall plaques, vases, statuettes. For years these products of the goldsmith's craft traveled from court to court as judges tried to determine whether they were truly works of art or gold hoards in disguise.

Though mines were now forbidden to send bullion out of the country some of them still sold their gold on the higher-paying London market. They managed the evasion by exporting barrels of amalgam and zinc precipitate which the London bullion dealers refined.

Despite the gold that escaped, enough was collected to swell the government reserve to $2.5 billion, at the official government price of $20.67 an ounce. Abroad, on the free exchanges, gold was valued higher and the dollar lower. The exchange rates on both changed daily.

In a fireside chat, on October 22, 1933, President Roosevelt explained: "Our dollar is now too greatly influenced by the accidents of international trade, by the internal policies of other nations and by political disturbances in other continents. Therefore the United States must take firmly in its own hands the control of the gold value of our dollar . . . . As a means to this end I am going to establish a government market for gold."

As it did on the free exchange, the price of gold in the new government market changed each day, moving upward. It was determined every morning in the President's bedroom. While the President breakfasted, he conferred with his fiscal advisers. These included Henry Morgenthau, of the Farm Credit Administration; Jesse Jones, of the Reconstruction Finance Corporation; and Professor George F. Warren who, with Professor Frank A. Pearson, both of Cornell, had proposed the monetary adjustment.

In *The Coming of the New Deal,* Arthur Schlesinger, Jr., reported how one day's rise in the price of gold was established. A disagreement was resolved when the President wrote out a morning's "chit" setting the increase at twenty-one cents. Because, he said, "Twenty-one is a lucky number. It's three times seven."

In January, 1934, the price of gold was stabilized at $35 an ounce, where it has remained since. This lowered the gold content of the dollar by forty percent. Roosevelt called it a "commodity dollar." Critics labeled it a "rubber dollar" and a "baloney dollar." Since there was no gold coinage, it was printed, not minted.

These men are pouring melted gold into molds to make the standard gold bar, which is four inches wide, about two inches high, and weighs thirty-five pounds. It is worth almost $20,000.

Bureau of the Mint, Washington, D.C.

Though the new dollar and the new price of gold did not please everyone at home, both were popular abroad. Gold began to flow toward America as foreign markets paid for United States exports. By October, 1939, the country had gathered in more than seventeen billion dollars worth of gold. This exceeded the value of United States currency in circulation and represented well over half the world's stock of gold.

Long before this, the storage and protection of the mounting hoard had posed a problem. Both nature and men have agreed that the safest place for gold is in the ground. So in 1935, at the cost of a million dollars, underground vaults were prepared to secure the nation's treasure.

The new Bullion Depository was located at Fort Knox, Kentucky, near Louisville. Writing about it at the time it was built, reporters padded out the sparse facts available with amazed comments that the vaults and the fortress that protected them were so small.

The bars of gold the vaults were built to receive vary slightly in size but average about seven inches in length. They are four inches wide, about two inches high, and weigh thirty-five pounds apiece. Each one is worth almost twenty thousand dollars and you could easily tuck a couple of them in a child's shoe box. All the gold in the United States at that time, about six billion dollars worth, could have been stored in your double garage.

The vaults at Fort Knox made up for their small size with the ingenious automatic devices that protected them. The twenty-ton steel door leading to the gold underground was equipped with a locking mechanism that no man could operate alone. An attempt to cut or burn through it could trigger jets of poison gas. The square steel and concrete building that covered this entrance to the bullion room was fitted with sensitive reactors that responded at once to unusual noise, movement, or changes in light or temperature.

This elaborate system was augmented with round-the-clock sentries at each corner of the building, an electrified steel fence, and a force of over a thousand officers and men patrolling the surrounding thirty-thousand-acre reserve. Nevertheless, people worried about the safety of the gold.

We were putting too many goldbricks in one basket, one columnist warned. Such a prize might inspire the Communists or

Bureau of the Mint, Washington, D.C.

Gold bars are weighed as a policeman stands guard.

the Fascists to take over the country. Others doubted that so much gold should be controlled by one man and reported, erroneously, that the key to the Fort Knox stronghold hung on the President's office wall in the White House.

It is unlikely that at any time the Bullion Depository held all the government's gold reserve. Then, and now, there is ordinarily more gold in the vaults of the mints and the Federal Reserve banks. There is also gold belonging to the United States in banks abroad and gold belonging to other countries in the Federal Reserve banks here.

This gold passes from country to country without ever leaving its place of safekeeping. The transfers are effected at the end of each day by moving the bullion from the vault assigned to one country to the vault assigned to another. The next day it may be moved back again.

Wherever it was, during the Second World War the bulk of the world's gold belonged to the United States. With dollars, it flowed into the government's vaults to pay for war supplies and was then immobilized. Like army goldbricks, the goldbricks in the vaults did not do any work.

After the war Europe needed working gold to pay for American materials to repair the damaged continent. There was none in sight. With some justification, the United States was held responsible for the shortage.

In her vaults $24 billion worth of gold lay buried. This was three quarters of all the gold in the world. Her mines, which had once replenished the world's gold supply with an annual production second only to that of South Africa, were idle. They had been closed by government order in 1942.

Not all our gold is at Fort Knox. In this photograph, staff members of the Federal Reserve Bank of New York are stacking gold bars in a vault eighty feet below street level.

Wide World Photos

ENDURING SPECIE

NOT ALL THE GOLD that is taken from the earth each year is listed in the official production figures. A surprising amount is spirited out of mines, mills, and refineries, smuggled over borders and oceans, and sold for many times the exchange quotation in the world's black markets.

The war and postwar inflation that cut American gold production by three quarters and world production by one half, increased the demand for under-the-counter gold and boomed the output of the hi-graders. These are the men who steal gold from the mining companies that employ them. Immediately after the war their illegal harvest rose to an estimated $200 million worth of gold a year.

Hi-graders get their name from their practice of stripping gold from high-grade ore deposits. In mines where the ore is low grade they find a greater opportunity in mills and refineries.

In the old Homestake stamp mill the stamps pounded wet ore to a pulp which released its gold as it flowed over copper plates covered with mercury. In the clean-up room this amalgam was heated to distill the mercury and free the gold. Ore assays predicted how much gold would be obtained.

When the yield dropped suddenly and sharply below the assay figure, suspicions were aroused. They were confirmed when several mill workers dropped too, with an ailment the men in the clean-up room called the "mercury shakes," a trembling paralytic condition indicative of mercury poisoning.

A dreaded occupational hazard of the clean-up room, the mercury shakes struck down only men who handled mercury too long or carelessly. The ailing mill workers had been doing both, grabbing fistfuls of amalgam as they passed the copper plates. Since then all Homestake amalgamators have been covered and locked.

Gold underground is not so easily guarded. In the dark labyrinth of the mine, men work in pairs in widely separated stopes. Close supervision is impossible. Even a low-grade ore mine like the Homestake has experienced underground thefts, but hi-graders usually concentrate in mines where the ore is rich in free gold. Many of the nonoperating California mines are of this type and continue to suffer property damage at the hands of trespassing hi-graders.

Underground hi-graders do a great deal more than they are paid to do. They not only drill and blast and muck the rock, they also mill it. Their equipment is often as crude as the first that was ever used—rock to crush rock. Or they may employ drill or pick to flake or grind rich ore. They work only the ground that contains chunks or grains of free gold.

These may be smuggled out of the mine in clothing, snuffboxes or pie cans, as the miners call their lunch buckets. More often the natural hiding places in the human body are used, since, when he reaches the top of the shaft, every miner must go through the rooms known as the dry, where he showers and changes clothes. At this time anything he has worn or carried out of the mine is subject to inspection.

The profits in stolen gold are great, but so are the risks. The hi-grader can never be sure whether he is really successful or whether he is being used to lead federal agents to the men who buy his product at three times the market price. These are the refiners. Behind the front of a legitimate business, they gather gold from many sources, melt it into convenient forms and keep it safe until the shipper calls for it.

Gold is smuggled onto trains, ships, and planes, and passed through customs, hidden in every kind of cargo, from cheese, to firewood, to automobiles. Detection isn't difficult.

In any quantity, weight gives gold away. All along its route people have to be paid not to notice that the carton of bonbons is heavier than a carton of books or that the consignment of new cars weighs more than a similar number of army tanks. These costs, and the attendant risks, spiral the price of gold on the black market.

Gold smugglers have grown fat in the past decade but the hi-graders have suffered a depression. Since 1954 the black-market dealers have been able to buy gold at cheaper prices and in greater quantities from the London bullion market.

During and after the war, when gold was scarce, the Bank of England sold it on a priority basis which favored governments and central banks and left the smugglers to find gold where they could. By 1954 South African production was on the rise, and through the bullion market the increasing supply of gold was available to everyone.

The London bullion market is one of the oldest of the world's exchanges where gold is bought and sold. Since it handles gold from the Commonwealth countries, it has controlled the larger share of the world's new gold supplies for more than a century and has dominated the gold market.

In the 1930's, currencies tumbled daily as buyers and sellers of gold on the London exchange moved the price up and down each morning. Today the ritual remains the same, but the price of gold is controlled by the Bank of England and is generally predictable.

The market convenes every morning at precisely 10:30 A.M. in an austere and gloomy upper-story room in the House of Rothschild in London's financial district. Bullion dealers, some from firms that are centuries old, arrive punctually and seat themselves around a large central table. Before each one is a telephone and a small Union Jack on a stand.

The Rothschild representative presides, as agent for the Bank of England which, in turn, represents the Reserve Bank of South Africa through which South Africa's billion dollars worth of gold is marketed each year. The flags are lowered and raised as trading starts and stops. Bids and offers are relayed by telephone to the firms and banks the buyers and sellers represent.

The Bank of England, as principal seller, rejects the bids or causes them to rise or fall by offering and withholding gold. When the supply from South Africa and other Commonwealth sources is not enough to bring the price down to thirty-five dollars an ounce, gold is fed to the market from British reserves which are replenished out of United States reserves.

When the day's official price has been established for publication the real trading begins, carried on by telephone or outside the doors of the bullion room, the gold changing hands at undisclosed figures. This is the larger part of the trading and supplies the private demand for gold.

Since 1958, the gold absorbed by industry, the arts, and private hoarding has consistently exceeded the amount added to monetary reserves. In 1962, more than a billion dollars in gold, four fifths of the world's output for the year, was purchased for private purposes. More than half of this went into personal gold hoards, much of it moving through the black market.

This bootleg business has grown steadily since the war, rising to peaks of activity at times of political or economic crisis. The black market was treated to world-wide booms by the demands of private hoarders as a result of the Korean War and the Suez Canal crisis in the 1950's. The 1960's opened with a fright over the price of gold and the value of the dollar. Gold hoarding was further stimulated with the Cuban trouble and the assassination of President Kennedy.

Changing conditions in different parts of the world shift the destination of black-market gold. In the 1940's the troubled countries of central Europe took the major part of the contraband gold. Stronger governments and currencies have weakened demands there while revolutions and inflation have upped gold sales in South America.

Not all the gold purchased for hoarding is buried in back yards and stuffed into mattresses. More of it represents sizable chunks of investment capital which has been frightened into hiding by stormy political and economic weather.

Nations attempt to prevent the flight of this working capital by passing laws against buying, selling, and possessing gold. For the most part these restrictions have only moved the bullion collections to Switzerland and increased black-market purchases. In Switzerland the private gold hoards are kept in safety deposit boxes and are said to total more than five times the amount of gold in the United States.

The oldest and most dependable markets for gold dealers catering to hoarders are the countries of the Near and Middle East. There nomadic tribes have worn their golden savings as ornaments for thousands of years. In India, gold jewelry is as important a status symbol as mink is in the United States. Indian marriages traditionally require gold as bride price and dowry.

Gold for the large Asian market is bought on the London exchange and shipped to dealers in Beirut. There it is melted into convenient forms for transport by Arab smugglers. Small, flat pieces, weighing just under four ounces, are easily carried and slipped from hand to hand.

The dealers in Beirut stamp these little squares of gold with their marks. Through centuries, some of the marks have established enviable reputations as honest guarantees of the quality of the product. Bars of gold not so favored are still tried on the touchstone or nicked and tested by fire.

Since the war, India has fought a valiant but losing battle against gold smugglers and hoarders. Despite firm laws, stiff penalties, and stepped-up police activity, the gold hoard keeps increasing and now totals close to four billion dollars. Spent on consumer goods or invested in industry, this money would circulate, enriching the economy by much more than its present value. Hoarded, it neither builds nor buys, robbing the country of needed capital and markets for its products.

Where restrictions prevent the possession of gold in other forms, hoarders often patronize their jewelers. This has ballooned the requirements for gold in the arts at the same time that the space age has been finding new uses for the metal in industry.

In the United States alone, industry and the arts have tripled their consumption of gold since 1955. As the country's production of the metal continues to fall, two thirds of this gold is drawn from the government reserve. This represented a reserve loss of $82,500,000 in 1962.

Strangely, in the technology of today gold has regained a utility value it has not known since the Stone Age. The price of the metal is partly responsible. While everything else has gone up, the price of gold has remained the same for thirty years, rendering it comparatively cheaper and economically attractive for industrial use. Of more importance are characteristics which make the metal a valuable aid in man's attempt to conquer both space and the atom.

Chemically inactive, gold can be counted on to endure despite exposures that would destroy other metals. This durability is combined with an extreme pliability. Gold wire, finer than thread, adds

Du Pont Company

In the space age, the gold covering on this suit protects a rocket worker from dangerous chemicals and sudden high temperatures. It is flexible and light, weighing only five and a half pounds.

minimum bulk to the small transistors and diodes needed by modern computers and missiles. Gold sheathing, thin as film, adds little weight to the spacecraft and aircraft it protects from heat and exposure. Clothing surfaced with gold remains flexible as it protects workers from the chemical and flash-fire hazards of handling rocket fuels.

These same qualities have long given gold more prosaic duties in amplifiers for telephone cables, sensitive electrical instruments, and dentistry. The use of radioactive gold to trace and treat cancer has increased the medical demand.

The metal that endures in the heart of a nuclear power reactor endures also in time. The gold that one civilization leaves behind, another collects and reshapes for old uses and new. A part of the gold in your wedding ring may once have been worn by Helen of Troy. And the gold that flashes in the sun's rays as a man-made satellite spins through space quite possibly glittered as brightly thousands of years ago from the top of a Sumerian ziggurat.

BARBAROUS RELIC

"IN TRUTH, the gold standard is already a barbarous relic," declared the British economist J. M. Keynes in 1923. Thirty-eight years later, Professor Robert Triffin, of Yale, wrote:

"It would seem paradoxical and ludicrous to claim that the most rational economic system of international settlements conceivable in this second half of the twentieth century consists in digging holes, at immense cost, in distant corners of the world for the sole purpose of extracting gold from them, transporting it across the oceans and reburying it immediately afterward in other deep holes especially excavated to receive it and heavily guarded to protect it."

Professor Triffin has his own Triffin Plan for replacing gold in the world of finance. In 1944, at the economic conference of nations held in Bretton Woods, New Hampshire, Professor Keynes offered his Keynes Clearing Arrangement based on an international monetary unit called "bancor." It was one of many alternatives to gold presented at Bretton Woods.

It seemed a good time to dispense with the metal, then in short supply. The war had knocked out production. The United States and private hoarders had buried most of the accumulated stock. But the men who had to carry on the world's business would not be swayed from their traditional reliance on gold.

To effect a compromise, the gold exchange standard of the 1920's was resurrected with modifications and innovations and a repetition of the same basic mistake that sent it to an early grave thirteen years before. War-inflated currencies, including the dollar, were given prewar valuations. The dollar was made convertible to gold at its 1934 measure of one thirty-fifth of an ounce. With the pound sterling, it was used to stretch gold in monetary reserves.

As an aid to the establishment and maintenance of economic order, the International Monetary Fund was set up to succor currencies in temporary difficulties and regulate international finance. It was not strong enough to help the British pound.

In a five-week period, in 1947, Britain lost a billion dollars from her monetary reserve as the overrated pound was exchanged for gold and dollars. The pound was made inconvertible and then devalued. By 1949 most of the world's monetary units had been adjusted downward, to the disadvantage of the dollar.

This key currency, with about half its prewar purchasing power, was still worth its weight in gold from the United States reserve. Dollars from abroad began to claim their share of America's treasure hoard.

The country's stockpile, worth almost $25 billion in 1949, has lost more than $9 billion in gold in the years since. This leaves the nation with $15.5 billion in gold today. The amount is one third the world's total, but less, by $3 billion, than the gold that would be needed to cover the claims outstanding against it.

The 1949 devaluation of currencies that set gold gushing from overstuffed United States vaults also stimulated gold production in South Africa. While output in other countries continues to decline, squeezed between rising costs and a set price, the mines of the Rand and of Russia have succeeded in lifting annual additions to the world's gold accumulation to above their prewar peak.

South Africa's 1963 production was just under a billion dollars. In second place, Russia's yearly take is variously guessed at from $350 million to $600 million.

None of this abundance has been added to U.S. reserves, but it has helped to meet the growing demand for gold in the London market and has made it less difficult for the United States to defend the gold valuation of the dollar by spending gold to keep the price of the metal pegged at thirty-five dollars an ounce. Defending the convertibility of an inflated currency against the inexorable judgments of the historic gold standard has always been expensive in terms of gold. Great Britain tried it twice and failed. Despite severe gold losses, the United States is still optimistic.

With both Russian and South African production feeding into the London bullion market in the 1950's, the price was easily regulated by means of a gold bridge between England and America. When the supply of new gold available on the exchange failed to meet the demand, gold was released from Britain's reserve and replaced from U.S. stock. Until 1960 this arrangement kept the price of gold at the desired level.

In the fall of that year Russia stopped selling gold in London. This dropped the available supply by $20 million a month. The price of gold began to rise until it reached $40 an ounce. To bring it down again and to restore confidence in the dollar, the United States released $200 million in gold in October and $500 million in November.

Since then the gold bridge has been strengthened with a gold pool, a loose agreement among the central banks of nations in the International Monetary Fund. These banks help the United States channel gold to the London market. When the demand for the metal threatens to exceed the supply at the dollar price, members of the gold pool meet their own needs by accepting other currencies and U.S. debt certificates in place of gold.

As a result, immediate losses from the United States reserve have been reduced by increasing potential future claims against it. As the U.S. gold pile dwindles and promises to pay gold increase, the promises, in any form, become less acceptable in monetary reserves.

Nations struggling against a lack of confidence in their own currencies at home and abroad have found it necessary to increase the proportion of gold in their reserves. Despite the gold pool, one third of the increase in monetary reserves in the free world continues to come from the United States.

Other nations, France and India among them, have had their hands full keeping the black-market and free-exchange price of gold at home from devaluating their currencies. To do this they have had to buy and sell gold on their own bullion markets at prices ranging from ten to fifteen dollars above the price in London.

This price difference has been used to advantage by Russia to increase her gold holdings, presumed to be second only to those of the United States and growing steadily. When the world's bankers met in Russia in the spring of 1963 the visitors learned that between August, 1962, and March, 1963, the U.S.S.R. sold twenty million dollars worth of gold in India. Through intermediaries, the rupees they received in payment were converted into gold from the United States at a net profit of five million dollars in gold.

France regularly buys half a billion dollars worth of gold from the United States reserve each year while paying her debts in dollars. The gold that isn't needed to back the franc is sold for a profit on the free exchange and minted into gold napoleons which sell for three times their monetary value. An increasing number of nations, including Great Britain, South Africa, and the tiny South Pacific island monarchy of Tonga, have found gold coins an excellent source of revenue.

The United States makes no profit on the gold sold by the treasury, nor can it be replaced. In defense of the dollar the country must keep selling gold at a bargain price that has closed out its suppliers. As the costs of mining rise, gold production continues to decline in every country using free labor, though total world output has never been higher.

This puts the United States and the rest of the free world in the hypocritical and precarious position of denouncing slavery and communism while depending on them to supply the world with gold. From a purely practical point of view it would seem shortsighted to count on an uninterrupted flow of gold from a country carefully planting seeds of internal strife and another collecting weapons in a cold war that might well be settled on the economic front.

Defending the dollar by expending gold that is never replaced can only be a short-term proposition. Eventually the destiny of the dollar and America's economic future will be decided by those who control the world's gold.

In the spring of 1962, after a serious economic crisis that forced a devaluation of the Canadian dollar, Canada took the first step toward regaining an adequate and continuing supply of gold for her monetary reserve. Through the Emergency Mines Assistance Act the government offered a premium price of forty-five dollars an ounce to gold producers who needed assistance to resume mining or increase output.

Reviving an industry which has been depressed for more than twenty years is necessarily a slow process. Realizing this makes it even more imperative that a future need for gold should be anticipated now.

In an ideal world, digging gold from the ground to bury it again as a monetary reserve might not be necessary. In a world of cold and hot wars, revolutions, shifting political alliances, unsteady governments, and fluctuating currencies, gold remains the one stable ingredient in a volatile economic brew. Men, banks, and nations trust it as the ultimate monetary reserve and the most acceptable international currency.

In view of gold's continuing importance, the advice George Bernard Shaw once addressed to intelligent women bears consideration by heads of governments and monetary authorities as well:

"The most important thing about money is to maintain its stability, so that a pound will buy as much a year hence or ten years hence or fifty years hence as today, and no more. With paper money this stability has to be maintained by the government. With a gold currency it tends to maintain itself even when the natural supply of gold is increased by discoveries of new deposits, because of the curious fact that the demand for gold in the world is practically infinite. You have to choose (as a voter) between trusting to the natural stability of gold and the natural stability of the honesty and intelligence of the members of the Government. And, with due respect for these gentlemen, I advise you, as long as the Capitalist system lasts, to vote for gold."

Glossary

ADIT. A nearly horizontal tunnel from the surface into the earth.

ALKAHEST. An imaginary liquid sought by alchemists because of its reputed ability to dissolve all substances and separate them into their constituent elements.

ALLUVIAL GOLD. "Placer gold;" any gold found associated with water-worn material.

AMALGAM. An alloy of mercury, especially one containing silver or gold. In *amalgamation,* gold is recovered from rock by exposing the ore to mercury, which unites with the gold but not with the other rock materials. Later distillation releases pure gold from the amalgam.

BACK. Ore-bearing part of the ceiling of a drift (tunnel) or stope. Often used interchangeably (but incorrectly) with ROOF.

BAR DIGGINGS. Sand bars of rivers that could be worked only during low tide or by use of cofferdams.

BASE METALS. Metals inferior in value and more chemically active than the NOBLE METALS of gold, silver, or platinum.

BASTARD QUARTZ. Bull quartz; any white, coarse-grained vein devoid of mineralization.

BEACH PLACER. An alluvial gold deposit on present or ancient sea beaches, formed by the continuous washing action of the tides which separated the heavier rock from the lighter. This "panning" by Mother Nature formed the fabulously rich beach placers in Nome, Alaska.

BEDROCK. The solid rock underlying placer deposits or any other unconsolidated rock or soil.

BIMETALISM. Concurrent use of gold and silver as legal money.

BLANKETING. Using blankets to capture gold from sands or slimes. Putting blankets in sluices becomes "blanket sluicing."

BONANZA. Spanish for "fair weather." In miners' parlance a high grade orebody.

BOOMING. Damming up water, then suddenly discharging it for placer mining.

BULLION. Solid gold as distinguished from any imitation.

CAKE GOLD. The mass of gold remaining from distillation of mercury from amalgam; also *sponge gold.*

CARAT. The measurement of fineness of gold alloy and meaning one-twenty-fourth. Fine gold is 24-carat gold. The standard of the goldsmith trade is 22-carat: 22 parts gold, 1 part silver, 1 part copper.

CAT GOLD. An obsolete term for mica reflecting a gold color.

CEMENT GOLD. Mass of gold precipitated from solution.

CHLORINATION PROCESS. Used to separate gold from metal sulfides. This technique requires roasting of the ores to drive off the sulfur, followed by saturation with chlorine gas which combines with the gold to form water-soluble gold chloride. The gold is subsequently precipitated from solution to form the purified cement gold.

CLEANUP. The collection of all gold production during a given period.

COLD NOSE. Mining "experts" of the late 19th century who underestimated the value of a mine. The opposite, favorable, term "nose for ore" is in use today.

CONCENTRATE. Ore which has been enriched by the removal of waste rock (gangue) in a *concentrator.*

CONGLOMERATE. Rock consisting of rounded waterworn pebbles cemented together by fine-grained material.

CONTRACT MINER. Any miner who is paid by the tonnage produced or distance or drift advancement, rather than by wages.

COUNTRY ROCK. Rock into which mineral veins have been intruded.

COUSIN JACK. In the Western U.S., any miner who emigrated from Cornwall, England.

COYOTING. An American term for mining in small, eroded, irregularly planned tunnels. Also known as *gophering,* this unsophisticated type of mining has, on occasion, been very productive and efficient.

CRADLE. A wooden box mounted on rockers which, when rocked back and forth, concentrates gold at the bottom, leaving lighter sand and gravel above.

CROSSCUT. Any horizontal underground passage driven at right angles from one main drift to another, or from a drift to an intersection with a vein.

CURSING IN WORK. Canadian term for falsifying an affidavit of the amount of assessment work done on a mining claim.

CUTCH. A pack of vellum leaves between which gold sheets are beaten into leaf.

CYANIDATION. Process of recovering gold by dissolving it in sodium or potassium cyanide, then precipitating the gold by adding zinc dust.

DIGGERS. An obsolete term for *miners,* it is now used in some parts of the English Commonwealth as slang for miners' work clothes.

DIGGINGS. In the U.S., placer workings; elsewhere, any mine.

DIP. Angle at which veins, faults, or rock formations are inclined from the horizontal.

DISCOVERY CLAIM. The claim which contains the site of the original mineral discovery.

DOODLEBUG. Any machine used in prospecting.

DOUBLE JACKING. Rock drilling in which one man holds a drill and another man swings a sledgehammer. Obviously faith, courage, and a good sense of humor are assets for the holder.

DRIFT. A nearly horizontal underground passage which follows a vein or serves as a main passageway as compared to a *crosscut* which intersects a drift or vein.

FACE. The end of a drift or stope where rock can be extracted.

FAULT. A fracture in a rock along which there has been displacement of the two sides relative to each other.

FINE GOLD. Almost pure gold. The value of bullion gold depends on its percentage of fineness.

FLOAT GOLD or FLOUR GOLD. Gold flakes so small that they can float on or be carried away by the water.

FLOTATION. A concentration process in which finely crushed and ground ore is submersed in a chemical solution containing special reagents that have an affinity for either the metallic mineral or the waste rock and separate one from the other.

FOOL'S GOLD. Pyrite, a gold-colored, common iron sulfide.

FOOTWALL. The solid rock beneath a lode, vein, or fault.

FOSSICKER. An old Australian term for a person who reworks old waste piles and tailings for the remaining gold content. A *night fossicker* was someone who robbed gold-diggings under cover of darkness. Fossicking is still a common term in some English Commonwealth countries for "prospecting."

FREE GOLD. Gold which occurs in its elemental (native) state.

GANGUE. Valueless waste rock.

GOGO. A plant growing in the Philippines whose juices are believed by natives to catch fine gold.

GOLD BEATER. A person who makes gold leaf by pounding very malleable gold in an especially prepared press composed of skins.

GUINEA GOLD. Twenty-two-carat gold of which the English guineas were coined.

HANGING WALL. Upper wall overlying a vein, lode, or fault.

HEADFRAME. The hoisting tower overlying a shaft.

HEAVY GOLD. Old Australian term for gold particles the size of gunshot.

HEAVY GROUND. Rock that tends to cave in.

HIGH-GRADING. Pilfering of gold ore by mine workers.

HOPPERINGS. Gravel retained in the hopper of a cradle or rocker.

HUNG SHOT. Explosive which failed to explode when fired.

ITAMBAMBA. A Brazilian plant whose juices are supposed to capture fine gold.

"IT'S DEEP ENOUGH." The American miner's traditional way of announcing the final shut-down of a mine.

JACKHAMMER. A power hammer used to drill rock.

JEWELER'S SHOP. Australian term for a rich pocket of gold.

JIG. A machine that concentrates ore on a reciprocating screen.

LAGGING. Planks or laths placed between timber roof supports to prevent rock fragments from sloughing off into the tunnel.

LAKE BED PLACERS. Placer deposits occurring in the beds of present or ancient lakes.

LEVEL. A horizontal drift in a mine. In the U.S., levels are usually designated by their depth (measured in feet) below the surface (*i.e.,* 100 level, 1500 level, 230 level).

LODE. Derived from the Cornish term for the verb "lead," it denotes a tabular-shaped vein.

MAN CAGE. A special platform designed for transporting miners up and down a mine shaft.

MANWAY. A small tunnel serving as a passageway for miners.

MATURATION. The alchemists' ultimate goal—the conversion of a base metal into gold.

MILL. Buildings that house crushing and grinding equipment.

MOSS GOLD. Gold exhibiting tree-shaped patterns.

MOTHER LODE. Main quartz vein from which placer gold deposits were derived. The term is best known as the name of the great gold-producing region of eastern California.

MUCK. Rock that is blasted down in a mine. A miner that loads the rock is a *mucker* and his shovel is a *muck stick.*

NOBLE METALS. Gold, silver, and platinum—metals which under normal circumstances are virtually inactive chemically. See BASE METALS.

NUGGET. A rounded, water-worn piece of native gold of appreciable size.

OPEN PIT. Excavating ore on the surface of the earth. Techniques and size and type of equipment vary greatly from that used in underground mining. This term does not apply to placer mines.

ORE. Rock containing minerals that can be mined at a profit.

ORE SHOOT. A relatively large and rich zone of ore trending somewhat vertically in a vein.

OVERBURDEN. Waste rock overlying an orebody. This term is usually applied to open pit mining and strip mining.

PAINT GOLD. A thin occurrence of gold which has crystallized on the surfaces of other minerals.

PLACERS. Glacial or alluvial deposits containing heavy valuable minerals.

POCKET HUNTER. In California, a prospector seeking small gold deposits on the surface.

PROVE UP. To determine the value and tonnage of an orebody.

RAISE. Underground passage driven upward, usually from one level to a higher level.

REEF. Australian term for a lode or vein. Introduced by sailors who left their ships during the Australian gold rush of 1851, the term was applied to quartz outcrops that rose above the surrounding surface in the manner of rock reefs projecting out of ocean water.

RETORTING. Distilling mercury from AMALGAM.

RIFFLES. Wooden slats placed across the bottom of a sluice or cradle to catch gold particles.

RIMROCK. Bedrock forming a boundary about a placer deposit.

ROASTING. Heating sulfide ore until the sulfur is driven off.

ROOF. Rock lying above an ore vein. Sometimes it is incorrectly used for the term BACK.

ROUND. A charge of explosives set in drill holes of a mine face and detonated, an act which miners call "pulling a round."

RUSTY GOLD. Native gold which does not amalgamate readily because it has a thin cover of iron oxide or other substance.

SCORIFIER. A furnace used in the process of capturing waste gold and silver from sweepings.

SHAFT. A vertical or inclined tunnel for hoisting and lowering men and material underground or for ventilation purposes.

SHIFT BOSS. Foreman of a mining crew.

SHOWING. Surface exposure of mineralized rock.

SINGLE JACKING. Drilling done by one man using a drill and light hammer.

SINK ON A PROSPECT. To excavate a small test shaft.

SLUICE. A long, inclined trough through which water and gold-bearing sands are run; also the heavy minerals captured by riffles, blankets, or other equipment.

SPANGLE GOLD. Australian term for smooth, flat flakes of gold.

STAMP MILL. A machine that uses descending pestles (stamps) to break up rock.

STOPE. Underground excavation where ore is mined.

STRIKE. The direction of an inclined vein; also commonly used to denote a discovery of ore.

STRINGER. A very narrow vein or thin filament of mineral traversing a rock mass of different material.

STULL. A timber prop used to support a mine opening.

SWEEPS. Dust from the workshops of jewelers, goldsmiths, silversmiths, and assayers and refiners of gold and silver.

SYLVANITE. See TELLURIUM.

TAILINGS. Waste from a concentration process.

TALMI-GOLD. Brass which looks like gold; also known as *Abyssinian gold.*

TELLURIUM. A rare element which has the unusual ability to bond chemically with gold to form the following naturally occurring minerals:

Petzite, $(Ag, Au)_2Te$

Sylvanit, $(Au, Ag)Te_2$

Kremmerite, $(Au, Ag)Te_2$

Calaverite, $AuTe_2$

Muthmannite, $(Ag, Au)Te$

Nagyagite, a gold-lead sulfo-telluride.

TIBIR. Spanish term for gold dust found on the African coast.

WASHING STUFF. Any gravel or soil containing enough gold to warrant washing the material in sluice boxes or other devices.

WEDGE ROCK. Miner's slang in the Comstock Lode for low-grade ore.

WINNOWING GOLD. Concentrating gold from dry powdered material by allowing air currents to blow away the lighter waste. Called "dry-blowing" in Australia.

WINZE. A vertical or inclined excavation driven downward within a mine, usually from one underground level to another.

Bibliography

GENERAL

AGRICOLA, GEORGIUS, *De Re Metallica,* trans. by Herbert Clark Hoover and Lou Henry Hoover, New York, Dover, 1950. The Hoovers' footnotes are a running commentary on the sixteenth-century text. The result is a carefully documented history of mining and metallurgy from ancient times to the twentieth century. Rich in gold lore. Agricola presents and comments on conflicting philosophical arguments for and against man's quest for gold.

COMSTOCK, J. L., *A History of the Precious Metals,* New York, 1849. The kind of enthusiastic book that swelled the gold rushes. More salesmanship than science, but historically interesting.

DEL MAR, ALEXANDER, *A History of the Precious Metals,* London, 1880. As free men searched for golden fortunes around the world, this mining expert propounded the unpopular thesis that mining for precious metals was profitable only when slave labor was available.

HOGG, GARRY, *Lust for Gold,* London, Robert Hale, Ltd., 1960. A disjointed, "believe it or not" account of large and small adventures and misadventures experienced by individuals and nations throughout history because of man's lust for gold.

MUMFORD, LEWIS, *Technics and Civilization,* New York, Harcourt, 1934. A profound analysis of the influence of the mine on modern civilization.

RICKARD, T. A., *Man and Metals,* 2 vols., London, McGraw-Hill, 1932. By the former editor of the *Mining and Engineering*

Journal. Since publication of this book, more than thirty years ago, the archaeologists have pushed back many of Mr. Rickard's prehistory dates but continue to find evidence to support his theories. In the meantime no work has replaced this comprehensive study of the part metals, including gold, have played in the development of civilization. Authoritative and highly readable.

SINGER, CHARLES; HOLMYARD, E. J.; HALL, A. R.; ed., *A History of Technology,* 5 vols., London, Oxford, 1954–59. Encyclopedic summary of technological changes from ancient times to the present, with much excellent material on mining, metallurgy, alchemy, goldsmithery, and industrial uses of gold.

SUTHERLAND, C. H. V., *Gold, Its Beauty, Power and Allure,* London, McGraw-Hill, 1959. A beautifully illustrated history of the metal from antiquity to the present, particularly informative on the subject of gold coinage and the gold mines of the Rand.

TABORI, PAUL, *The Natural Science of Stupidity,* Philadelphia, Chilton, 1959. Interesting oddities are related in a long section devoted to gold.

THE TIMES (London), reprint of *Gold,* a special issue first published June 20, 1933. A potpourri of articles on gold, its history, uses, and economic role.

CHILD OF THE SUN

APOLLODORUS, *Library,* The Loeb Classical Library, Cambridge, Harvard Univ. Press, 1951.

BIBBY, G., *The Testimony of the Spade,* New York, Knopf, 1956.

BREASTED, JAMES H., *A History of Egypt,* New York, Scribner's, 1909.

———, *The Conquest of Civilization,* New York, Harper, 1926.

CARRINGTON, RICHARD, *A Guide to Earth History,* New York, New American Library, 1956.

CARTER, HOWARD, AND MACE, A. C., *The Tomb of Tut-ankh-amen,* London, Doran (Doubleday), 1927.

CARY, M., AND WARMINGTON, E. H., *The Ancient Explorers,* London, Univ. of London Press, 1929.

CERAM, C. W., *Gods, Graves and Scholars,* trans. by E. B. Garside, New York, Knopf, 1961.

CHILDE, V. GORDON, *Man Makes Himself,* New York, New American Library, 1951.

———, *What Happened in History,* London, Penguin, 1942.

CLARK, GRAHAME, *World Prehistory,* London, Cambridge Univ. Press, 1961.

COTTRELL, LEONARD, *The Anvil of Civilization,* New York, New American Library, 1962.

———, *The Lost Pharaohs,* London, Evans, 1950.

DUNN, E. J., *Geology of Gold,* London, Griffin, 1929.

DURANT, WILL, *Our Oriental Heritage,* New York, Simon & Schuster, 1935.

HAMILTON, EDITH, *Mythology,* Boston, Little, Brown, 1940.

HERODOTUS, *The Histories,* trans. by Aubrey de Selincourt, London, Penguin, 1954.

HOYLE, FRED, *The Nature of the Universe,* New York, Harper, 1960.

KUHN, HERBERT, *On the Track of Prehistoric Man,* trans. by A. H. Broderick, New York, Random House, 1955.

KUMMEL, G., *History of the Earth,* San Francisco, Freeman, 1961.

LUCRETIUS, *Of the Nature of Things,* trans. by William Ellery Leonard, New York, Dutton, 1957.

LUDWIG, EMIL, *Schliemann: The Story of a Goldseeker,* Boston, Little, 1931.

MEADOWCROFT, KIRK, *Apes, Ivory and Jade,* New York, Smith (Longmans), 1936.

MONTAGU, ASHLEY, *Man: His First Million Years,* New York, World (Harcourt), 1956.

NEWBERRY, J. S., "The Genesis and Distribution of Gold," New York, *School of Mines Quarterly,* 1881.

PAYNE, ROBERT, *The Gold of Troy,* New York, Funk & Wagnalls, 1959.

PETRIE, SIR W. FLINDERS, *Social Life in Ancient Egypt,* London, Constable, 1932.

SCHENK, GUSTAV, *The History of Man,* Philadelphia, Chilton, 1961.

SCHLIEMANN, H., *Ilios: The City and Country of the Trojans,* New York, Harper, 1880.

———, *Troy and Its Remains,* London, 1880.

SCHREIBER, HERMANN, *Merchants, Pilgrims and Highwaymen,* New York, Putnam, 1962.

SCHREIBER, HERMANN AND GEORG, *Vanished Cities,* New York, Knopf, 1957.
SCOTT, NORA, *Home Life of the Egyptians,* New York, Metropolitan Museum, 1944.
SMITH, WILLIAM S., *Ancient Egypt,* Boston, Museum of Fine Arts, 1960.
WOOD, R. W., "The Purple Gold of Tut'Ankamun," London, *Journal of Egyptian Archaeology,* Vol. XX, 1934.
WOOLLEY, C. LEONARD, *Excavations at Ur,* London, Faber, 1926.
———, *The Sumerians,* London, Clarendon Press, 1929.

ROYAL METAL

BAINBRIDGE, HENRY C., *Peter Carl Faberge,* London, Batsford, 1949.
BOYLE, ROBERT, *The Sceptical Chemist,* London, J. Crooke, 1661.
BRADFORD, ERNLE, *Four Centuries of European Jewellery,* New York, Philosophical Library, 1953.
BURGESS, FRED W., *Chats on Old Coins,* London, Benn, 1913.
BURY, J. B., *A History of Greece* (1900), New York, Modern Library.
CELLINI, BENVENUTO, *The Life of Benvenuto Cellini,* trans. by John Addington Symonds, New York, Scribners, 1927.
———, *The Treatises,* trans. by C. R. Ashbee, London, 1898.
CENNINI, CENNINO, *The Craftsman's Handbook,* 2 vols., trans. by Daniel V. Thompson, Jr., New Haven, Yale Univ. Press, 1932–33.
DOBERER, K. K., *The Goldmakers,* trans. by E. W. Dickes, London, Nicholson & Watson, 1948.
DURANT, WILL, *Caesar and Christ,* New York, Simon & Schuster, 1944.
———, *The Life of Greece,* New York, Simon & Schuster, 1939.
FARNHAM, PAUL, *The Adams Gold Vase,* New York, Tiffany, 1896.
FINLEY, MOSES, *The Greek Historians,* New York, Viking, 1959.
GEBER (JABIR), *Jabir Ibn Hayyan, The Arabic Works,* ed. by E. J. Holmyard, Paris, Geuthner, 1928.

GEBER, *The Works of Geber,* trans. by Richard Russell, London, Dent, 1928.

GRANT, MICHAEL, *The World of Rome,* New York, World (Harcourt), 1960.

HOLMYARD, E. J., *Alchemy,* London, Harmsworth, 1957.

———, "Makers of Chemistry," London, Clarendon Press, 1931.

JABIR (*see* GEBER).

JAFFE, BERNARD, *Crucibles, The Story of Chemistry,* New York, Simon & Schuster, 1957.

MARTIN, J. B., *The Grasshopper in Lombard Street,* London, 1892.

MARYON, H., "Metalworking in the Ancient World," *American Journal of Archaeology,* 1949.

PLINY THE ELDER, *Chapters on Chemical Subjects,* K. C. Bailey, ed., 2 vols., London, Arnold, 1929–1932.

QUIGGEN, A. HINGSTON, *A Survey of Primitive Money,* London, Methuen, 1949.

READ, J., *Prelude to Chemistry,* London, G. Bell, 1939.

RIDGEWAY, W., *The Origin of Metallic Currency and Weight Standards,* Cambridge, 1892.

ROSTOVTZEFF, J. J., *Social and Economic History of the Hellenistic World,* London, Oxford, 1941.

———, *Social and Economic History of the Roman Empire,* London, Oxford, 1957.

TAYLOR, F. SHERWOOD, *The Alchemists: Founders of Modern Chemistry,* New York, Schuman (Abelard-Schuman), 1949.

YAN, LIEN-SHENG, *Money and Credit in China,* Cambridge, Harvard Univ. Press, 1952.

YARYON, H., *Metalwork and Enameling,* 4th ed. rev., New York, Ryerson Press (Appleton), 1959.

WORLD CONQUEROR

AGRICOLA, GEORGIUS, *De Metallica* (*see* previous listing under General Bibliography).

———, "De Natura Fossilium," trans. by M. C. and J. A. Bandy, Geological Society of America, Nov., 1955.

BLACKER, IRWIN R., AND ROSEN, HARRY M., *The Golden Conquistadores,* New York, Bobbs-Merrill, 1960.

BLOM, FRANZ, *The Conquest of Yucatan,* Boston, Houghton Mifflin, 1936.

BRAINERD, GEORGE W., *The Maya Civilization,* Los Angeles, Southwest Museum, 1954

CATHERWOOD, F., *Views of Ancient Monuments in Central America, Chiapas and Yucatan,* New York, 1844.

DIAZ DEL CASTILLO, BERNAL, *The Discovery and Conquest of Mexico,* trans. by A. P. Maudslay, New York, Farrar, Straus, 1956.

DIBNER, BERN, *Agricola on Metals,* Norwalk, Conn., Burndy Library, 1958.

GALLENKAMP, CHARLES, *Maya,* New York, McKay, 1959.

GANN, T. W. F., and THOMPSON, J. E. S., *The History of the Maya,* New York, Scribner's, 1931.

HAGEN, VICTOR W., "Realm of the Incas," New York, Mentor (New American Library), 1957.

HIBBEN, FRANK C., *The Lost Americans,* New York, Crowell, 1947.

HIRTH, FRIEDRICH, *Ancient History of China,* New York, Columbia Univ. Press, 1923.

KIRKPATRICK, F. A., *The Spanish Conquistadores,* New York, World (Harcourt), 1962.

KNIGHT, M., *Economic History of Europe to the End of the Middle Ages,* Cambridge, Harvard Univ. Press, 1926.

LATOURETTE, K. S., *The Development of China,* Boston, Houghton Mifflin, 1946.

MACGOWAN, KENNETH, *Early Man in the New World,* New York, Macmillan, 1950.

MORLEY, S. G., *The Ancient Maya,* Stanford, Calif., Stanford Univ. Press, 1946.

PIRENNE, HENRI, *Economic and Social History of Medieval Europe,* trans. by I. E. Clegg, New York, Harcourt, 1937.

POLO, MARCO, *Travels of Marco Polo,* ed. by Manuel Komroff, New York, Boni & Liveright, 1926.

PRESCOTT, WILLIAM H., *History of the Conquest of Mexico,* London, 1843.

———, *History of the Conquest of Peru,* New York, 1847

STEPHENS, JOHN L., *Incidents of Travel in Central America, Chiapas, and Yucatan,* ed. by Richard L. Predmore, New Brunswick, N. J., Rutgers Univ. Press, 1949.

VAILLANT, GEORGE C., *The Aztecs of Mexico,* New York, Doubleday, 1941.

FOR EVERYONE

ANZIER, R. C., *Klondike Gold Rush,* New York, Pageant, 1959.

AVERILL, C. V., *Placer Mining for Gold in California,* San Francisco, Calif. Dept. of Natural Resources, 1946.

BANCROFT, HUBERT HOWE, *The Works of H. H. Bancroft,* San Francisco, The History Company, 1887–88.

BENNETT, ESTELLINE, *Old Deadwood Days,* New York, Scribner's, 1935.

BERTON, PIERRE, *The Klondike Fever,* New York, Knopf, 1958.

BINGHAM, E. R., ed., *California Gold,* Boston, Heath, 1959.

BRYAN, JERRY, *An Illinois Gold Hunter in the Black Hills,* Springfield, Illinois State Historical Society, 1960.

CHALFANT, W. A., *Gold, Guns and Ghost Towns,* Stanford, Calif., Stanford Univ. Press, 1947.

DE QUILLE, DAN (WILLIAM WRIGHT), *History of the Big Bonanza,* Hartford, Conn., 1872.

DOWNIE, MAJOR WILLIAM, *Hunting for Gold,* San Francisco, Calif. Pub. Co., 1893.

EISSLER, M., *The Metallurgy of Gold,* Princeton, N.J., Van Nostrand, 1900.

FRENCH, L. H., *Seward's Land of Gold,* New York, Montross, Clarke and Emmons, 1900.

GOLD FIELDS OF SOUTH AFRICA LTD., CONSOLIDATED, *The Gold Fields,* London, 1937.

GREGORY, JOSEPH W., *Guide for California Travellers via the Isthmus of Panama,* New York, Nafis and Cornish, 1850.

HOMESTAKE MINING COMPANY, *Annual Reports,* Lead, S. D.

———, *The Homestake Story,* Lead, S. D., 5th ed., 1960.

———, *Sharp Bits,* Lead, S. D.

HULBERT, ARCHER BUTLER, *Forty-Niners,* Boston, Little, Brown, 1931.

JACKSON, JOSEPH HENRY, *Anybody's Gold,* New York, Appleton, 1941.

JACOBSSON, D., *Fifty Golden Years of the Rand,* London, Faber, 1936.

JEFFERSON, R. L., *Roughing It in Siberia,* London, 1897.

KLAPPHOLZ, LOWELL, *Gold! Gold!,* New York, McBride, 1959.

LANGFORD, NATHANIEL PITT, *Vigilante Days and Ways,* New York, D. D. Merrill, 1893.

LEWIS, OSCAR, *Sea Routes to the Gold Fields,* New York, Knopf, 1949.

MACDONALD, ROBERT M., *Opals and Gold,* Philadelphia, Lippincott, 1928.

MINERS' NEWS, *All About the Klondike Gold Mines,* New York, Miners' News Pub. Co., 1897.

MORRELL, W. P., *The Gold Rushes,* New York, Pioneer Histories, 1941.

PAUL, RODMAN W., *Mining Frontiers of the Far West,* New York, Holt, 1963.

PEATTIE, RODERICK, ed., *The Black Hills,* New York, Vanguard, 1952.

PETROV, VLADIMIR, *Soviet Gold,* trans. by Mirra Ginsburg, New York, Farrar, Straus, 1949.

QUIETT, GLENN C., Pay Dirt, New York, Ryerson Press (Appleton), 1936.

RICKARD, T. A., *A History of American Mining,* New York, McGraw-Hill, 1932.

———, *The Romance of Mining,* Toronto, Macmillan, 1947.

ROSENTHAL, ERIC, *Gold Bricks and Mortar, Sixty Years of Johannesburg History,* Johannesburg, Union of South Africa, 1946.

SHINN, CHARLES H., *Mining Camps, a Study in American Frontier Government,* New York, Knopf, 1948.

SMITH, GRANT H., *The History of the Comstock Lode,* Reno, Univ. of Nevada, 1943.

Sunset Editors, *Gold Rush Country,* Los Angeles, *Sunset Magazine* Discovery Book, 1958.

TAYLOR, BAYARD, *Eldorado,* London, Richard Bentley, 1850.

TOOLE, K. ROSS, *Montana: An Uncommon Land,* Norman, Univ. of Oklahoma, 1959.

TWAIN, MARK, *Roughing It,* Hartford, Conn., 1872.

WEBB, TODD, *Gold Strikes and Ghost Towns,* New York, Doubleday, 1961.

WELLMAN, PAUL, *Glory, God and Gold,* New York, Doubleday, 1954.

WYMAN, W. D., *California Emigrant Letters,* New York, Bookman Associates, 1952.

YOUNG, GEORGE J., *Elements of Mining,* New York, McGraw-Hill, 1916.

COINED AND CONDEMNED

BUSSCHAU, W. J., *Gold and International Liquidity,* Johannesburg, The South African Institute of International Affairs, 1961.

CHANDLER, LESTER V., *The Economics of Money and Banking,* New York, Harper, 1948.

DENIAU, J. F., *The Common Market,* New York, Praeger, 1960.

DILLARD, DUDLEY, *The Economics of John Maynard Keynes,* Englewood Cliffs, N. J., Prentice-Hall, 1948.

FERRIS, PAUL, *The City,* New York, Random House, 1961.

GEORGE, HENRY, *Progress and Poverty,* New York, Modern Library.

GRUCHY, ALLAN G., *Modern Economic Thought: The American Contribution,* Englewood Cliffs, N. J., Prentice-Hall, 1947.

HAGUE, D. C., editor, *Inflation: Proceedings of a Conference Held by the International Economic Association,* New York, St. Martin's, 1962.

HAHN, L. ALBERT, *The Economics of Illusion,* New York, Squier, 1949.

HARRIS, SEYMOUR E., *The Dollar in Crisis,* New York, Harcourt, 1961.

HARROD, ROY, *The Dollar,* New York, Harcourt, 1954.

HEPBURN, A. BARTON, *A History of Currency in the United States,* New York, Macmillan, 1915.

KEYNES, J. M., *A Tract on Monetary Reform,* London, Macmillan, 1923.

———, *The General Theory of Employment, Interest, and Money,* New York, Harcourt, 1935.

KORTEWEG, S., and KEESING, F. A. G., *A Textbook of Money,* New York, Longmans, 1959.

LONDON, KURT, *The Permanent Crisis,* New York, Walker, 1962.

MCCONNELL, CAMPBELL R., *Elementary Economics,* New York, McGraw-Hill, 1960.

MACDOUGALL, SIR DONALD, *The World Dollar Problem,* London, Macmillan, 1957.

MYRDAL, GUNNAR, *An International Economy,* New York, Harper, 1956.

NATIONAL INDUSTRIAL CONFERENCE BOARD, *The Economic Almanac,* New York, 1962.

———, *The New Monetary System of the United States,* New York, 1934.

PECK, H. AUSTIN, *International Economics,* New York, Crowell, 1957.

RIST, CHARLES, *The Triumph of Gold,* trans. by Philip Cortney, New York, Philosophical Library, 1961.

ROGERS, JAMES HARVEY, *America Weighs Her Gold,* New Haven, Conn., Yale Univ. Press, 1931.

SCHERMAN, HARRY, *The Real Danger in Our Gold,* New York, Simon & Schuster, 1940.

SHANNON, IAN, *The Economic Functions of Gold,* Melbourne, Cheshire, 1962.

SMITH, ADAM, *The Wealth of Nations,* Modern Library (Random House), 1937.

TRIFFIN, ROBERT, *Gold and the Dollar Crisis,* New Haven, Conn., Yale Univ. Press, 1961.

U.S. BANKING AND CURRENCY COMMISSION, *Gold Reserve Act of 1934, Hearings,* Washington, U.S. Government Printing Office, 1934.

U.S. TREASURY DEPARTMENT, *Gold Regulations,* Washington, U.S. Government Printing Office, Jan. 16, 1961.

WARD, BARBARA, *The Rich Nations and the Poor Nations,* New York, Norton, 1962.

———, *The West at Bay,* New York, Norton, 1948.

WOYTINSKY, W. S., and WOYTINSKY, E. S., *World Commerce and Governments,* New York, Twentieth Century Fund, 1955.

ZIMMERMAN, E. W., *World Resources and Industries,* New York, Harper, 1951.

Index

Temple Juno Moneta
Athena Parthenos
Troy
Cyrus
Ziggurat
Roman mines
Croesus
River Pactolus
Persepolis
Ur
Tutankhamen's tomb
Karnak
Happy Arabia
Miserable Kush
Zimbabwe
Johannesburg
Rand mines